Bromance

Stefan Robinson · Eric Anderson
Bromance
Male Friendship, Love and Sport

Stefan Robinson
Wantage, UK

Eric Anderson
Basingstoke, Hampshire, UK

ISBN 978-3-030-98609-4   ISBN 978-3-030-98610-0 (eBook)
https://doi.org/10.1007/978-3-030-98610-0

© The Editor(s) (if applicable) and The Author(s), under exclusive license to Springer Nature Switzerland AG 2022
This work is subject to copyright. All rights are solely and exclusively licensed by the Publisher, whether the whole or part of the material is concerned, specifically the rights of translation, reprinting, reuse of illustrations, recitation, broadcasting, reproduction on microfilms or in any other physical way, and transmission or information storage and retrieval, electronic adaptation, computer software, or by similar or dissimilar methodology now known or hereafter developed.
The use of general descriptive names, registered names, trademarks, service marks, etc. in this publication does not imply, even in the absence of a specific statement, that such names are exempt from the relevant protective laws and regulations and therefore free for general use.
The publisher, the authors and the editors are safe to assume that the advice and information in this book are believed to be true and accurate at the date of publication. Neither the publisher nor the authors or the editors give a warranty, expressed or implied, with respect to the material contained herein or for any errors or omissions that may have been made. The publisher remains neutral with regard to jurisdictional claims in published maps and institutional affiliations.

Cover illustration: Jacob Lund/Shutterstock

This Palgrave Macmillan imprint is published by the registered company Springer Nature Switzerland AG
The registered company address is: Gewerbestrasse 11, 6330 Cham, Switzerland

Contents

1	**Introduction**	1
	Origins of the Modern Bromance	3
	Research Methodology	8
	The Dodgeball Profile	9
	Situating the Researchers	13
	References	14
2	**Friendship**	17
	Sociological Perspectives on Friendship	17
	Evolutionary Perspectives on Friendship	21
	Online Friendship	24
	Defining Love	25
	Love Without Sex	28
	Chapter Conclusion	30
	References	31
3	**Homosociality**	35
	Homosociality	35
	Homosociality as Dangerous	38
	Homosociality in Sporting Culture	39
	Homosocial Intimacy	42

Expression and Love Between Men in the Late
Twentieth Century ... 48
Twenty-First Century Expressions of Love ... 51
Chapter Summary ... 53
References ... 54

4 Theorizing Masculinity ... 61
Social Constructionism ... 62
Hegemonic Masculinity ... 63
Critiques of Hegemonic Masculinity ... 65
A Third Wave of Masculinity Theorizing ... 69
Inclusive Masculinity Theory ... 70
Three Cultural Conditions to Inclusive Masculinities ... 73
   Stage 1: Homoerasure ... 74
   Stage 2: Homohysteria ... 76
   Stage 3: Inclusivity ... 79
Chapter Conclusion ... 82
References ... 83

5 Illustrating the Bromance ... 89
Illustrating the Bromance in Film ... 90
Illustrating the Bromance in Sociological Studies of Men ... 93
Illustrating the Bromance in This Ethnography ... 96
Bromances Compared to Friendship ... 98
Distinguishing Bromances from Romance ... 101
The Difference is Sex ... 101
Bromance and Non-exclusivity ... 104
Chapter Summary ... 106
References ... 107

6 Building the Bromance ... 111
Shared Interests ... 112
Emotional Intimacy ... 116
Love ... 121
Positive Mental Health Impacts of Having a Bromance ... 123
Chapter Summary ... 125
References ... 126

7	**Cuddling and Spooning**	129
	When Two Guys Share a Bed	132
	Cuddling Other Men, This Study	134
	Chapter Summary	138
	References	139
8	**Kissing**	141
	The First Study of Straight-Men Kissing, England	142
	The Second Study of Straight-Men Kissing, Australia	143
	The Third Study of Straight-Men Kissing, America	143
	The Fourth Study of Straight-Men Kissing, This Study	147
	Three-Way Kissing	151
	Frequency of Kissing	153
	Chapter Summary	156
	References	158
9	**Popularity and Banter in a Bromantic Culture**	161
	Humor	161
	Banter	163
	The Precarious Nature of Humor	167
	Codifying Banter	170
	Behavioral	170
	Cultural	171
	"No One is Unpopular"	171
	Athletic Ability	172
	Sociability	174
	Aggression	177
	Chapter Summary	179
	References	180
10	**Bromances and Gay Men**	183
	Inclusivity	184
	Kissing Gay Men	187
	Curious but not Concerned	188
	Gay Discourse	189
	Chapter Summary	190
	References	191

11 Sexuality — 195
Sexual Identity — 196
Pushing Heterosexual Boundaries — 200
Group Sex — 206
Nudity — 210
Sexual Bravado — 211
Chapter Summary — 213
References — 214

12 Privileging the Bromance — 217
Romance as Problematic — 218
Competing Priorities — 221
Chapter Summary — 223
References — 224

13 Discussing the Bromance — 225
Enduring Bromances — 229
Emotional Health and Well-Being — 231
Inexact Sexualities: "Boys Being Boys" — 234
Renovating Lad Culture — 237
Cross-Sex Socialization and Regulation — 239
Gender Equality — 241
Generalizability — 241
Theoretical Implications — 243
References — 246

References — 255

About the Authors

Stefan Robinson completed his Ph.D. on the study of Men and Masculinities at the University of Winchester, UK. He has published works across a range of topics and publishers and is currently working to develop robust and meaningful public policy in UK Local Government.

Eric Anderson is the leading authority on the changing nature of heterosexual men's masculinities, and is currently Professor of Sport, Masculinities, and Sexualities at the University of Winchester, UK. He has published over 20 books and nearly 100 peer-reviewed research articles related to sport, masculinities, and sexualities.

List of Figures

Fig. 3.1	A typical cuddle experienced by young men in the present day (Pekic/E + via Getty Images)	45
Fig. 4.1	Stage model of homohysteria	74
Fig. 13.1	Data collected from the Office for National Statistics (2015) overlaid with Anderson and McCormack's (2014) time series graph concerning the rise and decline of homohysteria	233

1

Introduction

Young and good-looking, athletic, and intelligent, Patrick and Rick met in college. They were assigned into dormitory halls with four other males, each room centrally connected by a kitchen. They bonded instantly. Patrick was unpacking when he realized that he had forgot to pack his facial moisturizer to take to college. Rick offered Patrick use of his, but Patrick was used to a more expensive brand.

The next day, Rick accompanied Patrick into the city's high street to purchase the moisturizer, the two stopped for coffee, and took their drinks to a communal green space, where they sat on the ground and compared interests. They found mutual joy in shared music and popular culture. They each wore skinny jeans, so tight they looked painted on, and short socks that left an inch of ankle showing.

They felt an immediate closeness that afternoon: a feeling that grew in the weeks and months of their first year at university. In fact, the two grew inseparable. They didn't give their relationship a name, but it was recognized by others in their social network. When someone invited Patrick to an event, they also asked him to bring Rick. The same was true of invitations for Rick.

The guys shared a love of cooking together, creating extravagant meals by university standards. On nights out, they were also excellent dancers, with such unison it looked rehearsed. After their first night out dancing together, they returned to Patrick's room, cuddling each other to sleep.

Months later, the two traveled to Thailand together for several weeks, posting images of themselves on social media to signal to their friends and family the joy they were having. One of those pictures included them showering in a steamy room together, and others showed them feeding each other with chopsticks.

The following academic year, they grew even closer; creating an enduring relationship that posed the difficult question after graduation: what now? One of the guys wrote about the moment, "I've always been quiet, but around him I light up. My whole three years at university were defined by meeting him that day." Given the depth of their love, the answer was to stay together, renting an apartment and looking for work.

The relationship lasted several more years, until Patrick told Rick that he was going to have to move out because his girlfriend wanted to live with him. You see, neither Patrick nor Rick is gay, nor do they identify as bisexual. They are heterosexual.

If you read into their description of a gay couple, you might need to examine the culture of contemporary male friendship, and your own preconceived ideas—precisely what this book is about.

The above vignette is a composite of actual student lives—manufactured to a degree, yes—but it is nonetheless recognizable to the young men that Professor Eric Anderson teaches at university in the Southern part of England. The type of relationship that Patrick and Rick portray does have a name: it's called, bromance.

Bromance is a term with cultural resonance among men of their generation. As one of the participants in this study describes, "a bromance is having a best friend and it's seen like a marriage; like a relationship." He adds, "I have a bromance with Ronnie…we are so connected…we're like an old married couple."

This type of relationship is nothing like most people think adolescent male friendships are. Male friendships have moved on since the twentieth century. Yet, there is very little academic attention on the topic. With this book, we address that need.

This is a book about the history, development, and benefits of bromantic relationships. It is fundamentally a story about over-turning preconceived ideas of limited male emotionality, to show just how far matters have changed.

Origins of the Modern Bromance

Research into the lives of men and their masculinity began in earnest in the late 1970s. By the 1980s a body of research emerged with findings that endured for the next two decades. It highlighted the social problems of masculinity. It found that men were primarily concerned with social status among other men; and that social status was achieved by being tough, stoic—and above all—not in the slightest bit gay. Compared to women, men were thought to have less interest in caretaking, to have less desire for emotional expressionism, and to lack empathy. This was thought to impact upon their friendships. It was not socially desirable for men to show love or confide emotional distress to other men. Men did not explicitly tell other men that they were friends: instead, they knew they had a friend when they played sports or drank beer together.

The concept of friendship is also well-examined in the social sciences literature (Hruschka 2010). Whilst friendship is primarily experienced by individuals as a complex psychological phenomenon (Poplawski 1989), its dimensions, behavioral requisites, and prohibitions are nonetheless socially defined and regulated (Van Duijn et al. 2003), making the study of friendship an interdisciplinary matter. This is to say that the feelings we experience in friendship are biopsychological, but the conditions upon which we feel them are somewhat socially regulated.

In an early account of the problem of male friendship, Lewis (1978) wrote:

> [Men] have not known what it means to love and care for a friend without the shadow of some guilt and fear of peer ridicule… most of these friendships are not close, intimate, or characterized by self-disclosure. (p. 108)

The social stifling of male friendship meant that men had a low threshold for recognizing that they had a friend. Men were thought to have a friend when they engaged in activities together, like playing, watching, or talking about sports (Seiden and Bart 1975). Conversely, women were found to have a friend when they shared secrets or vulnerabilities together. This meant that women's friendships were based on something emotionally deeper, and perhaps something more meaningful; certainly, something that is better for one's mental health. Yet this more progressive style of friendship was not socially available to men. In fact, men prevented it.

Michael Kimmel (1994), a now emeritus sociologist, and one of the founding scholars of the field of masculinities, argued that men had to prove and reprove their masculinity on a continuing basis. One act could not prove masculinity indefinitely, and one could not be socially titled "masculine" for life. Instead, men's masculinity was always suspect. It therefore needed to be continually established to maintain, or elevate, one's ranking above other men.

Scholars following in Kimmel's footsteps, mostly used unformulated concepts such as patriarchy, as drivers for these types of behaviors among men, but this was too simplified. This version of explaining men's masculinity was vested in men performing together for the sake of rule over women. It took a few decades and hindsight before masculinity scholars began to understand the more important driving mechanism of men's masculinity in the late twentieth century—homophobia—(e.g. Plummer 1999) and its constituent fear of being thought gay, which generated "homohysteria" (Anderson 2009).

Examining the use of homophobia as a driver of masculinity shifted the question away from an idea of men working together to maintain rule over women, to one of the men struggling among each other to maintain dominance over each other. Homophobia was a weapon to stratify men: so that not all were treated with fraternal equality. The degradation of men that were either known or perceived to harbor same-sex sexual interests essentially made heterosexuality, or the pretense of heterosexuality, compulsory for young males. The idea was first made popular by Adrienne Rich (1980) about women's sexuality, but soon found value in men's studies (Frank 1987).

Drawing on dozens of studies of men in and outside of sport, Eric Anderson (e.g. 2008a, 2009) conceptualized the importance of homophobia in masculinity-making through a more sophisticated analysis, using the concept of homohysteria. This concept explains when and how homophobia regulates men's gender performance. In cultures of high homophobia, like America in the 1980s, men acted in orthodox ways; ways that we might today call "toxic masculinity." However, a few decades later, in a contemporary culture that looks favorably upon gay men, masculinity is radically transformed.

The fear of being thought gay can be rationalized in homophobic times, particularly during the decades in which masculinity studies flourished, the 1980s and 1990s. After all, just as Kimmel described masculinity as always needing to be proven, Anderson argued that so would heterosexuality during this epoch. In other words, heterosexuality, like homosexuality, is a feeling (in this case the direction of sexual desire) that, unlike race, is not socially visible. It must be told, symbolized, for others to know what one's internal desires are. Whereas there is an assumption of heterosexuality, the wrongdoing of gender could question that sexuality. This was because it was the 1980s which saw the highest rates of homophobia in western history (Keleher and Smith 2012). High rates of homophobia necessarily meant that men feared being thought gay, too.

In 2008, Anderson laid the conceptual groundwork for homohysteria with his "one-time rule of homosexuality." Simply stated, heterosexuality has no physical identifiers, and the mere existence of the closet tells us that people may be lying about their heterosexuality. In other words, people can say that they are straight when they are not. This means that heterosexuality is established on faith.

Men who fear being thought gay in a homophobic culture, he argues, feel compelled to repeatedly establish their heterosexuality, and they do this by being macho, sexualizing women, and expressing homophobia. They do this vigilantly, and consistently, with such repetition that it becomes part of their gender. They do this because even one "slip" could result in a man being socially perceived as gay.

Illustrating this with sexual behaviors, Anderson (2008b) suggested that in the 1980s and 1990s, a dozen sexual experiences with women did not make a self-identified gay man socially straight, or even bisexual, but that one simple sexual experience with another man would dismiss a lifetime of heterosexual activity and loss of social credibility of heterosexuality for a self-identified straight man. Another way to view this is to say that in a homohysteric culture, individuals do not have the power to label their sexualities, their dominant culture does.

Related to friendship, in a homohysteric culture, Anderson (2009) suggested that the panoptic gaze of homophobic and emotionally distant peers dramatically limited the frequency and intensity of close relations between men (Lewis et al. 2015; Morman et al. 2013). Because emotional expressions were feminized, being open about fears or loves would cast serious social suspicion onto the men's heterosexuality. Men had good reason not to disclose secrets, to show vulnerability or express platonic love for another man, that could lead them to be thought gay. Remember, they do not have full control over how their sexuality is perceived. In a culture that looked very unfavorably upon gay men, this was powerful motivation to remain stoic and distant in friendship, in order to try and sway one's peers to viewing them as heterosexual.

By 2010 however, it was homophobia that was most highly stigmatized in many parts of the Anglo-American worlds, and not homosexuality. The relatively smaller scale of homophobia and wider acceptance of homosexuality meant that men had less reason to establish their heterosexual identity with other men; and consequently, less reason to establish their masculine identity. In other words: it is not masculinity which drives homophobia, it is homophobia which drives masculinity.

As we will show in this book, the stigmatizing of homophobia in the 1980s and 1990s was so intense that the very notion of "loving" another male in a platonic manner was to commit an act which earned social suspicion of homosexuality. It was an act that defied the strictures of masculinity. However, among millennial men, and those of the generation before them, the very concept of masculinity is stigmatized, and an increasing percentage of young men are now identifying as "mostly" heterosexual instead of "exclusively" heterosexual (McCormack and Savin-Williams 2018; Savin-Williams 2017). They no longer collectively desire to be perceived as exclusively masculine, nor do they necessarily desire to be perceived as totally heterosexual (Johnston and

Bradford 2019). Men and masculinities have become far more fluid, diverse, and free in how they operate, and this is even true of teamsport athletes who historically suffered the most distant same-sex relations (Anderson and Magrath 2019).

If young men today are less interested in being perceived as masculine and straight, and are motivated to avoid being perceived as homophobic, it is possible for closer and more intimate friendships with other men to develop (McCormack 2012). These newly practiced friendships, which often embrace impassioned emotion and physical affection, have recently been popularized under the rubric of the "bromance."

Although recent research has discussed the emergence of bromances and explored some elements of how contemporary men's friendships connect to male culture (Anderson 2014; Chen 2011; Hammarén and Johansson 2014; Ralph and Roberts 2020), there have been no systematic examinations of the bromance in terms of its conceptualization, behavioral requisites, or limitations, outside of what the authors of this book have published (Robinson et al. 2018). Instead, its meanings have been culturally mapped through comedy movies and television programs popular with the 16 to 25-year-old male demographic (DeAngelis 2014).

For all its comedic connotations and depiction, social scientists have, with only a few exceptions (see Ghaziani 2010; Way 2011, 2013) failed to consider the bromance as a serious and legitimate relationship type and ignored its importance in the everyday lives of young men. Instead, male relationships often continue to be defined by their simplicity in much of the research literature, lacking nuanced and dynamic perspectives. Equally important, there is very little cultural dialogue about the degree to which men's friendships have changed. Instead, there seems to be increasing antipathy for men and their masculinity (Kimmel and Wade 2018). It is only now that toxic masculinity is rare, that we have devised the concept of toxic masculinity. Prior to the current epoch, it was just, masculinity.

Our approach in this book is to examine how bromances operate to strengthen men's friendships. To accomplish this, we provide a coherent and comprehensive assessment of how these relationships strengthen male relations through the adoption of traditionally feminine friendship traits. These include physical elements, too. Thus, we detail extensive semi-sexual acts among men in bromances: kissing, cuddling, and loving are most often part of the package (Anderson and McCormack 2015; Anderson et al. 2019).

These nuances in male intimacy can then be assessed for their intersecting relationship with wider cultural issues, such as decreasing male power in society as women progress at pace toward equality (Rotolo and Wharton 2004).

In its broadest sense, this research is concerned with thoroughly documenting and examining the way in which young men experience and play out their masculine identities, and same-sex friendships. It is concerned with promoting men's intimacy as today being on par with women's intimacy. That is what this research and scores of related research tell us about adolescent masculinity in the early twenty-first century. Politically, we want other men to feel comfortable to engage in such intimacy, in the knowledge that it is a legitimated practice among contemporary men.

Research Methodology

This research is concerned with thoroughly documenting and examining the way in which young men experience and play out their masculine identities, and homosocial relationships, within the context of a university sports team. Based on a year-long observational study of a university society sports team, in which the first author, Stefan Robinson, was an active participant, training, competing, and attending student parties, it explores the shifting nature of homosocial boundaries within a masculine peer group.

Specifically, the study focusses on the ways in which young men invoke physical tactility, emotional disclosure, and sporting comradery to facilitate and pioneer closer, more intimate, and more loving same-sex friendships than previously experienced in the late twentieth and even the early twenty-first century.

This research is primarily based on observational data collected from a university society sports team, totaling approximately 600 hours. The research setting included training sessions, inter-university matches, weekly social events, dinners, lunches, evenings in town, and a weeklong team holiday.

Supplementing the primary source of enquiry, this project combines the use of semi-structured interviews with 20 male participants in the team to unearth how they understood, experienced, and validated the behaviors that were observed over the course of the year. Subsequent analysis examines the ways in which the men understand and experience love, sexuality, and bromances in their peer relations.

The project had university ethics approval. All participants knew that the primary author was researching. They had the right to have removed any descriptions of their observed behaviors, and if interviewed, their written word. None did. Also, all quoted speech is verbatim with exception of fixing errors. Some quoted speech comes directly from interviews, and others from researcher notes. These notes were taken in situ with help of a mobile phone.

All participants names have been changed to pseudonyms and we have waited three years from the data collection to assure that all participants are no longer at this university. The original dissertation was embargoed to protect the anonymity of the participants, too.

The Dodgeball Profile

Teamsport athletes have been traditionally thought to be the emblems of masculinity (Anderson 2005). It is our methodological reasoning that if we can show that physically brave men, who are willing to take masculine risks with their bodies in the name of sport, are willing to be emotionally vulnerable, we can perhaps better generalize that: men who are not partaking in such masculine endeavors are more inclusive in their masculinity, too.

Accordingly, a great deal of research has examined rugby, soccer, American football, and other athletes in highly masculinized sports. Anderson's (2014) book, *21st Century Jocks,* details dozens of them. Anderson has suggested that inclusive masculinities have been forged by teamsport athletes with high masculine capital. His theorizing holds that, because teamsport athletes of the 1980s and 1990s were so endowed with heterosexual capital, they had liberty to break heterosexual social strictures of gendered behaviors first. In other words, the very masculinity which helped fuel homophobia among teamsport athletes in the 1980s and 1990s was responsible for undoing that homophobia, and thus that masculinity.

Supporting Anderson's claims, research shows that teamsport athletes today have the same rates of acceptance of male homosexuality as non-athletes (Anderson et al. 2016; Roberts et al. 2017). Concluding a decade of longitudinal study on incoming university athletes and their attitudes toward homosexuality, Magrath et al. (2021), show rates of antipathy remain constant, exceptionally low, on a standardized instrument of homophobia. Backing this up, the second author of this book, Eric Anderson, along with the help of Outsports.com have shown that, among 1000 coming out experiences of openly gay, lesbian, bisexual, and transgender high school and university athletes in North America, 5% have had a bad experience (Outsports 2021).

Regardless of athletic status, young men are engaging in more affectionate, emotional, and physical relationships with their same-sex friends (Anderson and McCormack 2015; McCormack 2012; Scoats 2017). Anderson (2009) explains that young men today are now "rapidly running from the hegemonic type of masculinity that has been privileged for the past twenty-five years" (p. 115).

Dodgeball, the sport under investigation in this book, is a relatively new sport in the United Kingdom, with its first governing body, the United Kingdom Dodgeball Association (UKDBA), being founded in 2005 (now British Dodgeball). The sport has been popular in American institutions of education as a method of physical education but has received some criticism for facilitating bullying in the classroom because people would consistently throw balls at the same person (Fagogenis 2010).

At the turn of the century, the sport was phased out of some schools in America for this reason. However, the highly successful comedy movie *Dodgeball: A true underdog story*, which came out in 2004, starring Ben Stiller and Vince Vaughn, popularized the sport, with Naveed et al. (2013) describing the sport as a craze being taken up by younger people.

What likely facilitated the uptake of participation is the way the movie portrayed the sport. The movie's premise is about a random assortment of socially awkward people partaking in a dodgeball tournament against the most elite of athletes. Their team was aptly named "Average Joes" which illustrates the inclusive nature of the sport as depicted in the film. The UKDBA similarly championed inclusion, stating on their website:

> Through education and training, support and expertise we aim to ensure there is an excellent participation environment for players at schools, colleges, universities and clubs in the community. We believe that dodgeball is an extremely inclusive sport and that it creates an opportunity for all sporting abilities.
>
> At the UKDBA we are committed to Dodgeball as a 'Sport for All'. That is why we are working closely with experts in the field to develop new opportunities for Dodgeball to be played by young people and adults with disabilities.

The majority of open and league competitions that take place in the United Kingdom are dominated by either university teams, or people that have recently graduated from university. There are few community and school teams who have not been through the university system. The majority of players in the United Kingdom are between 18 and 30 years of age.

At the university where this research took place, dodgeball was often referred to as the largest sports club, although this is unverified it rings true to us. It is evident that compared to many mainstream sports that operate closed academy structures (Manley et al. 2012), there is opportunity for competitive participation in dodgeball by people of varying abilities. It is also mixed sex for training, and some competitions.

Key to this research, dodgeball players do not seem to be endowed with the same masculine script that rugby or football players—though many of them were also part of the university's football team. The very fact that they train with women, combined with the fact that movies portray dodgeball players as being geeky, highlights that this is not a masculine enterprise in the same way as boxing or rugby. This therefore makes dodgeball a unique team to study for the same types of behaviors that are found among players on more masculine teams because, essentially, we are looking to see if the same behaviors present in masculinized team sports are also present in geeky teamsport. In finding identical friendship patterns and masculinity preferences, it shows the extent of the liberalizing project of changing masculinity and its resultant impact on adolescent friendship more thoroughly.

The university dodgeball club observed constituted of 21 men and 16 women, as observed at the end of the 2015/2016 academic year. The structure of the dodgeball team incorporated the following at the end of the 2015/2016 academic year:

1. Social members—those who train for participation and attend team socials, but do not compete for a team, except when filling in for absences (6 members).
2. Competitive members—the majority of team members who are involved in inter-university competition and are a member of one of the five teams: men's 1st, 2nd and 3rd, women's 1st and 2nd. These teams incorporate a range of abilities from first time athletes to first team players (26 members).
3. Elite members—those in international teams (5 members).

As outlined, there was a broad range of participation abilities within the team. Training sessions were a mix of entirely gender and ability integrated, and team separated sessions, dependent on the competitive calendar (competitive teams would train against one another in the week prior to a competition). Training sessions occurred twice a week, with at least one day being a completely integrated training session of social, competitive, and elite members of both genders. Training usually totaled five hours per week. Inter-university competitions occurred roughly once a month for all competitive teams, and all members took part in two charity tournaments.

The year concluded with a weeklong holiday abroad for most of the team. This popular trip, named "Tour" involved a 26-hour bus and booze-drinking journey to Spain, where other university sports teams would also meet for a week of sports, drinking, and partying. Fancy dress (costumes) and dares were common activities, but the trip was largely unstructured and the activities entirely organic. Some of the data in this study were collected from this environment, too.

Situating the Researchers

In order to understand how this study emerged, it is important to understand the relationship between the authors. Stefan Robinson is the primary author of this book. He conducted his PhD, in England, under the supervision of Professor Eric Anderson. However, that is not where the two met.

Eric Anderson was an academic at the University of Bath, England between the years 2005 and 2010. It is during this time that he found data about males in his ethnographic, interview, and quantitative data that showed men at his university behaving in ways not previously found in modern times. Specifically, he taught on a Coaching Education degree, which brought in about 60 students a year (half male) from a variety of sporting backgrounds. He conducted his research on these students, and found heterosexual men being: (1) very gay friendly and inclusive; (2) expressing physical tactility and even kissing with each other; and (3) declaring themselves to having bromances. He formulated Inclusive Masculinity Theory (2009) based on this data.

Stefan was one of Eric's undergraduate students at the time. He was not, however, part of Eric's studies. Years later, he was in a gym when he recognized his old lecturer. The two began talking and Stefan informed Eric that his experiences in the university rowing team, one that he was captain of, showed little of this intimacy. Eric was fascinated and wondered what was so different about Stefan's experience at university that prohibited male intimacy from occurring the way he found it occurring among other students. A PhD was born.

Stefan, not much older than undergraduates now, returned to do his PhD with Eric a few years later. He was dubious that he would find what Anderson says he found earlier at Bath University. He chose dodgeball as an alternative to some of the traditionally mainstream sports, as he was more interested in the social elements of sport. Many other former sportsmen and women joined for the same reasons, and it quickly became an obvious place to conduct ethnography on male athletes.

Stefan found a whole lot of bromances occurring in his study.

References

Anderson, E. (2005). *In the game: Gay athletes and the cult of masculinity.* New York: University of New York Press.

Anderson, E. (2008a). Inclusive masculinity in a fraternal setting. *Men and Masculinities, 10*(5), 604–620.

Anderson, E. (2008b). "Being masculine is not about who you sleep with…:" Heterosexual athletes contesting masculinity and the one-time rule of homosexuality. *Sex Roles, 58*(1–2), 104–115.

Anderson, E. (2009). *Inclusive masculinity: The changing nature of masculinities.* New York: Routledge.

Anderson, E. (2014). *21st century Jocks: Sporting men and contemporary heterosexuality.* New York: Macmillan.

Anderson, E., and Magrath, R. (2019). *Men and masculinities.* Routledge.

Anderson, E., and McCormack, M. (2015). Cuddling and Spooning Heteromasculinity and Homosocial Tactility among Student-athletes. *Men and Masculinities, 18*(2), 214–230.

Anderson, E., Magrath, R., and Bullingham, R. (2016). *Out in Sport: The Experiences of Openly Gay and Lesbian Athletes.* New York: Routledge.

Anderson, E., Ripley, M., and McCormack, M. (2019). A mixed-method study of same-sex kissing among college-attending heterosexual men in the US. *Sexuality and Culture, 23*(1), 26–44.

Chen, E. (2011). Caught in a bad bromance. *Texas Journal of Women and Law, 21*(2), 241–267.

DeAngelis, M. (2014). *Reading the Bromance: Homosocial relationships in film and television.* Detroit: Wayne State University Press.

Fagogenis, B. (2010). In defense of Dodgeball. *Physical and Health Education Journal, 76*(2), 32.

Frank, B. (1987). Hegemonic heterosexual masculinity. *Studies in Political Economy, 24*(1).

Ghaziani, A. (2010). The reinvention of heterosexuality. *Gay and Lesbian Review, 17*(3): 27–29.

Hammarén, S., and Johansson, T. (2014). Homosociality in between power and intimacy. *SAGE Open, 4*(1), 1–11.

Hruschka, D. (2010). Friendship: Development, ecology, and evolution of a relationship (Vol. 5). Berkeley: University of California Press.

Johnston, C., & Bradford, S. (2019). Alternative spaces of failure. Disabled 'bad boys' in in alternative further education provision. *Disability & Society, 34*(9–10), 1548–1572.

Keleher, A., and Smith, E. (2012). Growing support for gay and lesbian equality since 1990. *Journal of Homosexuality, 59*, 1307–1326.

Kimmel, M., and Wade, L. (2018). Ask a feminist: Michael Kimmel and Lisa Wade discuss toxic masculinity. *Signs: Journal of Women in Culture and Society, 44*(1), 233–254.

Lewis, D., Al-Shawaf, L., Russell., E., and Buss, D. (2015). Friends and happiness: An evolutionary perspective on friendship. *Friendship and Happiness*, 37.

Lewis, R. (1978). Emotional intimacy among men. *Journal of Social Research, 34*(1), 108–121.

Magrath, R. Batten, J. Anderson, E., and White, A. (2001). Five-year cohort study of White British Male student-athletes' attitudes toward gay men. *Journal for the Study of Sports and Athletes in Education.* https://doi.org/10.1080/19357397.2021.1989277.

Magrath, R., Batten, J., Anderson, E., and White, A. J. (2021). White. *Journal for the Study of Sports and Athletes in Education*, 1–15.

Manley, A., Palmer, C., and Roderick, M. (2012). Disciplinary power, the oligopticon and rhizomatic surveillance in elite sports academies. *Surveillance and Society, 10*(3/4), 303–319.

McCormack, M. (2012). *The declining significance of homophobia: How teenage boys are redefining masculinity and heterosexuality*. New York: Oxford University Press.

McCormack, M., and Savin-Williams, R. (2018). Young men's rationales for non-exclusive gay sexualities. *Culture, Health and Sexuality, 20*(8), 929–944.

Morman, M, Schrodt P, Tornes, M. (2013). Self-disclosure mediates the effects of gender orientation and homophobia on the relationship quality of male same-sex friendships. *Journal of Social and Personal Relationships, 30*(5), 582–605.

Naveed, M., Malal, J., Guisasola, I., and Dunn, A. (2013). Dodgeball: A true sporting story! A typical presentation of an osteochondroma of the scapula. *European Orthopaedics and Traumatology, 4*(3), 183–185.

Outsports. (2021). https://www.outsports.com/out-gay-athletes/2021/10/4/22706376/out-in-sports-study-lgbtq-athletes-high-school-college-acceptance. October 4th, 2021.

Plummer, D. (1999). *One of the boys: Masculinity, homophobia, and modern manhood*. New York: Routledge.

Poplawski, P. (1989). *Psychological and qualitative dimensions of friendship among men: An examination of intimacy, sex-role, loneliness, control and the friendship experience*. PhD diss. Temple University.

Ralph, B., and Roberts, S. (2020). One small step for man: Change and continuity in perceptions and enactments of homosocial intimacy among young Australian men. *Men and Masculinities, 23*(1), 83–103.

Rich, A. (1980). Compulsory heterosexuality and lesbian existence. *Signs, 5*(4), 631–660.

Roberts, S., Anderson, E., & Magrath, R. (2017). Continuity, change and complexity in the performance of masculinity among elite young footballers in England. *The British Journal of Sociology, 68*(2), 336–357.

Robinson, S., Anderson, E., and White, A. (2018). The bromance: Undergraduate male friendships and the expansion of contemporary homosocial boundaries. *Sex Roles, 78*(1–2), 94–106.

Rotolo, T., and Wharton, A. (2004). Living across institutions: Exploring sex-based homophily in occupations and voluntary groups. *Sociological Perspectives, 46*(1), 59–82.

Savin-Williams, R. C. (2017). *Mostly straight: Sexual fluidity among men*. Harvard University Press.

Scoats, R. (2017). Inclusive masculinity and Facebook photographs among early emerging adults at a British university. *Journal of Adolescent Research, 32*(3), 323–345.

Seiden, A., and Bart, P. (1975). Woman to woman: Is sisterhood powerful? In Glazer-Malbin, N. (Ed.), *Old family/New family*. New York: Van Nostrand. Pp. 189–228.

Van Duijn, M., Evelien, A., Zeggelink, P., Huisman M., Stokman, F., and Wasseur, F. (2003). Evolution of sociology freshmen into a friendship network. *Journal of Mathematical Sociology, 27*(2–3), 153–191.

Way, N. (2011). *Deep secrets*. Illinois: Harvard University Press.

Way, N. (2013). Boys' friendships during adolescence: Intimacy, desire, and loss. *Journal of Research on Adolescence, 23*(2), 201–213.

2

Friendship

Sociological Perspectives on Friendship

Friendship is normally defined as the exchange of long-term mutual support, loyalty, and positive emotions between two people. This is perhaps a durable understanding. Aristotle's perspective (350BC), for example, was reflective of the modern interpretation, writing in 350 BC "to be friends, then, they must be mutually recognized as bearing goodwill and wishing well to each other (MacLean 2016, p. 2)."

In this capacity, friendship is not altogether different from what it means to be in a familial relationship, like a brother or sister. Friendships, though, are not sanctioned by law (O'Connor 1998). Instead, friendships are sanctioned socially and freely chosen.

The lack of legal recognition of friendship has advantages. It provides people with the ability to choose and unfriend their friends. One cannot, after all, choose their biological family. People can therefore select certain friends that fulfill certain psychological or social needs, something Weston shows that gay and lesbian people used to do considering homophobic family members (1997). The point is, with biological family members, you get what you get; with friendships you get what you choose and make.

We understand that friendship is more complex than that. Friendships are not purely choice alone. They are the result of socialized, and sometimes compelled by parents, coaches, or bosses. Similarly, families are more complex than we portray. But we think the idea of family being not of choice, and friendship being of choice, illustrates important differences that are mostly true.

The ability to select and deselect friends is perhaps the greatest strength of this type of relationship. If genuine affection is not retained, by both or multiple parties in the friendship, it is relatively easy to leave. There are no formal requirements to remain friends, and friendships often easily dissolve once people move away or are no longer structured together for other reasons.

In his book, *Kinship and Friendship in Modern Britain* (1996), after studying modern perspectives on informal relationships, Graham Allan suggests that kinship solidarities are increasingly complex in modern Britain. He suggests that there are multiple types of friendships, each with varying obligations and commitments. Above all, and consistent with our thesis, is that Allan views of kinship and friendship as economic exchange.

Friendships are thus formed and preserved mostly through indications of goodwill between the members—reciprocity. This is to say that each member must derive something beneficial to them for it to continue. The exchange may be emotional support for emotional support, or emotional support for financial or other material benefits, or laughter, or any number of things that make people happy. But if the exchange ceases to be viewed as beneficial to one of the members in the dyad, it will begin a process of gradual or rapid termination. In this sense, friendships are equivalent to a month-to-month lease, whereas having children is a form of love that is like taking out a mortgage. Yes, there are still some ways out of a mortgage, but they come with serious costs. Not renewing a lease is far easier. All of this is to say that friendships operate off the principle of reciprocity (Ezzy 1998). Enough reciprocity, over a long enough period of time, results in an enduring friendship that is somewhat balanced in the give and the take.

Trivers (1971) argues that the exchange of social support, gifts, and positive emotions are reciprocally altruistic behaviors in friendships. Other scholars have deformalized this to be a model of "tit-for-tat" accounting (Axelrod and Hamilton 1981). This is to say that if one member of the friendship determines an imbalance exists between what is given and what is received from a friend, they are likely to end the friendship.

These currencies are not easily measured. Emotional support represents an exchange that is subjective (Hruschka 2010). Moreover, this tit-for-tat idea of friendship does not account for feelings of happiness that many people experience when helping a friend, where people do not expect to be rewarded for their help (DeScioli and Kurzban 2009).

The point is that friendships are sustained only for as long as these behaviors continue or are perceived to continue. This condition might also exist among long-term friends that see each other rarely. The friendship will no longer be reliant upon frequency, but reciprocity must also exist. The temporal nature of friendships means that the mere existence of friends is a declaration of that friendship: it serves as evidence of affection in a way that the declaration of spouse does not. After all, romantic relationships may often continue out of structural necessity, even if the two partners dislike each other.

Although lacking legal status, friendship formations are culturally celebrated. There have been, and continue to be, myriad ways in which friends publicly or privately indicate their commitment to one another. For example, mutual blood-letting rituals were conducted between Zambian farmers in the nineteenth century as a means for the affirmation of friendship (Wood 1868); legally binding contractual ceremonies were held in fifteenth-century France (Tulchin 2007); and today the publishing of physically intimate photographs on Facebook serve as a public declaration of friendship (Scoats 2017); as does listing a best male friend as "brother" on social media.

Principally, research on women's friendships shows that, traditionally, they offered a safer space for confiding and a safer place of social security. They functioned with less judgment, have traditionally had less boundaries, and an increased capacity to resolve conflicts constructively. These types of friendships provided emotional support in times of need; friends would listen and give advice with fewer vested interests than family members. However, this is not to suggest that this is a simple binary. Women's friendships can also be fraught with in-group/out-grouping, secrecy, issues of popularity and bullying (Hey 1997).

Geoffrey Greif's (2008) leading research identifies that men have a lot to learn from the positive aspects of women's friendships and how they operate. His profiling of men across all age groups unpacks the importance of close male friendships, and men's aspirations to emulate and regain many of the positive characteristics traditionally associated with women's friendships, such as intimacy and disclosure. This critical work provides a detailed account of how a cultural shift in male friendships is enabling happier and healthier living among men across all generations.

The evidence of the benefit of friendships is also found in the consequences of not having friends. People are social creatures. We require friendship for our psychological health. When people are not able to have these important social exchanges, this disrupts one's ability to negotiate social situations, which can lead to isolation, individual economic ruin, depression, and even neuropsychiatric disorders (Baron and Markman 2003).

None of this is to suggest that friendships are monolithic. One can certainly have more and less valued friends. The general principle here is that the more important a friendship is, the more resource intensive it is: particularly in the early phases of that friendship. As the close friendship matures, it may continue without as much effort, and with less balance in reciprocity. Close friendships offer the individuals a form of insurance, in times of need. Requena (1995) maintains that:

> Compared to acquaintances, close friends are more likely to be responsive to one's troubles, to sense the nature, degree, and source of one's distress, and to engage in supportive behavior that is appropriate to one's needs, even if costly in time or effort. (p. 272)

Some argue that in long-standing, close friendships, the "norm of reciprocity" is less monitored. Boster et al. (1995) showed that close friends have a complete absence of expectation to reciprocate material rewards. Indeed, when people are asked about their close friendships, they almost always deny that they are based on measured exchanges (Silk 2003; Xue and Silk 2012). We are suspicious of this supposition, however. It sounds more virtuous to signal that one is in friendship for the give and not the take: if it's all given, for years on end, we doubt the friendship would survive.

Because close friends generally require a significant outlay of time and emotional investment from both people involved (Lewis et al. 2015), the commitment required to achieve these *good* friendships will inevitably limit the number of friends one can have. Hays (1984) suggests that we are limited to the number of close friends we can maintain relationships with; and that those we cannot are relegated to casual friendships. These occur more through mutual liking rather than reciprocity. When we feel an affinity for someone, we are more likely to consider them a friend, even if we have not labored for them.

Even these forms of casual friendships are however limited. Research suggests that we are only able to keep about 200 people within our social lives (Hruschka 2010). Proof of this comes from examining the phone numbers in your smart phone and determining what percent you have spoken to in the previous year. The same can be said with Facebook friends. How many have you messaged in the last year? This research, among others, shows that the ability to establish and maintain friendships has come about from some relatively simplistic evolutionary processes.

Evolutionary Perspectives on Friendship

The study of friendship has appealed to a cross section of scholars, from anthropologists and gender scholars to evolutionary psychologists. Each academic discipline brings its own perspective on the developmental purpose and processes of the relationship. This section considers the impact that friendship and cooperation has had on the structuring of society, and the impact society has had on the structure of friendships. In other words, we examine why friendship is important not just to the individuals involved, but to society as a whole.

The approach that evolutionary psychologists take in understanding the origins of friendships is to examine how the personal desire and social need to form friendships comes about from survival needs. Lewis and colleagues (2015) write:

> Friendships were almost certainly recurrently linked to survival and reproduction during human evolutionary history... An evolutionary perspective can offer insight into how specific types of friendship would have benefitted ancestral humans in both the currency of natural selection—reproductive success—and the currency of subjective wellbeing, happiness. (p. 1)

Friendships provided our ancestors with the ability to cooperate, form allegiances, and have allies. Its evolution enabled humans to develop complex social support networks that positively facilitate feelings of motivation and happiness (Cosmides and Tooby 2000); feelings that lead to increased self-satisfaction and reciprocate similar feelings to others (Hruschka 2010).

These effects of friendship are seen in other species, too. Baboons maintain tactile relationships which have a positive impact on their wellbeing (Silk et al. 2010). Ryan and Jethá (2010) note that bonobos engage in hand holding and kissing as a sign of affection and social security, among other primates, reflecting the customs of human interaction. Various species of birds have been shown to have complex communication networks, with specific calls being used as a way of identifying danger, and others to identify friends (Williams 1966; Boeckle and Bugnyar 2012). Those who live in a socially active society, but do not possess the ability and social awareness to collaborate in friendships, risk being excluded; a process that Darwin (1871) defined as natural selection.

Nowak (2006) explains that "evolution is based on a fierce competition between individuals and should therefore reward only selfish behavior" (p. 1560). An example of Nowak's thinking can be seen through analyzing human friendships, too.

Humans have such an advanced and reflexive understanding of their friendships, that they can often fake them, for the sake of maintaining other, more superior and self-rewarding relationships (Hruschka 2010).

Trivers (1971) explains that friendships in modern society operate from the same principles of ancient human cultures. In the hunter-gatherer context, a diversity of talents promoted the tribe's overall wellbeing. One person may be the best maker of a tool, and another may be the best user of that tool; and the best hunter may not be the best at cooking the meal. Buss (2004) and Hill and Hurtado (1996) both highlight that teamwork and cooperation are required to hunt large game animals, that would otherwise be too dangerous for humans to pursue on their own.

This act of hunting provides a grounding narrative for the development of friendship: The shared success of slaughtering large game will be highly rewarding. They will share the meal with those who made the tools to kill the animal and those who cooked the meat; and then they will sit together in a shared shelter to eat. Perhaps they will tell stories, share knowledge, and impart wisdom to one another.

Over the expanse of human history, individuals have collectivized into units of civilization. This occurs through a vast web of exchanges and alliances made through complex social networks over time, which in some unique instances has led to the formation of vast empires. We employ economists to administrate our exchanges, enforcers to reprimand those who exchange unequally, and educators to teach specialist talents.

All of this is to say that a network of friends can benefit individuals and all those in the network. You might call this kinship. Kinship is particularly important in a society that does not have money for which to exchange for goods and services. With the invention of money, however, people need smaller kinship networks: they can use money to purchase what they need. With money, one can buy goods and services, including services that are biological in how they make people feel better, like sex workers or massage. With money, one can even purchase people who will listen to you and make you feel validated for your feelings. We call them psychologists.

In a modern context, and with the infusion of the complexities of money, friendships help with contemporary problem solving, whilst saving money: like asking a friend for help in how to use a computer program instead of hiring a guy to do that. Modern friendships help teams succeed, whether they be in sport or business. Whereas emotional needs, like disclosure, may be best fulfilled by close friends, the importance of casual friendships helps in daily matters.

Some scholars, and particularly some sociologists (e.g., Putnam 2000), argue that kinship networks are becoming more complicated as a result of modernity. Putnam argues that, today, we no longer live within tight kinship networks and that this has promoted a loss of a sense of community. He uses quantitative data to show that people are less organized around civic duties, and social clubs than ever before. Conversely, others, like Spencer and Pahl (2006) suggest that all we are seeing is a change in the way friendship networks operate. Digital communities complicate this. One might, today, feel affinity for an individual who one has never met in person.

Online Friendship

A modern understanding of friendship necessitates the inclusion of online and offline friendships: friendship has changed in the digital age. Offline friendships are what we principally refer to in this monograph. We are concerned with the material realities of how they grow and manifest in face-to-face interactions, individually and within groups. This is not to diminish online friendships: they, too, have value.

In a study comparing the two (Chan and Cheng 2004) show that offline friendships involve more interdependence, breadth, depth, code change, understanding, commitment, and network convergence than exclusively online friendships. Conversely, online friendships are found to be more conducive of cross-sex friendships than offline. Chan and Cheng show that qualities of cross-sex online friendships were higher than that of same-sex online friendship.

For purposes of this research, we highlight that we report upon friendships that exist offline. This does not also preclude them from existing online, but it is to say we were interested in studying traditional friendship with this research.

Defining Love

What is not discussed in the friendship literature much, however, is the role that the interjection of love into a friendship has. Anderson (2014) has shown that youth today frequently express their homosocial love for their male friends. This opens questions about what love is, how it may or may not manifest differently in sexual versus non-sexual relationships, and what impact love has on the value of reciprocity.

Defining social phenomena is always a difficult task. Unlike the natural sciences, where things can often be measured and discretely described, social matters are often invisible. We develop surveys and questionnaires in attempt to understand them, but these are not exact, open to opinion, and constantly change. Perhaps one of the most difficult social matters to define is love. Part of this difficulty stems from the fact that it exists as a relatively unmeasurable emotion or set of emotions that vary in intensity and longevity; and that vary from individual to individual. Part of this difficulty is because there will be/are so many types of love. Finally, love, like friendship is both conditional and transient.

The ancient Greeks helped to classify the complexity of love. These categorizations are crude, but helpful. They spoke of four types of love: *philía*, *éros*, *agape*, and *storgē*. Although the precise meanings are hard to interpret because these terms are contextualized according to our current culture, the basic notion is that *philía* refers to the love of a friend; *éros* refers to sexual passion; *agape* refers to the romantic love of one's partner; and *storgē* refers to the love of a child or life partner. This framework of love has somewhat stood the test of time, being referenced throughout modern literature (Osborne 1994; Anderson 2012).

Helen Fisher (2004), one of the foremost contemporary scholars in the study of love, argues that feelings of love are innate and that they have a role in facilitating long-term attachments such as friendships and romances. Like the ancient Greeks, she chooses to deconstruct love into three separate categories: Lust, Romantic Love, and Companionate Love.

Companionate love, Hruschka (2010) suggests, can also be interpreted as a friend-like love. In this section, contemporary conceptions of love are considered and contrasted against the characteristics of close friendship. We examine to what extent our understanding of love and friendship are different or similar, and what can be learned from each concept to comprehend the other.

Many scholars identify sexual desire in their descriptions of love (Fisher 2004; Sternberg 1986; Regan 2004). The desire for sexual gratification is perhaps the simplest to explain, at least in terms of its evolutionary origins. It is uniquely uncontested as a drive that is premised on the need to reproduce with an appropriate mate (Ryan and Jethá 2010). Ryan and Jethá (2010) explain, "Like bonobos and chimps, we are the randy descendants of hypersexual ancestors" (p. 1). We are shamelessly, undeniably, inescapably sexual (p. 46)." This desire for sex, can and does exist independent of love, or even liking; it is perfectly normal to want to have sex with someone whom you do not even know. However, "romantic love" refers to a combination of sex with affinity for the person sex is engaged with.

Romantic love is perhaps the most widely recognized version of love, being that it is propagated by an array of Hollywood films and romantic novels (Goldmeier and Richardson 2005). These cultural arenas, along with the wider media, have circulated a glorified and idealistic vision of romantic love (Fisher 2004) which is often premised on the understanding that sexual desire and love are intricately and mutually dependent on one another. Anderson (2012) agrees that popular culture excessively conflates sex with romantic love, highlighting that the narrative of the film *Titanic* epitomizes this transgression.

If romantic love is to be understood as dependent on sexual desire, then romantic relationships would not last long. This is because it is a long-standing sexological finding that sexual frequency and enjoyment diminishes among monogamous couples (Anderson 2012).

After the initial excitement and novelty of a new relationships, known as the "honeymoon period," sexual desire rapidly diminishes after one to two years (Fisher 2004; Schwartz and Young 2009; Anderson 2012; Ryan and Jethá 2010). Fisher (2004) therefore has a more holistic view of romantic love. She suggests that its presence is defined by one disrupting their habits for another, investing their wellbeing in another, and being involved in another's interests and social networks.

This is not at all dissimilar to our understanding of close friendships, being that both concepts involve interdependence, self-sacrifice, and shared interests (Hruschka 2010). In his research into monogamy and cheating, Anderson (2012) also offers a description of romantic love that challenges popular understandings of love-related sexual desire. He explains that a romance occurs between:

> Two consenting adolescence/adults, in which goods, services, emotions and needs are exchanged and met… it normally occurs with sexual activity, at least in the onset, but sexual activity is not required and quite often, long term romantic love – the type that lasts into old age… lacks a sexual component at all. (p. 54)

Here, most importantly, Anderson presents the notion that sexual desire is a temporary variable in a romantic relationship. Tennov (1979) similarly conducted a study on US men and women, asking them if there was "any need for sex" in their romantic relationships. Results showed that 61% of women and 35% of men said no. Furthermore, researchers conclude that deep infatuations and intimacies can occur in romantic relationships without the existence of sexual desire (Diamond 2000; 2003). Ryan and Jethá (2010) go as far to express that the desire for sex, and the experience of love, "are as different from each other as red wine and blue cheese… they get conflated with amazing, dumbfounded regularity" (p. 113). Indeed, Anderson (2014) points out that in the twenty-first century, love and sex are progressively being understood as separate constructs, owing to our gradual but increasing divorce from religiosity, our enhanced sense of self-liberty, the advancement of birth control, and the achievements of feminism.

Love Without Sex

This raises the question that, without sexual desire, what can definitively distinguish a romantic relationship from a close friendship, given that their characteristics are unarguably reflective of one another? The answer lies in the way culture perceives and represents the relationships, rather than in the way they are enacted. In other words, we argue that the difference between love of a close friend and love for a partner/spouse may be experienced the same by the individual involved but be interpreted different by others. The difference is thus social.

Friendships and relationships are separated and distinguished from one another principally through structural, legal, and cultural boundaries (such as marriage and housing arrangements); but the emotional and behavioral requisites of both reflect one another (Pahl 2000). It is therefore not surprising to note that, owing to the interrelated components of romantic relationships and friendships, it is very common for men and women in contemporary Anglo-American societies to refer to their romantic partners as their best friend (Pahl and Pevalin 2005). Hruschka (2010) appropriately supports the view that close friends are romantic partners operate relatively parallel to one another; "It seems that romantic partners are often more friend-like, in terms of feelings and behavior, than are one's closest friends (p. 115)."

Savin-Williams (2014) shows that young men today are versed at understanding that a romantic orientation is different than a sexual orientation. Simply put, some heterosexual men may find that they have better emotional joy and deep affection for another male, than for females. This does not mean that they sexually desire men. It is this ability to distinguish romance from sexual desire which he argues has fueled men's increasing adoption of describing themselves as "mostly" heterosexual, instead of exclusively. Savin-Williams (2014) and McCormack (2018), and Anderson and Magrath (2019) all suggest that the concept of heterosexuality itself is no longer in reference strictly to sexual desires.

We know that the term heterosexuality makes this confusing—after all it ends in "sexuality." Yet, what young men say in studies is that sexuality is more complicated than sexual desires alone. They thus say that sexual desires and romantic desires are different, and that, traditionally, heterosexuality coupled them. Hence, there is growing resistance to the use of the term. This resistance appears in young men complicating it with the term "mostly."

This is not to say that sexual desire/s do/does not assist in the development of romantic relationships. Indeed, sexual relationships have important social functions, extending beyond the need for physical gratification and reproduction (Ryan and Jethá 2010). However, it remains that traits associated within a romantic relationship, such as jealousy, physical touch, separation anxiety, and preoccupation, are all reflected in the emotional and behavioral dimensions of close friendship.

In the absence of sexual desire, Rotundo (1989) appropriately conceptualizes these relationships as "romantic friendships." Diamond (2003) and Fisher (1998) substantiate this view, explaining that the human hormonal system permits bonding without the need for sex, and sex without the need for bonding. Hruschka (2010) comprehensively broadens our perspective on the way in which romantic relationships and friendships become conflated:

> One can have a romantic relationship with no friendship, in which one is obsessed with a partner but lacks any degree of goodwill toward him or her. It is also possible to have a purely sexual relationship without romantic interest or the goodwill of friendship. At the same time, sexual and romantic relationships can come to include friend-like feelings and behaviors, and friendship can unfold into sexual or romantic interests. More research is necessary on the topic, but it may even be possible to have "romantic friendships," which involve intense devotion to (and jealousy over) a partner but lack sexual desire or activity. (p. 120)

In the case of romantic and lustful love, most scholars offer the view that successful relationships (defined by longevity), which are initially characterized by romance and sexual desire, eventually transform into a more settled and less obsessive state of love, characterized by long-term commitment, companionship, intimacy and life sharing (Ryan and Jethá 2010; Anderson 2012; Fisher 2004, 2006). This *philía* type of love plays an important role in long-term relationship stability, representing "a wider and more embracing love" (Nelson 1988, p. 54) which permits more diverse means of affection giving beyond sexual and material exchange.

This is not to say that sex is unlikely to be part of a long-term relationship, but that the feelings of love for one another are progressively based on mutual compatibility and companionship, and not sex or sexual desire. The chronology of this shift in experiencing love types is perhaps best exemplified by the honeymoon period of a relationship, moving into a state of marriage. Hruschka (2010) suggests that "there is sufficient evidence in the research that those not attracted to each other in a sexual or romantic capacity, can bypass this [honeymoon period] and transgress directly to companionate love; the type of love displayed by long-term close friends (p. 112)."

We think that the findings of our research, the existence of the bromance, support the idea that love of a close friend can exist in the same perspective and intensity, as love for a sexual partner or spouse. This reality contravenes the traditionally narrow cultural discourse that presents love as being achievable only within the confines of heterosexual, romantic, and sexual relationships.

Critically, for our research into the bromance, the exploration of love raises a key question in the pursuit of understanding friendships and bromances: if romantic and companionate love can exist between two people without sexual desire, then can it exist without discrimination toward gender and sexuality? Can it exist between two heterosexual men or women? We believe our results show that it does. We are not alone in suggesting this, either.

Chapter Conclusion

This chapter sought to provide the groundwork for understanding what friendship is: how it is created, maintained, and terminated. We examined this mostly through the exchange of material, economic, or socio-emotional goods; suggesting that both the psychological and sociological views of friendship highlight the importance of exchange.

Friendship is more than an advantage between two people, however. Sociologists, anthropologists, and evolutionary psychologists all agree that friendship patterns that are connected create kinship, community, and that communities can create shared values which can rise to the level of national culture.

Key to this research is that friendship and love are not easily disentangled, and because they are invisible social constructs, they are very difficult to measure. Of importance for our work is that friendship provides an exchange of goods, and that those goods can be emotional support. Men's friendships were once thought to lack in this, at least compared to women's friendships (Greif 2008). Our research will show this is no longer true. Broadly speaking, we suggest in this book that the friendships we describe as bromances, are more akin to what scholars would call love. Love need not be sexual.

References

Allan, G. (1996). *Kinship and friendship in Modern Britain.* Oxford: London.
Anderson, E. (2012). *The monogamy gap: Men, love, and the reality of cheating.* Oxford University Press
Anderson, E. (2014). *21st Century Jocks: Sporting Men and Contemporary Heterosexuality.* New York: Macmillan.
Anderson, E., and Magrath, R. (2019). *Men and masculinities.* Routledge.
Axelrod, R., and Hamilton, W. (1981). The evolution of cooperation. *Science, 211*(4489), 1390–1396.
Baron, R., and Markman, G. (2003). Beyond social capital: the role of entrepreneurs' social competence in their financial success. *J. Business Venturing, 18*(1), 41–60.
Boeckle, M., and Bugnyar, T. (2012). Long-term memory for affiliates in ravens. *Current Biology, 22*(9), 801–806.
Boster, F., Rodriguez, J., Cruz, M., and Marshall, L. (1995). The relative effectiveness of a direct request message and a pregiving message on friends and strangers. *Communication Research, 22*(4), 475–484.
Buss, D. (2004). *Evolutionary psychology: The new science of the mind (4th ed.).* Boston: Allyn and Bacon.
Chan, D. K. S., & Cheng, G. H. L. (2004). A comparison of offline and online friendship qualities at different stages of relationship development. *Journal of Social and Personal Relationships, 21*(3), 305–320.

Cosmides, L., and Tooby, J. (2000). Evolutionary psychology and the emotions. In Lewis, M., and Haviland-Jones, J (Ed.), *Handbook of emotions* (2nd ed.). New York: Guilford. Pp. 91–115.

Darwin, C. (1871). 2003. *The descent of man.* London: Gibson Square.

DeScioli, P., and Kurzban, R. (2009). The alliance hypothesis for human friendship. *PloS One, 4*(6), e5802.

Diamond, L. (2000). Passionate friendships among lesbian, bisexual and heterosexual women. *Journal of Research on Adolescence, 10*(2), 191–209.

Diamond, L. (2003). What does sexual orientation orient? A bio-behavioural model distinguishing romantic love and sexual desire. *Psychological Review, 110*(1), 173–192.

Ezzy, D. (1998). Theorizing narrative identity: Symbolic interactionism and hermeneutics. *The Sociological Quarterly, 39*(2), 239–252.

Fisher, H. (1998). Lust, attraction and attachment in mammalian reproduction. *Human Nature, 9*(1), 23–52

Fisher, H. (2004). *Why we love: The nature and chemistry of romantic love.* New York: Henry Holt and Company.

Fisher, H. (2006). The drive to love: The neural mechanism for mate selection. In Steinberg, R., and Weis, K. (Ed.), *The new psychology of love.* New Haven: Yale University Press. Pp. 87–115.

Goldmeier, D., and Richardson, D. (2005). Romantic love and sexually transmitted infection acquisition: Hypothesis and review. *International Journal of STD and AIDS, 16*(9), 585–587.

Greif, G. (2008). *Buddy system: Understanding male friendships.* Oxford University Press.

Hays, R. (1984). The development and maintenance of friendship. *Journal of Social and Personal Relationships, 1*(1), 75–98.

Hey, V. (1997). *The company she keeps: An ethnography of girls' friendships.* McGraw-Hill Education (UK).

Hill, K., and Hurtado, A. (1996). *Ache life history: The ecology and demography of a foraging people.* New York: Aldine De Gruyter.

Hruschka, D. (2010). Friendship: Development, ecology, and evolution of a relationship (Vol. 5). Berkeley: University of California Press.

Lewis, D., Al-Shawaf, L., Russell., E., and Buss, D. (2015). Friends and happiness: An evolutionary perspective on friendship. *Friendship and Happiness,* 37.

MacLean, S. (2016). Alcohol and the constitution of friendship for young adults. *Sociology, 50*(1), 93–108

McCormack, M. (2018). Mostly straights and the study of sexualities: An introduction to the special issue. *Sexualities, 21*(1–2), 3–15.

Nelson, J. (1988). *The intimate connection: Male sexuality, masculine spirituality.* Westminster: John Knox Press.

Nowak, M. (2006). Five rules for the evolution of cooperation. *Science, 314*(5805), 1560–1563.

O'Connor, P. (1998). Women's friendships in a post-modern world. In Adams, R., and Allan, G. (Ed.), *Placing friendship in context.* Cambridge: Cambridge University Press. Pp. 117–135.

Osborne, C. (1994). *Eros unveiled: Plato and the God of love.* Oxford: Clarendon Press.

Pahl, R (2000). *On friendship.* Oxford: Blackwell Publishing.

Pahl, R., and Pevalin, D. (2005). Between family and friends: A longitudinal study of friendship choice. *British Journal of Sociology, 56*(3), 433–450.

Putnam, R. D. (2000). *Bowling alone: America's declining social capital.* In *Culture and politics.* Palgrave Macmillan, New York. Pp. 223–234

Regan, P. (2004). Sex and the attraction process: Lessons from science (and Shakespeare) on lust, love, chastity, and fidelity. In Harvey, J., Wenzel, A., and Sprecher, S (Ed.), *The handbook of sexuality in close relationships.* New York: Psychology Press. Pp. 115–133.

Requena, F. (1995). Friendship and subjective well-being in Spain: A cross-national comparison with the United States. *Social Indicators Research, 35*(3), 271–288.

Rotundo, A. (1989). Romantic friendship: Male intimacy and middle-class youth in the northern United States, 1800–1900. *Journal of Social History, 23*(1), 1–25.

Ryan, C., and Jethá, C. (2010). Sex at dawn. *The Prehistoric Origins of Modern Sexuality.* New York.

Savin-Williams, R. C. (2014). An exploratory study of the categorical versus spectrum nature of sexual orientation. *The Journal of Sex Research, 51*(4), 446–453.

Schwartz, P., and Young, L. (2009). Sexual satisfaction in committed relationships. *Sexuality Research and Social Policy, 6*(1), 1–17.

Scoats, R. (2017). Inclusive masculinity and Facebook photographs among early emerging adults at a British university. *Journal of Adolescent Research, 32*(3), 323–345.

Silk, J. (2003). Cooperation without counting. In Hammerstein, P (Ed.), *Genetic and cultural evolution of cooperation.* MIT Press. Pp. 37–54.

Silk, J., Beehner, J., Bergman, T., Crockford, C., Engh, A., Moscovice, L., and Cheney, D. (2010). Strong and consistent social bonds enhance the longevity of female baboons. *Current Biology*, *20*(15), 1359–1361.

Spencer, L., and Pahl, R. (2006). *Rethinking friendship*: Hidden solidarities today. Princeton University Press.

Sternberg, R. J. (1986). A triangular theory of love. *Psychological Review*, *93*(2), 119.

Tennov, D. (1979). *Love and limerance: The experience of being in love in New York*. Stein and Day, New York.

Trivers, R. (1971). The evolution of reciprocal altruism. *The Quarterly Review of Biology*, *46*(1), 35–57.

Tulchin, A. (2007). Same-sex couples creating households in old regime France: The uses of the affrèrement. *The Journal of Modern History*, *79*(3), 613–647.

Weston, K. (1997). *Families we choose: Lesbians, gays, kinship*. Columbia University Press.

Williams, G. (1966). Adaptation and natural selection. *The American Naturalist*, *100*(916), 687–690.

Wood, J. (1868). *Natural history of man: Africa*. New York: George Routeledge and Sons.

Xue, M., and Silk, J. (2012). The role of tracking and tolerance in relationship among friends. *Evolution and Human Behaviour*. *33*(1), 17–25.

3

Homosociality

Homosociality

During much of the twentieth century, investigations of friendship have drawn attention to the different ways in which men and women experience and constitute their same-sex friendships. Research has consistently documented two primary differences in the way male and female same sex-friendships function. There has historically been a broad consensus among scholars that men's same-sex friendships are organized around "doing things" together and sharing activities (Vigil 2007). As Curry (2000) explains:

> Social scientists studying masculinity note that a male bond is an affiliation link, but one that is based on activity rather than the expression of emotion, that is, men typically relate to each other through participation in activities rather than through intimate self-disclosures. (p. 164)

Contrasting to the friendship through activity model, women have both historically, and continue to, emphasize their same-sex friendships through emotionality, verbal communication, and the disclosure of personal secrets. Wright (1998) has a simple way of stating this: men's friendships operate side by side, whilst women's friendships operate face-to-face.

One reason for the variance in how friendships operate between males and females concerns structural segregation (Fehr 1996). For example, since the second industrial revolution and the introduction of wage labor, men predominantly took up positions in factories, workhouses, and on the production line, because men were perceived to be more physically durable workers. Meanwhile, women were consequently assigned to the domestic realm as caregivers (Cancian 1990). This exaggerated cultural stereotype favored men as stoic (read masculine) and women as emotive (read feminine).

Another reason for the variance between how male and female friendships operate concerns culture. Male friendships have historically taken precedent over female friendships, being seen as more noble and important (Rotundo 1994). It should be noted however that the vast majority of historical accounts have been about men, transcribed by men, and thus unsurprisingly depict the male version as supreme (Bourdieu 2001).

One consequence of men's over-representation in these arenas is that male friendships are seen as more loyal, trusting, and gallant (Nardi 1992). After all, men fight for each other in war; they labor for each other in sport; and they value loyalty in business. In line with men's inclination to create and maintain friendships through sharing activities and labor, some research suggests that men are accordingly more prone to engage in cooperative activities (Benenson 2013). Whether they share experiences of hunting, sports, or the military, they are shared endeavors. This makes sense, as men's valued friendship activities require cooperation on mass in order to achieve shared outcomes.

Some scholars (Geary et al. 2003) suggest that because men are structured into and culturally socialized to prefer side-by-side, cooperative friendship styles, men learn to be more tolerant of non-reciprocity than women. Others argue that men's friendships are able to resolve conflict better than women's (Beneson 2013), because they tolerate friendship stress better.

The loyalty of men to each other in battle, should not however prevent us from examining the social benefits that occur from people valuing each other in peace. Thus, in the late twentieth century scholars began to examine women's friendships as a legitimate scholarly activity.

Today, the female preference for maintaining friendships through sharing emotions, intimacies, and secrets is thus very well documented and promoted in old and new media (Winstead and Griffin 2001). Benenson (2013) goes as far to say that this understanding of same-sex female friendships has been "ubiquitously accepted across the social sciences" (p. 184).

The preference for social bonds with members of the same sex is referred to as homosociality, and it is a widespread historical phenomenon of friendships (Lipman-Blumen 1976). To bring together a simple perspective on the extent to which sex affects friendship preference, Bell (1981) concludes, "there is no social factor more important than that of sex in leading to friendship variations" (p. 55).

The ordering of society and its institutions is structurally homosocial. Thomas (2019) uses a national survey to show that friendships are mostly homosocial, and that they first evolve in formal education, then into work and occupation, and then finally into social and civic clubs. This might, at first, sound like the likelihood of males befriending females is as good as befriending other males: most schools are gender integrated. However, sex-segregated sports teams will impact upon friendship dyads. Joseph and Anderson have shown that even though both boys and girls play sport, because they do so separately, it has an impact on homosociality in employment; one that benefits men (Joseph and Anderson 2016).

Occupational segregation also occurs without direct discrimination. Women, it appears, are more likely to end up working in certain occupations than men. Whether this is the product of socialization or biology, or both, is not important to understanding that certain occupations, nursing, early education, and childcare sectors are dominated by women as caregivers who work in small teams (Cancian 1990) and thus women are more likely to befriend women in these sectors. Men, on the other hand, fulfill more physical, cooperative, and larger group roles in general (Anderson and Magrath 2019).

Another way to examine this is to say that women are attracted to working with people, and men with things. This is an international finding, and the more luxury of money that a country has, the more likely the two sexes are to exhibit this pattern (Su et al. 2009). This is something that continues upto the present day, and something that is more of a robust finding in socialist countries whose living wage provides males and females the opportunity to pursue the types of careers they desire (Stoet and Geary 2021).

Perhaps most important for homosociality, Anderson (2009) highlights that by raising men and women differently through binary assumptions about gender from a young age, people learn to associate only with their own gender. Simply put, people acquire the skills needed to relate better to their own sex out of necessity. Therefore, it is common for people to prefer same-sex socialization because they are altogether more comfortable with it. Nowhere is this more salient than in the world of sport.

Homosociality as Dangerous

In some regards, men's social bonding is viewed through a negative lens. In modernity, this stems from the fact that, as Anderson (2009) writes, "men control politics, religion, education, entertainment, news etc." (p. 127); all institutions that possess the power to vilify or verify men as supreme.

Thus, in recent decades, men's friendships have been looked upon by academics and cultural critics as suspicious. Ralph and Roberts (2020b) show that they are typically described as negative (harming each other) or about power over women. In short, they are perceived as toxic. There is a clear genre of belief that male friendships are bad for women.

We do not substantially engage with this argument in this work, as we do not think it represents an intellectually honest approach to examining men's friendships. Still, we understand why some might view men this way: this is particularly true if we consider violence and sexual assault committed by men against women whilst in packs of athletes. There is no question, for example, that male teamsport athletes of sports like football and basketball commit more violence than male teamsport athletes of lesser masculinized sports.

Homosociality in Sporting Culture

The sports field has historically provided a space for exclusively male relations. It is where male coaches have taught boys how to be men. This has little changed in the contemporary setting of Anglo-American sports today: sport mostly remains gender segregated and boys are almost always coached by males (Anderson 2014). This continues until adult levels of sport, too.

Anderson (2009) shows how structural gender segregation in sport encourages a preference for homosocial bonding between men and the exclusion of women:

> Boys and men learn to bond, relate to each other, work and solve problems all without the presence of girls and/or women in sport. And, because sport is gender segregated, it means that women are excluded from the domain in which this language and way of relating is learned. Women therefore have a harder time acquiring the cultural codes and behavioral conducts deemed necessary to impress masculine gatekeepers. (Anderson 2009. p. 124)

The experience of sharing hardships, adversity, failure, and success in sport is said to be the defining features that make sporting friendships successful. Here, men are able to express their friendships through having a collective goal, focusing their attention on sports instead of focusing on one another's emotional needs (Winstead 1986). Hall (2011) adds that, "Men and boys are more likely to organize their social environments hierarchically, wherein competition between males, once resolved, results in a stable coalition structure" (p. 5). Nowhere is this structure best illustrated than in sport.

However, it has been noted that friendships among teammates become problematized when this balance is disrupted, when the sporting environment becomes increasingly competitive and elite (Magrath 2016). This is because elite athletes often find that they are dependent on their sporting identity for social and sometimes financial mobility (Anderson 2009). The increased pressure on elite athletes to succeed as individuals can cause intra-team rivalry and competition for the top spot on the team. For example, in a comparative study between participatory and elite football players, Magrath (2016) found that the incentive of a professional football contract for academy-level players had a detrimental impact on the willingness of teammates to express emotions to one another, or to express vulnerability.

It is possible that this external pressure operates much in the same way that children or mortgages do in romantic and familial relationships, manipulating displays of resentment, love, or altruism for the purposes of satisfying another interest. Thibaut and Kelley (1959) explain that by being vulnerable with someone, power is given to the confident to control the discloser's social standing. Therefore, when a contract is available to an elite athlete, they may be less willing to be vulnerable with teammates for fear that their candidness may be used against them. In his investigations of the sporting context, David Riesman (1953) called this hostile intra-team environment, Antagonistic Cooperation.

Opportunity to participate in sport is ever-present in contemporary Anglo-American societies. Relevant to this research, opportunity to partake in university sport is also high. Sports teams/clubs, both orthodox and new, are popular in England. The mix and availability of clubs can provide a safe haven in which people can meet people who share similar interests. Team sports are very popular for young men attending university because they afford men a space to engage in their preferred method of friendship building with other males, shared interests and activities.

In the university setting, young men have a prevailing desire to form deep and meaningful bonds with their peers premised on self-disclosure and intimacy (Collins and Sroufe 1999). This yearning for intimate friendship arises as they search for new avenues of nurturing, seeking independence from their parents and new people for advice and companionship. In this time of transition, the attention and devotion that young people formerly received from their parents is gradually replaced by romantic partners and friends as their favored choice for support and socialization (Berndt 2004).

For students wanting to join a club in England, they are likely to encounter what Americans call hazing and what the British call an initiation ceremony. Here, young men wishing to join a social club or sports team, are usually required to perform an embarrassing or humiliating act as a symbol of their entrance and social acceptance into the club (Nuwer 1999). This has been noted as sometimes excessively deviant, abusive, and homophobic (Bryshun and Young 2007).

The withstanding of this abusive treatment serves two purposes: firstly, as a means of proving one's toughness, stoicism, and commonality in front of the team. Secondly, to show sacrifice and loyalty to the team (Anderson 2010). The characteristics expected of men in these initiations are those expected of traditionally masculine men, demonstrating resilience both physically and emotionally. Those who do not pass or conform to hazing expectations are likely to be socially excluded and even bullied.

In university culture, these ceremonies have become highly symbolic of entry into sports clubs, and universities actively create policies to renounce hazing and sanction clubs. In Anderson et al. (2012) longitudinal study, they conclude that the two most common forms of hazing activity have traditionally been excessive alcohol consumption and same-sex sexual activities.

Excessive alcohol consumption usually contributes to the social conditions that permit certain deviant activities to occur, with many students reporting alcohol-related unconsciousness and sickness because of hazing (Allan and Madden 2008). Indeed, Peralta (2007) notes that the consumption of alcohol itself contributes to the image of masculinity, and its consumption is a common part of male bonding practices.

The use of same-sex shaming behaviors used to be a way of lowering initiates capital and sustaining masculine hierarchies within a club (Anderson et al. 2012). However, in more recent works, same-sex sexual behaviors are rapidly losing their embarrassment factor because of the more liberal sexual attitudes and behaviors are being esteemed among young men. This was supported by Anderson et al. (2012) seven-year study on undergraduate men at a British university which showed a progressive decline in the use of same-sex hazing as form of humiliation, with some participants voluntarily engaging in same-sex kissing without being requested.

They conclude that use of physical touch of other males as a hazing practice will only work in cultural moments in which touch between men is stigmatized. This has not always been the case, however. Physical intimacy between men is not always looked upon in the same light.

Homosocial Intimacy

The level of physical and emotional intimacy expressed between same-sex heterosexual friends is dependent on a number of socio-cultural variables. For example, there was a time when homosocial emotional intimacy flourished between men (Deitcher 2001). Before the turn of the twentieth century, boys in boarding schools forged deep intimate friendships with other boys, which White and Vagi (1990) suggest was because they had lost the nurturance from their mothers.

Rotundo (1989) explains that, in this time, heterosexual men were able to develop highly intimate friendships which he describes as "romantic friendships." This historical finding might be odd for some. At face value, it can seem as if cultural homophobia has decreased gradually over decades, and it is equally easy to assume that men did not touch each other or experience romance with each other in non-sexual ways, until most recently. Both of these suppositions are false.

For example, Tripp (2005) highlights that, over the period of four years, President Abraham Lincoln shared a bed with his intimate male partner, Joshua Speed, and that President George Washington wrote endearing letters to other men. However, this intimacy that Tripp describes began to be strictly policed in the twentieth century, when the awareness of and subsequent fear of homosexuality grew. McKay and McKay (2012) provide a detailed description of how changing attitudes toward homosexuality came to limit men's friendships. They argue that, at the turn of the twentieth century:

> Thinking of men as either "homosexual" or "heterosexual" became common. And this new category of identity was at the same time pathologized — decried by psychiatrists as a mental illness, by ministers as a perversion, and by politicians as something to be legislated against. As this new conception of homosexuality as a stigmatized and onerous identifier took root in [Anglo] American culture, men began to be much more

careful to not send messages to other men, and to women, that they were gay. And this is the reason why, it is theorized, men have become less comfortable with showing affection towards each other over the last century. (McKay and McKay 2012. p. 1)

We know from research on men's literature and letters that men used to express deep emotional affinity for one another; but later to our understanding of men's intimacy came what was not in the written word—but evidenced in physical, tactile behavior. We have to thank for this addition to our knowledge of men and their physical tactility in friendship, Professor of American Studies, John Ibson (2002).

As a gay male scholar, Ibson thought he had hit the jackpot on gay history, when he found for sale photos taken at the dawn of professional photography; photos of men posed together. Although clothed, the men in the photos were positioned intimately. Recognizing them as gay ancestors, Ibson was delighted to learn that the vendor he purchased them from had many others to sell—all capturing a similar level of tactile intimacy between men.

The outright visibility of gay men a hundred years earlier fascinated Ibson. Had sexuality historians missed something about turn-of-the-twentieth-century-America? Were, contrary to historical accounts, gay men actually out of the closet and visible during this time? Ibson embarked on a quest to find more photographs, so that he could perhaps re-write gay history.

However, somewhere between collecting his first few photographs and his current collection of over 5,000, Ibson figured out that these were not necessarily gay men pictured. Instead, they were heterosexual men doing what heterosexual men did at that moment in American culture: expressing affection for a friend.

After years of careful analysis—and in what must be the most significant, yet underappreciated gender studies book ever written—Ibson (2002) uses his collection of 5,000 photos to describe the history of men's relationships from the 1880s until the 1980s. Ibson is very clear not to explain what the photographs mean to us today (that would be presentism), but rather what they meant to the subjects at the time the photos were taken. Specifically, Ibson uses the photos to illustrate the changing nature of physical intimacy between men in response to the cultural contextualization of homosexuality in modern society.

For example, his book contains images of athletes before the 1920s, as well as friends, servicemen, brothers, collegiate, and prep schoolboys in many settings. In different pictures, the boys and men are lavishly dressed, provocatively undressed, arms wrapped around each other, embracing, lying in piles, sleeping in the same beds, holding hands, and sitting on each other's laps—all to show their affection for one another.

It was these photos (and Ibson's astute analysis) that heavily influenced Anderson's thinking about the role of homophobia in producing gendered behaviors and men's masculinities (Anderson 2009). The photographs Ibson collected suggested that the gradual awareness of homosexuality as a static identity (not just an abhorrent behavior) resulted in an equal growth in cultural homophobia.

This was displayed in his photographs which, when organized by passing decades, clearly suggest that as American culture grew increasingly aware of homosexuality, men began to pry intimacy away from fraternal bonding. This mass awareness of homosexuality, combined with social homophobia, increased men's fear of being falsely homosexualized by their behaviors, attitudes, emotions, or associations. Accordingly, as the awareness of homosexuality grew (in the presence of homophobia), so did the space between men.

This growing distance between men is clearly illustrated through multiple subsets of Ibson's photographs. Thus, Ibson shows that cultural space has been added between men in many walks of public and private life. However, none is more germane to this book than Ibson's photographs of men's sport teams.

Here, Ibson uses images of teams to illustrate the evolution of the team portrait, and consequential growing rigidity that athletes displayed through the passing years. For example, prior to the 1920s, his photographs show athletes hugging, laying their heads in each other's laps, holding hands, or draping their arms around each other. Soon after, however, teams appeared in straight rows. Men first stand with their hands at their side, and years later their arms are folded across their chests. Men ceased to touch each other when being photographed.

3 Homosociality   45

Ibson's photographs provide visual evidence regarding the relationship between homohysteria and male intimacy. They help one understand that homohysteria has greatly limited the expression of gender and intimacy among all men. His photographs represented men before modern understandings of a gay identity, and the effect that this identity had on heterosexual men's gendered behaviors.

Today, this physical closeness of friends is understood to be an important part of forming friendships for other scholar's work on boys and men, too (McCormack 2012). Hruschka (2010) suggests that "one of the most honest ways of accepting vulnerability is getting close enough to a person to touch him or her and, perhaps even more important, to permit oneself to be touched" (p. 42).

Figure 3.1 shows a typical cuddle experienced by young men in the present day.

Whilst there have been fluctuations in the level of homophobia experienced across time (Anderson 2009), negativity toward homosexual men reached a cultural zeitgeist in the 1980s. The romantic friendships

Fig. 3.1 A typical cuddle experienced by young men in the present day (Pekic/E + via Getty Images)

between same-sex friends that Rotundo (1989) described became entirely limited to homosexuals and women because of a pervasive cultural shift in the condemnation of homosexuality (McCormack 2012). Anderson (2009) describes this as a state of homohysteria, whereby a moral panic emerged in response to the AIDS epidemic which was primarily associated with gay men.

In this epoch, straight men began to fear being thought of as gay for displaying physical or emotional intimacy, and this significantly interfered with their ability to develop close same-sex friendships (Morin and Garfinkle 1978). Instead of the closeness seen between men in the nineteenth century, by the late twentieth century, a hypermasculine discourse sought to severely restrict male intimacy. This developed in response to the mass cultural awareness of homosexuality among Western populations, particularly facilitated by the spread of the HIV/AIDS virus, which brought such cultural visibility that it solidified the notion that homosexuals existed in great numbers (Anderson 2009).

Research from this era shows that men began to emotionally distance themselves from other men. It is this zeitgeist, as described earlier in this chapter, in which young men knew that they had a friendship with another when they engaged in activities together, like playing sports, drinking, fixing things, or gambling. Lewis (1978) wrote:

> [Men] have not known what it means to love and care for a friend without the shadow of some guilt and fear of peer ridicule… Although males report more same- sex friendships than women do, most of these are not close, intimate, or characterized by self- disclosure. Many barriers exist to emotional intimacy between men, some stemming from the demands of traditional male roles in our society, such as pressures to compete, homophobia, and aversion to vulnerability and openness, as well as from the lack of adequate role models. (p. 108)

McCormack and Anderson (2014) more recently explained that the reason behind the physical and emotional alienation between straight male friends was that there was an overwhelming fear in the 1980s and early 1990s of being socially perceived as gay. Consequently, unlike the pictures unearthed by Ibson's (2002) study of men in the nineteenth century, men would physically distance their bodies from other men (except in the masculine proving ground of sports). Subsequently, they were culturally compelled to perform certain overtly heterosexual behaviors and avoid engaging in those that would feminize them. Anderson (2014) recalls his experience of same-sex intimacy, or rather lack of, in this time:

> I look back with sadness over the way in which the 1980s treated and conditioned me and my peers…The impact on our masculinity was horrific: we were denied physical touch with our male friends (outside of sporting or other aggressive activities), emotional expressionism, or even the ability to admit loving a same-sex friend. Our sexualities were also damaged. They were silenced, and we all told lies about them… We were all entirely heterosexual; we were all vehemently homophobic. (p. 2)

The primary difference between the early and latter stages of the twentieth century, concerned a growing recognition in the latter half that homosexuality exists as a static sexual orientation among a significant portion of the population, with corresponding antipathy toward it. Accordingly, Anderson (2009) theorizes that it was the fear of being thought gay that ended the physical and emotional intimacy that heterosexual men once shared, suggesting that by the 1980s, heterosexual men were severely regulated in their behaviors. The *General Social Survey* and the *British Social Attitudes Survey* also show that cultural homophobia peeked in the mid-1980s to early 1990s (Keleher and Smith 2012). Leading into this time, men further asserted their heterosexual identity by performing exaggerated versions of homophobia through both verbal and physical abuse (Morin and Garfinkle 1978).

The fear of being thought feminine, and subsequently gay, was omnipresent among both gay and straight men in the latter half of the twentieth century. A homophobic discourse circulated throughout cultural institutions of education and government (Ahmed 2013). The presence of homophobia in Anglo-American societies caused men to regulate themselves and others to ensure their heterosexuality was believed. The requirement for men to refrain from emotional vulnerability had filtered into almost all aspects of their personal lives.

Supporting Anderson's notions of how the awareness and dislike of homosexuality influence men's behaviors in friendships, Riesman (1990) notes that when people rate their ability to self-disclose and be emotional as low, they are less likely to have close friendships. Furthermore, Stokes et al. (1980) note that those people who are highly homophobic are much less likely to self-disclosure. Bank and Hansford (2000) agree that "it seems likely that individuals with high levels of homophobia will be less likely to form close and supportive same-sex friendships than those who are more comfortable with homosexuality" (p. 65). Simply put, homophobic conditions are understood to severely restrict men's friendships.

Expression and Love Between Men in the Late Twentieth Century

Writing in the decade that witnessed the height of homophobia, Cancian (1990) said that society has "a feminine conception of love. We identify love with emotional expression and talking about our feelings" (p. 69). Accordingly, male youth of this time would refrain from even using the word love to detract homosexual suspicion. They were structured into exceptionally narrow masculine identities that rejected emotionality (Kellner 1991). Instead, they aspired to the muscular, heterosexual, hostile, and patriotic action heroes that filled Hollywood (Pope et al. 2000).

Love and intimacy for men had no place in this era because it projected a feminine (read homosexual) image. Perhaps this is why, unlike Ibson's (2002) findings regarding an earlier century, Rands and Levinger (1979) found that women were much more likely to be physically tactile with each other than men were. Conversely, swearing, abuse, and readiness to fight were compulsory male characteristics of the time. Men did not kiss, cuddle or disclose their insecurities to other men, as the lost their freedom to express fear, weakness, uncertainty, or affection (Plummer 1999). For example, McGuffy and Lindsay Rich (1999) observed boys at a school, who, when talking about another boy crying, said "he would probably be gay when he grows up" (p. 116).

Pleck (1975) similarly found men of this era to be restricted in their expression, describing in detail the social confines of male intimacy and emotionality. He found that men were expected to exhibit greater control in their emotional behavior than women, being far removed from their feelings. He said that, "at the same time, men appear to become angry or violent more easily than women and are often rewarded for doing so… having greater fears about homosexuality than do women" (p. 156).

Men of this era were to avoid emotional intimacy with other men, too. Finding and expecting legitimate intimacy and companionship was only to occur within the confines of heterosexual relationships with women. In the 1980s and 1990s, any in depth conversations that men did have with same-sex friends would generally be limited to the masculine subject of sport (Aries and Johnson 1983), and even in their strongest friendships they could not experience the same intimacy that women had on a regular basis with many friends (Bank and Hansford 2000).

Restrictive masculinity found its routes in the lives of even very young boys. Exemplifying this, Pollack (1999) showed that fathers of this era would withhold their love and affection from their children, and before boys even reached their teenage years, they could be subjected to abusive and shaming torments from peers and teachers for performing feminine behaviors, such as skipping and poetry readings (Pollack 1999). Whilst fathers would withhold emotional care from their children, young boys would equally separate themselves from their mothers, being rather bereft of any emotional attention from either of their parents (White and Vagi 1990).

Whilst the broad consensus has been that women's friendships are more intimate and emotive (Lewis et al. 2015; Greif 2008), some scholars questioned the totality of this perspective. Firstly, they argued, it could be possible that men experience the same level of intimacy as women, but their willingness to express their emotionality to research observers or interviewers may be more limited (Wright 1998). Moreover, Walker (1994) found that whilst men and women identified with gender stereotypes (that men bond through physical activity and women through emotional disclosure), many participants gave examples of how they deviate from these characteristics. Some men reported bonding through emotional disclosure and some women through shared experiences in sports.

Secondly, whilst Cancian (1986) said that our conception of love is feminine, she also cautioned that this is only a conception. She explained that Anglo-American societies use a feminine ruler to measure the level of intimacy between friends, "based on feminine styles of loving, such as verbal self-disclosure, emotional expression, and willingness to report that one has close relationships" (p. 699). This "willingness" for women to report on the closeness of their friendships further substantiates the plausibility of Wright's (1998) claims that men self-limit their accounts of the intimacy in their friendships.

Taking Cancian's (1986, 1990) perspective on the feminine conception of love a step further, it could be argued that men experience heights of intimacy on the sports field, albeit under a more masculine characterization. For example, if a player becomes angry and abusive toward a referee in a match, a teammate who interjects to hold them back, calm them down and tells them to "walk it off" could be perceived as being highly intimate. They are managing their friend's emotions, being physically tactile, and helping them avoid further conflict. Critically, this example demonstrates how emotionality and expression can be engaged without femininity.

These exceptions to the men as side-to-side and women as face-to-face highlight that it is not definitive to say that men are inherently or predisposed to be less emotive and expressive than women; matters are more complex than that. First, the way the expression of love is culturally defined favors the way women are thought to show love, with tender words and caretaking activities. The way men have shown love, like providing for a family, is not defined as love (Cancian 1990) even though men's risk-taking and sacrifice is done out of love.

Next, historically, culture has predisposed their emotional boundaries to be more rigid. In the latter years of the twentieth century, and particularly in the 1980s, men were, for example, pressured by a prevailing homophobic and hypermasculine discourse to reject emotionality and embrace stoicism. This placed severe regulations on the intimacies of same-sex male friendship. It thus appears that men are not fundamentally less intimate than women, but, as Fehr (1996) explained, men had chosen to be in line with masculine archetypes, even when they may internally desire open, emotional, and tactile contact with other men in the way women have been socially prescribed.

Twenty-First Century Expressions of Love

In the following chapter we describe the history of masculinity theorizing. Here, however, we want to pick up on the archetypical form of modern masculinity, something known as inclusive masculinity, because it sits in opposition to restrictive, orthodox, hegemonic, or toxic version of masculinity—all similar nomenclature to describe men as opposite of what we show them to be in this study.

Anderson (2009, 2011, 2012) highlights that inclusive masculinities are plural, not singular. He and McCormack (Anderson and McCormack 2018) highlight that the concept of "inclusive" masculinity does not mean that men are inclusive of everything. They might still be racists; they might still be sexist; they might still be classist; but what counts for the theoretical examination of changing men's homosocial behaviors and expressions of intimacy is that, today, they are collectively inclusive of homosexuality.

This is the one variable which Anderson (2009) theorized to have the most impact on young men's homosocial behaviors. It is not, as Anderson points out, the only. Other variables include socioeconomics, geo-political struggles, and of course war. Anderson is also very clear to state that the newly emergent masculinities that he documented in 2005 (Anderson 2005a) have retained and strengthened their position in accord to decreasing levels of cultural homophobia. However, he argues that declining homophobia is an uneven social phenomenon.

Anderson and dozens of other scholars have documented the existence of inclusive masculinities among athletes, businessmen, and many others, in multiple countries (Anderson and McCormack 2018). There is no clear-cut definition of this, but the overriding variable is that inclusive masculinities can only emerge in a culture of low antipathy toward homosexuality. It is not important for every male to maintain positive attitudes toward gay men, but it is necessary for homophobia, not homosexuality, to be stigmatized. In such a culture men are shown to be:

- More physically tactile with each other
- More emotionally expressive with each other
- Less aggressive to each other
- Less willing to take unnecessary risks
- More willing to show weakness, fear, and to cry
- More willing to delay heterosexual coupling
- More willing to engage with fashion codes that were once feminized
- More willing to work in occupation sectors that were once feminized

Anderson (2005a, 2009, 2011) mapped much of this terrain in the study of both American and British Sportsmen. McCormack then contributed to this body of research by showing its existence in younger males, who were not sportsmen. A growing body of recent work has also pointed to the emergence of at least some of these changes in homosocial friendship practices among different groups of young men (e.g. Ralph and Roberts 2020a, b; Roberts 2018).

In his ethnography of an English sixth form, McCormack (2012) explores the shifting patterns of friendship among young men aged between 16 and 18. Rather than patterns of marginalization and subordination characterized as core processes of masculine interaction (Connell 1995), he found instead that popularity was organized through charismatic and authentic behaviors, the provision of emotional support, and the ability to have a diverse group of friends.

Whilst cliques existed, he showed that the young men valued the ability to have friends across different friendship groups and also privileged the ability to make small talk with acquaintances. Importantly, rather than the side-to-side discussions, these young men embraced the face-to-face emotional discussions and sharing of hopes, fears, and loves that have traditionally been classified as women's emotion. In doing so, McCormack (2012) added to the literature by suggesting that masculine hierarchies had mostly diminished. Instead, youth today very often value authenticity and collapse hierarchies.

In order to highlight that the behaviors Anderson first catalogued exist for men born around 1980 and later, but not before, Anderson and Fidler (2018) highlighted that there is limited research about homosociality and physical tactility between men born in the early to middle decades of the twentieth century. Accordingly, they utilized 27 in-depth interviews with heterosexual British men aged between 65 and 91 to explore their masculinity and homosociality, then and today. Participants were interviewed about (1) their recollections of masculinity and same-sex friendships aged 18; (2) their awareness of, and attitudes toward, homosexuality at this age; and (3) their current views regarding today's heterosexual male's gendered behaviors, inclusive of their kissing, cuddling, and loving other men.

Results found that men born between 1924 and 1951 lived in absence of, or desire for, homosocial affection. Even today they look upon the display of inclusive masculinities by today's male youth with disdain. The research therefore evidences that antipathy toward homosociality is reflective of elevated cultural homophobia and homohysteria of their youths. As this research on the bromance shows, everything has thus changed in recent decades.

Chapter Summary

This chapter highlights two aspects of friendship. The first is that most friendships are now, and appear to have historically, been dominated by same-sex dyads. The reasons for this are perhaps biological, in that males and females might retain different interests upon which to bond over (Anderson and Magrath 2019), but that they are certainly also socially structured. This structuring occurs in schools and occupations, and other social institutions.

Next, the chapter highlights that homosociality, or same-sex friendship patterns, are not stagnant in how they discuss and display their feelings for one another. The expressed endearment of affinity for other males has shifted in culture, in response to socio-political events. We evidenced that at one time in American history, for example, men were florid with the written word, and highlighted their affections in prose.

We also evidenced that men's tactile/physical elements of intimacy varied from what scholars thought men engaged in.

We evidenced photographic records which show that men, from the dawn of photography until the first half of the twentieth century displayed physical acts of intimacy: touch, cuddling, and bodily contact in their chosen photographed positions. Ibson (2002) showed us that this changed in the second half of the twentieth century. By the time most masculinity scholarship was conducted in the later decades of the twentieth century it appeared that men were monolithic in their desire for distance between their bodies and their emotions.

Anderson (2005b, 2009, 2011; Anderson and McCormack 2018) emerged into the masculinity scholarship to show us that university-aged men once again were growing closer in physical intimacy and that they were growing closer in expressing their emotional intimacy for their same-sex male friends. McCormack (2012) extended this work to younger males, aged 16–18. A new form of masculinity studies emerged: one that was based in empirical data of how young men behaved with their friends. What is not immediately clear, however, is the question: why did men who were presumably highly homophobic in the 1880s touch each other physically, but men who we know to be highly homophobic in the 1980s did not? Either, social scientists are wrong about cultural homophobia, historically; or is there another variable at play.

Anderson's theory of Inclusive Masculinity explained that extra-variable of importance: the belief that gay men actually exist among your friends, family, colleagues, or fellow church patrons. In other words, the later decades of the twentieth century made the omnipresence of the homosexual known. This Anderson and McCormack theorized (2014) changed everything. That is the topic of the next chapter.

References

Ahmed, S. (2013). *The cultural politics of emotion.* New York: Routledge

Allan, E., and Madden, M. (2008). *Hazing in view: College students at risk. Initial findings from the national study of student hazing* [Online].

Available at: http://www.stophazing.org/wp-content/uploads/2014/06/hazing_in_view_web1.pdf.
Anderson, E. (2005a). *In the game: Gay athletes and the cult of masculinity*. New York: University of New York Press.
Anderson, E. (2005b). Orthodox and inclusive masculinity: Competing masculinities among heterosexual men in a feminized terrain. *Sociological Perspectives, 48*(3), 337–355.
Anderson, E. (2009). *Inclusive masculinity: The changing nature of masculinities*. New York: Routledge
Anderson, E. (2010). *Sport, theory and social problems: A critical introduction*. New York: Routledge.
Anderson, E. (2011). Masculinities and sexualities in sport and physical cultures: Three decades of evolving research. *Journal of Homosexuality, 58*(5), 565–578.
Anderson, E. (2012). Inclusive masculinity in a physical education setting. *Journal of Boyhood Studies, 6*(1–2), 151–165.
Anderson, E. (2014). *21st Century Jocks: Sporting Men and Contemporary Heterosexuality*. New York: Macmillan.
Anderson, E., and Fidler, C. (2018). Elderly British men: Homohysteria and orthodox masculinities. *Journal of Gender Studies, 27*(3), 248–259.
Anderson, E., and Magrath, R. (2019). *Men and masculinities*. Routledge.
Anderson, E., and McCormack, M. (2014). Homohysteria: Definitions, Context and Intersectionality. *Sex Roles, 71*(3), 152–158
Anderson, E., & McCormack, M. (2018). Inclusive masculinity theory: Overview, reflection and refinement. *Journal of gender studies, 27*(5), 547–561.
Anderson, E., McCormack., and Lee, H. (2012). Male Team Sport Hazing Initiations in a Culture of Decreasing Homohysteria. *Journal of Adolescent Research, 27*(4), 427–448.
Aries, E., and Johnson, F. (1983). Close friendship in adulthood: Conversational content between same-sex friends. *Sex Roles, 9*(12), 1183–1196.
Bank, B., and Hansford, S. (2000). Gender and friendship: Why are men's best same-sex friendships less intimate and supportive? *Personal Relationships, 7*(1), 63–78.
Bell, S. (1981). *Worlds of friendship*. Newbury Park: Sage Publications.
Benenson, J. (2013). The development of human female competition: allies and adversaries. *Philosophical Transactions of the Royal Society B, 368*(1631).

Berndt, T. (2004). Children's friendships: Shifts over a half-century in perspectives on their development and their effects. *Merrill-Palmer Quarterly, 50*(3), 206–223.

Bourdieu, P. (2001). *Masculine domination*. Stanford University Press.

Bryshun, J., and Young, K. (2007). Hazing as a form of sport and gender socialization. In Young., and White., (Ed.), *Sport and Gender in Canada (2nd ed.)*. Oxford: Oxford University Press. Pp. 302–327

Cancian, F. (1990). *Love in America: Gender and self-development*. Cambridge: Cambridge University Press.

Cancian, F. M. (1986). The feminization of love. *Signs: Journal of Women in Culture and Society, 11*(4), 692–709.

Collins, W., and Sroufe, L. (1999). Capacity for intimate relationships. In W. Furman., B. Brown., and C. Feiring (Ed.), *The development of romantic relationships in adolescence*. Cambridge: Cambridge University Press. Pp. 125–147.

Connell, R. (1995). *Masculinities*. Berkeley: University of California Press.

Curry, T. (2000). Booze and bar fights: A journey to the dark side of college athletics. In McKay, J., Messner, M., and Sabo, D. (Ed.), *Masculinities, gender relations and sport*. London: Sage. Pp. 162–175.

Deitcher, D. (2001). *Dear friends: American photographs of men together, 1840-1918*. Michigan: Harry N Abrams Inc.

Fehr, B. (1996). *Friendship processes*. Thousand Oaks, CA: Sage.

Geary, D., Byrd-Craven, J., Hoard, M., Vigil, J., and Numtee, C. (2003). Evolution and development of boys' social behavior. *Developmental Review, 23*(4), 444–470.

Greif, G. (2008). *Buddy system: Understanding male friendships*. Oxford University Press.

Hall, J. (2011). Sex differences in friendship expectations: A meta-analysis. *Journal of Social and Personal Relationships, 28*(6), 723–747.

Hruschka, D. (2010). Friendship: Development, ecology, and evolution of a relationship (Vol. 5). Berkeley: University of California Press.

Ibson, J. (2002). *Picturing men: A century of male relationships in everyday American photography*. Illinois: University of Chicago Press.

Joseph, L. J., and Anderson, E. (2016). The influence of gender segregation and teamsport experience on occupational discrimination in sport-based employment. *Journal of Gender Studies, 25*(5), 586–598.

Kellner, D. (1991). Film, politics, and ideology: Reflections on Hollywood film in the age of Reagan. *Velvet Light Trap, 27*, 9–24.

Keleher, A., and Smith, E. (2012). Growing support for gay and lesbian equality since 1990. *Journal of Homosexuality, 59*, 1307–1326.

Lewis, D., Al-Shawaf, L., Russell., E., and Buss, D. (2015). Friends and happiness: An evolutionary perspective on friendship. *Friendship and Happiness*, 37.

Lewis, R. (1978). Emotional intimacy among men. *Journal of Social Research, 34*(1), 108–121.

Lipman-Blumen, J. (1976). Toward a homosocial theory of sex roles: An explanation of the sex segregation of social institutions. *Signs, 1*(3), 15–31.

Magrath, R. (2016). *Inclusive masculinities in contemporary football: Men in the beautiful game*. Routledge.

McCormack, M. (2012). *The declining significance of homophobia: How teenage boys are redefining masculinity and heterosexuality*. New York: Oxford University Press.

McCormack, M., and Anderson, E. (2014). The influence of declining homophobia on men's gender in the United States: An argument for the study of homohysteria. *Sex Roles, 71*(3–4), 109–120.

McGuffey, S., and Lindsay Rich, B. (1999). "Playing in the gender transgression zone": Race, class, and hegemonic masculinity in middle childhood. *Gender and Society, 13*(5), 608–627.

McKay, B., and McKay, J. (2012). Bosom buddies: A photo history of male affection [Online]. Available at: http://www.artofmanliness.com/2012/07/29/bosom-buddies-a-photo-history-of-male-affection/.

Morin, S., and Garfinkle, E. (1978). Male homophobia. *Journal of Social Issues, 34*(1), 29–47.

Nardi, P. (1992). *Men's friendships*. London: Sage Publications.

Nuwer, H. (1999). *Wrongs of passage: Fraternities, sororities, hazing and binge drinking*. Bloomington: Indiana University Press.

Peralta, R. (2007). College alcohol use and the embodiment of hegemonic masculinity among European American men. *Sex Roles, 56*(11), 741–756.

Pleck, J. (1975). Issues for the men's movement: Summer, 1975. *Changing Men: A Newsletter for Men against Sexism*, 21–23.

Plummer, D. (1999). *One of the boys: Masculinity, homophobia, and modern manhood*. New York: Routledge.

Pollack, W. (1999). *Real boys: Rescuing our sons from the myths of boyhood*. New York: Macmillan.

Pope, H., Phillips, K., and Olivardia, R. (2000). *The Adonis complex: The secret crisis of male body obsession*. New York: Simon and Schuster.

Ralph, B., and Roberts, S. (2020a). One small step for man: Change and continuity in perceptions and enactments of homosocial intimacy among young Australian men. *Men and Masculinities, 23*(1), 83–103.

Ralph, B., and Roberts, S. (2020b). *The Palgrave Handbook of Masculinity and Sport.* Pp. 19–38.

Rands, M., and Levinger, G. (1979). Implicit theories of relationship: An intergenerational study. *Journal of Personality and Social Psychology, 37*(5), 645.

Reisman, J. (1990). Intimacy in same-gender friendships. *Sex Roles, 23*(1–2), 65–82.

Riesman, D. (1953). *The lonely crowd.* New Haven: Yale University press.

Roberts, S. (2018). *Young working-class men in transition.* Routledge.

Rotundo, A. (1989). Romantic friendship: Male intimacy and middle-class youth in the northern United States, 1800–1900. *Journal of Social History, 23*(1), 1–25.

Rotundo, A. (1994). *American manhood: Transformations in masculinity from the revolution to the modern era.* New York: Basic Books.

Stoet, G., & Geary, D. C. (2021). Sex differences in adolescents' occupational aspirations: Variations across time and place. https://doi.org/10.1371/journal.pone.0261438.

Stokes, J., Fuehrer, A., and Childs, L. (1980). Gender differences in self-disclosure to various target persons. *Journal of Counseling Psychology, 27*(2), 192.

Su, R., Rounds, J., & Armstrong, P. I. (2009). Men and things, women and people: A meta-analysis of sex differences in interests. *Psychological Bulletin, 135*(6), 859.

Thibaut, J., and Kelly, H. 1959. *The social psychology of groups.* New York: Wiley

Thomas, R. J. (2019). Sources of friendship and structurally induced homophily across the life course. *Sociological Perspectives, 62*(6), 822–843.

Tripp, C. (2005). *The intimate world of Abraham Lincoln.* New York: Free Press.

Vigil, J. (2007). Asymmetries in the friendship preferences and social styles of men and Women. *Human Nature, 18*, 143–161.

Walker, K. (1994). I'm not friends the way she's friends: Ideological and behavioral constructions of masculinity in men's friendships. *Masculinities, 2*(2), 38–55.

White, P., and Vagi, A. (1990). Rugby in the 19th-century British boarding-school system: A feminist psychoanalytic perspective. In Messner, M. and

Sabo, D. (Ed.), *Sport, men and the gender order: Critical feminist perspectives.* Illinois: Human Kinetics. Pp. 67–78.

Winstead, B. (1986). Sex differences in same-sex friendships. In Winstead, B., and Derlega, V. (Ed.), *Friendship and social interaction: An introduction.* New York: Springer. Pp. 81–99.

Winstead, B., and Griffin, J. (2001). Friendship styles. In Worell, J. (Ed.), *Encyclopedia of women and gender.* Boston: Academic Press. Pp. 481–492.

Wright, P. (1998). Toward an expanded orientation to the study of sex differences in friendship. In Canary, D., and Dindia, K (Ed.), *Sex differences and similarities in communication.* Mahwah: Lawrence Erlbaum. Pp. 41–63.

4

Theorizing Masculinity

It is important to understand how men used to be theorized prior to the start of the twenty-first century. The chapter begins with an examination of social constructionism, before taking us into the dominant theoretical paradigm of the weaning decades of the twentieth century, Hegemonic Masculinity. We then detail how Inclusive Masculinity Theory was developed out of changing cultural times as both a refinement of Hegemonic Masculinity Theory, and a critique as well. We conclude that the field of masculinities has been too reliant upon Hegemonic Masculinity in the previous few decades, and now that it is dissipating, new ways of imagining masculinities are emerging.

This chapter thus not only explains how the dominating mid-level theories of a social-constructionist account of masculinity operate, but it reminds us that theories are products of their times, and that as times change, social theories often do too. In this case, the bromance forces scholars wedded to old views of men as stoic, homophobic, violent, and friend-lacking, to challenge their old views. This is no longer true.

Social Constructionism

Social constructionism is a concept which refers to theories that emphasize the socially created nature of our lives. The idea of social constructionism solidified in sociology with the publication of Berger and Luckman's (1966) influential text, *The Social Construction of Reality*. Since its publication, a sizeable number of theories and research projects centered on the idea that people are affected by and simultaneously affect their cultural worlds. Or, as Fairhurst and Grant (2010, p. 174) argue, "…taken-for-granted realities are produced from interactions between and among social agents."

Reality should also not be understood as one, universal and objective truth. Instead, social constructionism suggests that multiple realities exist, and that these are dependent on the social context in which one lives. Social constructionism also acknowledges the centrality of language and communication, and argues that language does not merely reflect reality, it constructs and creates it.

Theorizing of men has varied across disciplines. Psychology has largely argued that masculinity was socially constructed within the family unit and sociology has largely taken a social-constructionist perspective. There are however intersecting and competing factors which complicate this viewpoint from biological research (Gaston et al. 2018), which emerges from sociobiology or evolutionary psychology. What we engage with mostly here in this section is the sociological understanding of how masculinity and friendship develops, as the theory we utilize to explain the bromance is vested in sociology.

In 1987, a highly influential addition to sociology of gender scholarship occurred in the first edition of an academic journal founded by feminists, *Gender and Society*. Looking for a more sophisticated and critical study of gender, seminal feminist studies of the time galvanized around the explanation that gender was created not just through the top-down modeling that psychologists articulated occurred within the family structure, but that gender was created from the bottom-up, too.

The article's title alone, *Doing Gender* (West and Zimmerman 1987) was enough to suggest that gender isn't something that is done "to" someone; it is something we are *all* engaged with, and often make choices about. Simply put, gender was something that we "do." Indeed, in the article, they wrote that gender "is not simply an aspect of what one is, but, more fundamentally, it is something that one does, and does recurrently, in interaction with others (1987 p. 140)." This is to say that sociologists acknowledged that gender is established by institutional and cultural norms, but also focused on how it was reproduced and consolidated through social interactions.

This was further evidenced in Joan Acker's (1990) article, *Hierarchies, Jobs, Bodies: A Theory of Gendered Organizations* in *Gender and Society*. Here, Acker explained the ways in which organizations are gendered, where "advantage and disadvantage, exploitation and control, action and emotion, meaning and identity, are patterned through and in terms of a distinction between male and female, masculine and feminine (p. 146)."

Equally as important, more sociologists began examining gender specifically during the 1980s. With them came a more social constructionist understanding of gender—one which requires analysis at both the macro and micro levels.

The above approach to the study of masculinity really signals the end of the first wave of masculinity studies. This was approached by a blend of sex role theory, social constructionism, and evolutionary psychology. There was no one dominating theory. This would change with the second wave.

Hegemonic Masculinity

The second wave of masculinity scholarship was sparked by Raewyn Connell (1987/1995), who proposed a theoretical model of masculinity making that moved us further away from sex role theory for a few reasons. First, she took a sociological approach to the study of masculinity and accounted for the influence of institutions and the interactions that individuals have with those institutions—such as those outlined in the previous section. Second, she accounted for how gay men and men of color varied from dominant, white, and straight conditioning of masculinity. Equally important, Connell discussed how not all masculinities were equal.

Collectively, this created a more sophisticated cultural examination of masculinity, not based in ideas of the mother, and not based in the passive receiving of gender. Her ideas were conceptualized as Hegemonic Masculinity. While some call Hegemonic Masculinity a concept, we refer to it as a theory because, to some degree, it does maintain predictive power. Furthermore, because Hegemonic Masculinity Theory (HMT) explains social relations of gender it covers a range of processes and actions that, for us, make it too broad and expansive to be a concept.

The full application of HMT is vast. The theory viewed men's hierarchies as "configurations of practice," in order to accomplish its interrelated goals of understanding the social dynamics of men (their social organization and behaviors); and understanding how these dynamics reproduced patriarchy.

Related to the first, understanding the social stratifications of men, Connell applied the notion of *hegemony* to the study of masculinities. Hegemony is a concept developed by Italian philosopher and political prisoner Antonio Gramsci (1971). It refers to a particular form of dominance in which a ruling class legitimates its position and secures their acceptance —if not outright support—from those classes below them. While a feature to Gramsci's version of hegemony is that there is often the threat of rules or force structuring a belief, the key element to hegemony is that force cannot be the causative factor in order to elicit complicity. Rather, people must believe that their subordinated place is both *right* and *natural*. For example, hegemony is fortified when a slave believes his rightful place is that of slave (a racist society), when a woman believes she should be subservient to a man (a sexist society), when a poor person believes that he does not merit wealth (a classist society), or when a gay man believes he is undeserving of the same rights as a straight man (a heterosexist society). Hegemony has therefore been a key concept in understanding oppression of women ethnic and sexual minorities, and of the lower classes (Bradford et al. 2016).

This second aspect of Connell's work, an attempt to account for what establishes and reproduces patriarchy, is so strong in her theorizing that she defines hegemonic masculinity as being the study of it. In this capacity, it is clear that it is the explanation of men's power and privilege over women that she most concerned herself with. Her famous quote is:

Hegemonic masculinity is "...the configuration of gender practice which embodies the currently accepted answer to the problem of the legitimacy of patriarchy" (Connell 1995, p. 77).

Implicit in this definition, though, is also the configuration of gender practices of men. This is the aspect of her theory that most of all scholars using her theory have used Connell for, suggesting that the social ordering of men was inscribed through physical domination (or threat thereof), discursive marginalization (think homophobic discourse), and hegemonic oppression (see Demetriou 2001). Connell thus designated three categories of masculinities that, by definition, emerge "under" the hegemonic form: complicit, subordinated, and marginalized. Although Connell does not herself discuss this hierarchy explicitly, she alludes to it by suggesting that complicit masculinities keep the dominant form of masculinity (hegemonic masculinity) in power because they aspire to attain or at least mimic it; the "subordination of nonhegemonic masculinities" (Connell and Messerschmidt 2005 p. 846) also clearly implies a hierarchical structure.

Marginalized masculinities are said to categorize men subordinated by the hegemonic form of masculinity because of their race or class, and Connell (1995, 80) distinguished them from the "relations internal to the gender order." Finally, highlighting homosexual oppression as distinct, Connell labeled the masculinities of gay men as "subordinated," suggesting they were "the most conspicuous" (1995, 79) form—"subordinated to straight men by an array of quite material practices" (1995, 78). These categories provided an effective framework for understanding the hierarchical stratification of men in Western society in the 1980s and 1990s.

Critiques of Hegemonic Masculinity

Connell's work has been a major intervention in feminist theorizing of masculinities. It helped advance the study of masculinities, and it accurately captured the dynamics of many male cultures in the latter half of the twentieth century.

There have also been many critiques of Connell's theorizing. First, Connell envisioned the social organization of these loosely defined categories of masculinity as a structural mechanism for the reproduction of patriarchy. Yet she is unable to prove this. This notion is not falsifiable because it presumes men's actions reproduce patriarchy, without describing how or in what contexts. This aspect of her theory is thus grand theory—or philosophy—which means that it has less empirical validation than micro and meso theories; despite some scholars writing as if it is empirically proven. The other part of her theory, examining masculinities within a hierarchy has more utility. Yet, we argue that its utility is limited to making sense of the negative findings. It makes sense when examining men pursuing power over each other; but if you want to examine men's behaviors for any other purpose, the theory falls short.

It is for these reasons that little empirical evidence supports/ed this position (Demetriou 2001). Regarding the issue of gender inequality, hegemonic masculinity theory offers a one-dimensional answer to a complex problem that likely has multiple social roots (Bourdieu 2001; Roberts 2018), and this is why many sociologists employing it have looked solely at the intra-masculine stratifications, and how men behave.

Despite this failure, the original power and continued endurance of this theory comes from the fact that it was a very effective theory in understanding the social dynamics of men in the 1980s and early 1990s. This is particularly true because the 1980s marked an apex of homophobic attitudes in the Western world (Clements and Field 2014; Twenge, Sherman and Wells 2016). At this time, gay men were socially feminized and overtly stigmatized by mainstream society, meaning that Hegemonic Masculinity Theory was particularly well suited to the social organization of stratified masculinities (Grindstaff and West 2011).

Hegemonic Masculinity Theory was therefore largely successful in describing intra-masculine stratifications because it powerfully and pragmatically captured the masculine zeitgeist of the era in which it was conceived (Anderson 2009). Supported by a growing body of empirical research, Hegemonic Masculinity Theory soon became the primary way of analyzing all masculinity issues to the point that the theory itself seems to have become hegemonic in the new sociology of masculinities scholarship by the turn of the century (second wave). This is to say that even scholars who did not adopt the theory to explain their data still drew upon it (e.g., Messerschmidt 2012; Plummer 1999).

But the turn of the twenty-first century brought multiple other critiques of the theory. It was for this reason that Connell and Messerschmidt (2005) reformulated the theory in several ways. First, they recognized that members of subordinated groups have agency—rather than passively accepting their subordination. And in response to improving attitudes toward homosexuality, they argued that gay men were no longer necessarily at the bottom of the hierarchy, but that at best they can be both oppressed and tolerated at the same time. Still, they did not consider what happens if gay men achieve equality or something approximating it.

The revised Hegemonic Masculinity Theory therefore denies heterosexuals the ability to treat gays and lesbians equally (Moller 2007; Roberts 2018). The conceptual logic of saying that hegemonic masculinity will always exists, and that it requires the oppression of gay men, structurally traps gay men into perpetual subordination. Alongside limiting the times in which the theory can be applied, this also presents a very limited understanding of heterosexual men and stereotypes them as inherently homophobic.

Several other problems with hegemonic masculinity theory also persist. The theory still contends that a hegemonic version of masculinity explains patriarchy, yet there remains neither the empirical evidence nor conceptual logic to support this position. This also means that any challenges to hegemonic masculinity, such as the inclusion of gay people, are seen as unimportant in gender equality—yet the writing of equality of sexuality seems deeply flawed in understanding social equality more broadly.

The refined theory also remains steadfast in using complicit, subordinated, and marginalized categories of masculinities, yet never concisely defines them (McCormack 2012). Why are gay men seen as conceptually distinct from ethnic minorities, particularly now that it is accepted that gay men are not necessarily excluded from masculine consideration altogether?

Another problem is that the paradigmatic dominance has watered it down and damaged its utility as a theory (Moller 2007). Related to the previous point, the fact that hegemonic masculinity is dominant means that scholars looked for characteristics of masculinity (aggression, violence, banter, drinking) and use those individual behaviors as evidence for the broader social dynamic (Roberts 2018). Yet, as we argue, men can adopt some problematic behaviors (like drinking far too much) while being loving caring partners and friends.

Messerschmidt (2018) has recently yielded in further than his reformulation of the theory with Connell in (2005). In his (2018) book *Hegemonic Masculinity: Formulation, Reformulation, and Amplification* he sets out a variety of different types of hegemonic and non-hegemonic masculinities and describes "positive masculinities." This is a new theory than the original (1995) theory, and reads similar to orthodox and inclusive masculinities described by Anderson, 13 years earlier.

After this proposition, Messerschmidt then goes on to reject inclusive masculinity theory, which according to his own words would be precisely a definition of positive masculinity. He justifies this by picking one of the hundreds of published studies that use IMT, to state that Anderson's work with Magrath et al. (2015) for example (on adolescent academy football players) does not look at what happens outside a sport setting. Given that Roberts Anderson and Magrath do exactly this in a different paper (2017) with the exact same athletes and given that IMT is utilized across a broad spectrum of settings, there is no merit to Messerschmidt's outright dismissal. Instead, it sounds like the narcissism of small differences: Anderson was the first to capitulate the idea of multiple, non-hegemonic, masculinities in a setting, and after the utility of the idea of hegemonic masculinity wore off, Messerschmidt tried to reinsert himself as the harbinger of cutting-edge theorizing.

Hegemonic Masculinity Theory's reformulation and the accounting of positive and negative masculinities, loses theoretical specificity. It fails to explain how masculinities have changed. Hegemonic masculinity is thus just often used to recognize that women suffer from gender norms, or that masculinities exist in the plural (see Chapter 1). But these are fundamentals of the social study of masculinities, and they are not domain solely to HMT.

A Third Wave of Masculinity Theorizing

Hearn et al. (2012) indicates that we are in a third wave of masculinity theorizing. He suggests that we have moved from general ideas about social constructionism, into a hegemonic model of hegemonic masculinity, which we have then, collectively, eroded to the point that it is no longer distinguishable from the vagueness of social constructionism more broadly (Anderson and McCormack 2018). Borkowska (2018) describes this third wave as "Andersonian" (p. 3). This, she argues, is because recent masculinity research has shown a shift from hyper or orthodox forms of masculinity to those that are softer in their measurable presentations.

As outlined above, some of the critique of hegemonic masculinity came from the scholars who proffered it in the first place—in response to growing awareness of the primary theory to contest hegemonic masculinity, Inclusive Masculinity Theory (Anderson 2009). However, there are a plethora of other concepts as well.

For example, Demetriou (2001) introduced the notion of hybridity of masculinity. He argued that it was necessary to take account of the ways in which marginalized and subordinated masculinities are appropriated by dominant ones; arguing that men's practices form a "hybrid bloc that unites practices from diverse masculinities in order to ensure the reproduction of patriarchy" (p. 337).

Some scholars have also adopted Arxer's (2011) theorizing of hybrid masculinities ostensibly to develop hegemonic masculinity by more explicitly recognizing the changing nature of masculinities. Bridges (2014, 80) argues that straight men have started to embrace "gay aesthetics," but contends they do so "without challenging the systems of inequality from which they emerge."

We argue that unfounded claims that inclusive masculinities are not part of broader transformations that challenge inequalities deny the real social change that has occurred. This includes changes in laws related to LGB people (equal marriage, the removal of anti-sodomy laws, increased worker protection); the increased visibility of straight allies; the improving experiences of sexual minorities; the growing condemnation of overt homophobia; the increased acceptance of gay athletes; and many other social changes—all of which are supported by massive amounts of empirical evidence.

In addition to hybrid masculinities, a number of other concepts have been used to describe these new types of men empirically examined in the new millennia: personalized masculinities (Swain 2006); soft-boiled masculinities (Heath et al. 2003); cool masculinities (Jackson and Dempster 2009); caring masculinities (Elliot 2016); flexible masculinities; chameleon masculinities (Ward 2015); and saturated masculinities (Mercer 2017). These are useful concepts that undoubtedly speak to the diversification and multiplication of forms of masculinities, and support Hearn et al.'s (2012) claim that we are in a third phase of masculinities research.

Inclusive Masculinity Theory

A substantial body of recent research into masculinities has moved away from Hegemonic Masculinity Theory to understand the social dynamics of men today (Beasley 2008; Hearn 2004). Masculinity scholarship is today in the third wave, and primary here is the work of Eric Anderson, the architect of Inclusive Masculinity Theory (Borkowska 2018).

The derivation of this theory geminates from Anderson's PhD studies. Anderson began by using Hegemonic Masculinity in his examinations of openly gay male athletes (Anderson 2002). However, he found that the theory could not explain his results. Having experienced the incredibly homophobic 1980s as a teenager himself, he knew that Connell was right about homophobia driving a stratification of masculinity during that time. In that cultural context, in this historical moment, the idea of hegemonic masculinity accurately reflected what he experienced (Anderson 2000).

Further, his research on heterosexual college athletes continued to confound the assumptions of machismo and homophobia among male youth as well (Anderson 2005a, 2005b, 2008a, 2008b, 2012a, 2012b, 2014, 2015). He found that heterosexual males were not acting as one would predict using hegemonic masculinity theory (Anderson 2002, 2014; Anderson and McCormack 2018; Gaston et al. 2018; Magrath et al. 2017). Anderson suggested that the high levels of homophobia of that period were thus historically situated and contingent on a number of social factors. And, in order to understand the intersection of masculinities and decreasing homophobia, he realized we needed to account for the effect of how homophobia changes (Ibson 2002).

This is to say that Anderson realized that what drove men's social organizations (meaning which groups had power over other groups) was a social construction of masculinity that was related to varying levels of *homophobia*. Yet antipathy toward homosexuality alone did not explain matters. There was still a missing element.

Between the years 2003 and 2007, Anderson mused about cultural and theoretical differences, but he could not quite fashion a new social theory to explain what he was seeing with young men's rapidly changing masculinities. He knew that homophobia was key, but gender, and particularly homosocial tactility and intimacy, seemed to be displayed differently in countries that were high in homophobia. He then came across a book by John Ibson (2002), entitled *Picturing Men,* that showed how varying levels of the understanding that homosexuality exists in a culture impacts on how close men are willing to be with each other, emotionally and physically. In *Picturing Men,* Ibson (2002) shows that increasing cultural homophobia influences American heterosexual men to further police their homosocial tactility, while decreasing cultural homophobia has the opposite effect. Ibson's work was highly influential in the creation of Inclusive Masculinity Theory.

With Ibson's findings in mind, Anderson wanted a theory that that:

- Was a middle-range (meso) theory based on empirical studies.
- Was falsifiable.
- Included a stage model of masculinity that charted social change across time and cultures.
- Accounted for varying levels of cultural homophobia.
- Accounted for a culture's awareness that homosexuality exists.
- Was written in engaging and accessible language.
- Was precise about what the theory did and did not cover.
- Was open to revision by other scholars.

In 2009 he produced Inclusive Masculinity Theory (IMT). IMT emerged from research finding more inclusive behaviors of heterosexual men and the changing dynamics of male peer group cultures in the United States and United Kingdom. This body of research has shown that many young straight men: reject homophobia; include gay peers in friendship networks; are more emotionally intimate with friends; are physically tactile with other men; recognize bisexuality as a legitimate sexual orientation; embrace activities and artefacts once coded feminine; and eschew violence and bullying. His theory has been utilized in dozens of studies from across the social sciences to help explain these findings in other settings (Morales and Parsons 2017; Ripley 2018; Rumens 2017), including in a variety of digital realms (e.g. Caruso and Roberts 2018; Maloney et al. 2018, 2019).

In the absence of this policing mechanism, boys are permitted to engage in a wider range of behaviors without ridicule. This will include choices of clothes, expressions of friendship and emotional intimacy, hobbies, and pastimes, and who one chooses to be friends with. And as straight boys become friends with gay peers, they further undo their homophobia. McCormack (2012, 63) describes this as a "virtuous circle of decreasing homophobia."

Anderson argues that Connell's stratification of masculinity (from hegemonic, to complicit, to subordinated, and marginalized) no longer exists within a culture of inclusivity toward homosexuality. Instead, there exists a clustering of non-vertically arranged masculinity types, including football jocks, runners, band-members, preps, goths, emos, and computer geeks (see also McCormack 2011, 2012, 2014).

There are a few important conditions to Inclusive Masculinity Theory to keep in mind:

- Inclusive masculinity theory does not predict or intend to imply that all men within any given culture, or that every culture today is gay friendly. Instead, boys and men's behaviors will radically change if and when that culture does become accepting of homosexuality. The theory also predicts how men will behave in a culture of high homohysteria (here, adopting Connell's theorizing).

- Even if some individuals remain homophobic in an inclusive culture, they benefit from the larger context. It is when the majority of boys and men are no longer afraid to act in ways coded as feminine that the culture will change concerning what is acceptable masculine behaviors.
- Inclusivity does not refer to all forms of difference, but the form that was once exclusive to masculinity—homosexuality.
- A culture of changing masculinities occurs when straight men reduce their overt homophobia. Heterosexism still exists in these cultures, however.
- In a culture of inclusivity, dominance and privilege might still occur for certain men, this is mainly due to popularity. However, gay men are not excluded from achieving popularity, social dominance, or privilege.

Three Cultural Conditions to Inclusive Masculinities

Sociological research has demonstrated that masculinities in Western cultures have been closely related to personal and societal homophobia (e.g. Connell 1995; Plummer 1999). However, levels of homophobia do not in-and-of themselves explain changes in masculinities. Homophobia is only part of the social equation of importance to masculinity and sexuality. The cultural awareness of homosexuality existing within one's culture is also important.

Key to the understanding of Inclusive Masculinity Theory is homohysteria, which describes a culture where homophobia polices gendered behavior: A culture in which boys and men fear being socially perceived as gay because of the stigma they will receive as a result, and so alter their behaviors to avoid it.

Anderson suggests that there are three social conditions that must be met for a homohysteric culture to exist: (1) widespread awareness that homosexuality exists as an immutable sexual orientation within a significant portion of a culture's population; (2) high levels of homophobia in that culture; and (3) an association of gender atypicality with homosexuality. As each of these factors change, the level of homohysteria

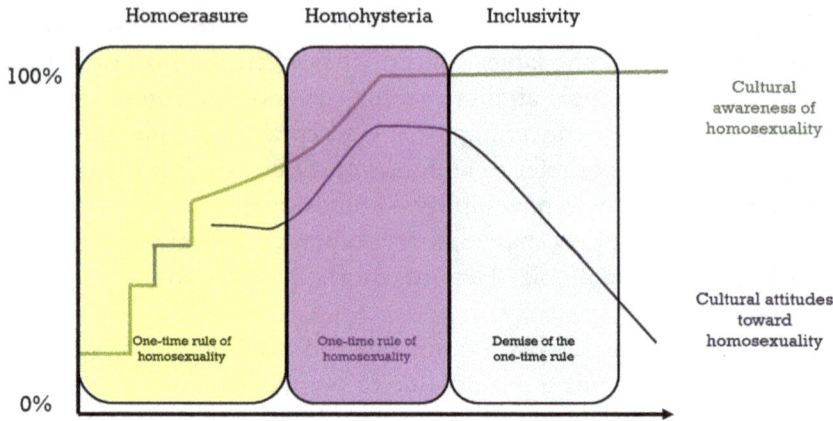

Fig. 4.1 Stage model of homohysteria

and the nature of gender dynamics in the culture will vary. Given that each of these factors can and do change, it is clear that there will be: temporal variation within any given culture; variation across cultures; and organizational variance within any given culture.

The above figure provides a visual representation of homohysteria as a stage model (see Anderson 2009; Anderson and McCormack 2018) (Fig. 4.1).

Stage 1: Homoerasure

Anderson (2009) argued that homohysteria is a product of modernity, and that the conditions for a culture to be homohysteric are the result of the discourses of gender and sexuality that emerged from the second industrial revolution in the West (see Cancian 1986). Recognizing that contemporary taxonomies of sexual identity are the result of specific historical, social, and intellectual circumstances (Greenberg 1988), the modern understanding of gay identity is pivotal to the emergence of homohysteric cultures. There is only evidence supporting homohysteria in modern cultures, and homohysteria does not apply to cultures that have no understanding of sexual identities, such as pre-modern Western civilizations.

Prior to urbanization, the majority of the population lived in rural areas and males with same-sex sexual desire were unlikely to encounter others with similar desires. However, the migration to the cities of the second industrial revolution provided a population density that enabled individuals with same-sex desire to organize socially (Bullough 2019). This included the emergence of sexual subcultures of gay men.

Related to the censure of these identities, new forms of labor that included long working hours structured men away from their families (Cancian 1986), influencing Freud's (1905) theorizing of same-sex sexual desires as a form of gender inversion. Near contemporaneously, sexological thinkers of the time, like Westphal, Ulrichs, and Krafft-Ebing, sought to classify homosexual acts as belonging to a *type* of person—a gender invert (Halperin 2000).

The emergence of sexual identities was supported by developments in the public and political sphere. The 1895 conviction of Oscar Wilde for "gross indecency" was particularly important: So extensive was the media coverage around the trial of Britain's celebrated playwright, it became emblematic of the gay male identity. The case consolidated the conflation of gender atypicality with same-sex attraction, the image of the male homosexual as effeminate. It was reported that many men fled to France after Wilde's conviction (Halperin 2000). Thus, the first wide-scale social recognition and awareness of same-sex sexuality as a static and relatively immutable sexual identity was accompanied by social and legal oppression of same-sex sexual acts. Ibson (2002) provides evidence that this British phenomenon influenced American men's behaviors, too.

This stigmatization of same-sex sexual identities was also consolidated through the medicalization of homosexuality (Greenberg 1988). Corresponding with an increasing criminalization of male same-sex sex doctors sought to define these acts within a medical framework as a way of consolidating their own emerging respectability as a profession. As a result, homosexuals were considered mentally ill or morally depraved (Greenberg 1988).

While sub-cultures organized around same-sex desires existed in the early twentieth century, threat of social and legal censure kept these cultures mostly underground, and the general population was unaware that such cultures existed. Where there was knowledge of same-sex desire, it was greatly stigmatized, and the general population rejected the notion that same-sex sexual identities were legitimate (Johnson 2003). These were thus cultures of *erasure*, where homophobia was so extreme that social and legal persecution forced sexual minorities to conceal their sexual desires and identities, preventing identity politics from occurring.

In this stage of erasure, gendered behaviors are not regulated by homophobia and men did not find their behaviors policed in the way we often think of today. In the latter decades of the nineteenth century and early part of thetwentieth, men exhibited a great deal of physical intimacy, posed for photos while sitting on each other's laps and gently hugging, and expressed themselves emotionally in letters (see Ibson 2002). These cultures were homophobic, but not homohysteric.

Stage 2: Homohysteria

Anderson (2009) and Anderson and McCormack (2018) developed the concept homohysteria as part of Inclusive Masculinity Theory in order to explain the power dynamics of changing homophobia on the masculinities of heterosexual men. While earlier scholarship demonstrated that high levels of cultural homophobia influence individuals to distance themselves from social suspicion of homosexuality through the avoidance of gender atypical behaviors (Ibson 2002), there was less attention paid to how changing social norms would influence these behaviors. Anderson used the term homohysteria to situate this scholarship within specific social and historical conditions, arguing that homophobia only operates this way in *homohysteric* settings. In other words, homophobia only influences gendered behaviors in particular social and historical contexts.

Homohysteria is particularly useful for understanding different attitudes toward homosocial tactility in homophobic cultures. We ask, why can men hold hands in Iran without being socially perceived as gay, but in America they are? The difference occurs because it is simply not accepted within Iran that homosexuality exists (Afary 2009)—the first condition of homohysteria mentioned earlier. Instead, homosexuality is claimed to be a Western, imperialist phenomenon. From this cultural perspective, homosexuality is considered an aberration and combined with extreme homophobia, homosexuality is effectively erased.

Iran, and other similar cultures in Africa and the Middle East are thus highly homophobic but they are not homohysteric. This is why homophobia does not regulate these men's gendered behaviors. Supporting this, news reports that document the persecution of gay men in these countries tend to report that the men were found engaging in same-sex sexual acts—they are not identified through their gendered behaviors. Thus, homohysteria provides an explanation for the differences between the intersections of homophobia, masculinity, and men's tactility in differing contemporary cultures, explaining why homophobia retains the ability to regulate gender in one culture but not another.

In the West, despite the liberalizing trend in the 1960s and 1970s, a combination of social factors led to an upsurge in homophobic attitudes in the mid-1980s (Loftus 2001). This, combined with a closing-down of inclusivity that had resulted from the feminist movements and beat neck politicking of the 1960s and 1970s (Hall 2011), occurred for three reasons:

1. HIV/AIDS

HIV/AIDS made visible the notion that homosexuals were present in the population in large numbers (Shilts 2007), giving cultural credibility to Kinsey's figure of 10%. Iconic figures dying of AIDS-related illnesses, like Robert Reed (Mr. Brady of the Brady Bunch) and Rock Hudson, also highlighted that homosexuality existed in men who seemed to embody masculinity and heterosexuality. In this culture, homosexuality was pathologized as a danger to physical health (Weeks 2007) and AIDS-phobia was exacerbated by a media panic. Rumors persisted that AIDS could be caught by a handshake or sneeze. Health care professionals, schools, and even airlines denied service to those with HIV/AIDS; some undertakers refused to bury those who had died from illnesses related to the disease. The image of the effeminate homosexual was replaced by that of the emaciated one (Weeks 2007).

2. Fundamentalist Christianity

A body of research shows that Fundamentalist Christianity grew increasingly concerned with and opposed to homosexuality and bisexuality in the 1980s, positioning them as threats to the nuclear family while conveniently using this fear to increase donations to the church in an age in which church attendance began to decline. This corresponded with an increasingly old-fashioned moral outlook more broadly. As Loftus (2001, 765) describes, "From the 1970s through the mid-1980s, Americans held increasingly traditional religious beliefs, with more people supporting prayer in school, and believing the Bible was the literal word of God."

3. The Integration of Fundamentalist Christianity and Politics

Politicians adopted the religious right's culture war against homosexuality, realizing that elections could be won through inspiring traditional Christians to vote (see Sherkat et al. 2011). These drew on fears of homosexuality and bisexuality and HIV to foster a moral panic about sexuality, social change, and so-called traditional family values (Lugg 1998).

It was in this epoch that awareness of homosexuality as a static identity in America was near-total and attitudinal homophobia reached its apex. Evidencing this, data from the 1987 General Social Survey (GSS) documented 77% of Americans stating that homosexual sex was *always wrong*, a rise from the previous decade. Following from the emergence of modern sexual identities and the conflation of gender and sexuality, these conditions proved to be a perfect storm for homohysteria. In this homohysteric culture, where femininity in males was conflated with homosexuality, men had to distance themselves socially and attitudinally from homosexuality (Floyd 2006; McCreary 1994). They aligned their gendered behaviors with idealized and narrowing definitions of masculinity.

Men used culturally endorsed sports to consolidate their masculine standing (Burton-Nelson 1994), and demonstrated masculinity through anger and violence, while denying fear and weakness (Kimmel 1998). They also stopped engaging in homosocial intimacy (Pollack 1999). Derlega et al. (1989) found undergraduate heterosexual males rated photos of men hugging as significantly more "abnormal" than photos of men standing alongside each other; conversely, they did not rate mixed-sex couples or women hugging as abnormal.

However, while HIV/AIDS led to the hysteria of the 1980s, it also served as a catalyst for identity politics and more inclusive attitudes. Given the power of social contact in improving social attitudes (Smith et al. 2009), the increased numbers of openly gay and bisexual males that resulted from the visibility of HIV/AIDS began to improve cultural attitudes among heterosexual communities in the early 1990s, particularly with Bill Clinton's advocating for gays to serve in the military in 1992. This is a trend that continues today (Anderson 2014). As homophobia decreased, so did the hysteria and homophobia gradually grew less effective in policing gendered behaviors—something McCormack (2012, 63) describes as a "virtuous circle of decreasing homophobia."

Stage 3: Inclusivity

The decrease of homophobia in British and American cultures accelerated in thetwenty-first century (e.g. Baunach 2012; Clements and Field 2014). Today, we live in a culture where people with positive attitudes toward homosexuality are in the majority, and where there is widespread recognition of homosexuality as a sexual identity. This is a culture of *inclusivity*. This does not mean that these cultures are inclusive in general, as there may well be issues related to class, ethnicity, and disability among other forms of discrimination. *Inclusivity* refers to attitudes toward gay men and lesbians, and even here heteronormativity may persist.

The key driver of decreasing homohysteria during this stage has been the improving attitudes toward homosexuality. The late 1990s and first decade of the new millennium saw the political labor of feminist and LGBT identity politics come to fruition. During this period, in which homohysteria decreased but homophobia was still used as a political tool, men started to lose some of the hypermasculinity of the 1980s. One of the most visible elements of this was the emergence of the metrosexual (Coad 2008).

In the late 1990s, metrosexuality emerged as a counter-cultural trend among young men who cared about their appearance and had a sexualized image of themselves. McNair (2002, p. 157) described metrosexuality as "a homosexualized vision of masculinity, in the sense that this studied narcissism and attention to self-grooming are traditionally associated with gayness." The metrosexual was interpreted as a conscious rejection of more traditional male norms where such expressionism was strictly censured. The metrosexual is such an important figure in understanding decreasing homohysteria because metrosexuality was used by heterosexual men as a way to engage in a softer form of masculinity without being socially perceived as gay.

During this time Anderson (2002, 2005a) also found that openly gay men were being accepted on their sporting teams, challenging dominant forms of masculinity by being the *best* on their teams. Furthermore, he found other sporting teams where *competing* versions of masculinity held equal sway. A style of masculinity that was inclusive of gay men and valued the voice of women was valued by as many people as the once-dominant misogynistic and homophobic version (Anderson 2005b). At a similar time, metrosexuality moved from the counterculture to be embraced in sports that were considered highly masculine (Anderson et al. 2016) and among men who use make-up but perceive themselves to be part of mainstream culture (Adams 2011). These findings were supported by research showing the increasing inclusion of sexual minorities in a range of contexts (Savin-Williams 2005; Parry et al. 2021).

These shifts in masculinity corresponded with the sustained decrease in homophobia that continues to the present day. General Social Survey (GSS) data show the proportion of the US population condemning homosexuality has steadily declined since 1987. In a statistical analysis of this data, Keleher and Smith (2012, 1232) contend that "willingness to accept lesbians and gays has grown enormously since 1990." While more progressive attitudes toward homosexuality are partly due to generational replacement (Loftus 2001), Keleher and Smith show that all demographic groups analyzed became more tolerant, and, importantly, that all age cohorts became more tolerant at the same rate; arguing that "we are witnessing a sweeping change in attitudes toward lesbians and gay men" (p. 1324).

Pew (June 13, 2013) research found that 70% of those born after 1980 support same-sex marriage, and 74% of these Americans believe that "homosexuality should be accepted by society." Highlighting the speed of social acceptance, when the same questions were asked just seven years earlier, 46% said they would be less likely to vote for a homosexual candidate" (see also Baunach 2012).

It is also important to stress that decreasing homophobia is an uneven social process. The visibility of gay and bisexual men is, for example, still restricted in professional sports, among senior politicians, within organized religions, and among elementary and high school teachers (Anderson 2011). Notwithstanding this variance, considerable evidence documents a markedly improved environment for sexual minorities.

The masculinities of men in this stage of inclusivity have changed dramatically (McCormack 2012). In general, adolescent males are no longer police their gendered behaviors to avoid being socially perceived as gay; or do so to a much lesser extent.

Inclusive masculinity theory argues that there will be a relationship between these above-mentioned behaviors and the social organization of masculinity types. In a culture of extreme homohysteria boys and men will align, vertically, in a homophobic-hegemonic stratification similar, or perhaps identical, to the one Connell alludes to, while restricting the above-mentioned categories to what is perceived to be heterosexual. But, in a culture of inclusivity—when a "so what" attitude exists around male homosexuality—a vertical, hegemonic, stratification of masculinity types will not exist. Instead, multiple masculinity types will proliferate without inequality.

The primary contribution of Inclusive Masculinity Theory is that it connects men's gendered behaviors with the social trend of decreasing homophobia, explaining variance between cultures and generations.

Anderson also ties sexuality studies in more explicitly with masculinity studies. As Chapter 5 shows, his theory suggests that cultures with high antipathy toward homosexuality will have more prescriptive views on what men can permissibly do sexually, and that in a culture of inclusive masculinity, multiple forms of sexual interactions and sexual identities (like bisexuality) that were once highly stigmatized become socially acceptable (Anderson and McCormack 2018; Maloney, Roberts and Caruso 2018).

Chapter Conclusion

This chapter has examined social theories that try to explain the social construction of masculinity. It highlighted that a first wave of masculinity scholarship relied on both family structure and social constructionism. Then, Connell's notion of hegemonic masculinity (1987, 1995) dominated the literature concerning masculinities until the last decade or so.

The third wave is that of theories looking to the multiplicity of masculinity types within any given culture. Chief among them, Anderson's (2009) Inclusive Masculinity Theory has been taken up by a host of younger scholars, whose experiences of masculinity do not reflect what Connell described. Anderson's theory has not, however, become hegemonic, the way Connell's has. In fact, it has opened up a flurry of new ideas about masculinities.

Masculinity scholars have never been freer to introduce new models of masculinity-making, and even more free to establish new archetypes of masculinity. In the last decade we have seen masculine archetypes flourish within the masculinity literature: personalized masculinities, soft-boiled masculinities, hybrid masculinities, cool masculinities, caring masculinities, flexible masculinities, chameleon masculinities, pastiche masculinities, styled masculinities, saturated masculinities, and orthodox masculinity, among others. Non-academic labels include metrosexuality and toxic masculinity. Some of these may be theorized as to their emergence and others not.

Although these "types" have not caught on with other scholars to the same extent as Connell's theorizing, they are still pervasive. This proliferation of ideas nonetheless highlights that the field of masculinities has moved far away from the one, homogenized, type of masculinity offered by Sex Roles, and the four types offered by Hegemonic Masculinity.

We highlight that Inclusive Masculinity Theory does not list "types." It instead, recognized that a plurality of masculinity types can now exist. This means that scholars using this theory are freer to investigate the nuanced complexities of particular types of masculinity. There is, we believe, a bourgeoning understanding of masculinities, in the same way that Chapter 5 will show that there is a bourgeoning understanding of sexualities among millennial men, too.

Of relevance to the bromance, Inclusive Masculinity Theory proves to have more utility than any other masculinity theory for one reason: it explains why, historically, men have moved from a disposition of emotional and physical intimacy in the nineteenth century and early twentieth century (Ibson 2002), to one of physical and emotional distance in the later decades of the twentieth century (Connell 1987, 1989, 2000, 2005); to again being able to have physical and emotional intimacy in the twenty-first century. No other theory does this.

References

Acker, J. (1990). Hierarchies, jobs, bodies: A theory of gendered organizations. *Gender and Society*, 4(2), 139–158.

Adams, A. (2011). Josh wears pink cleats: Inclusive Masculinity on the Soccer Field. *Journal of Homosexuality*, 58(5), 579–596.

Afary, J. (2009). *Sexual politics in modern Iran.* Cambridge: Cambridge University Press.

Anderson, E. (2000). *Trailblazing: The true story of America's first openly gay track coach.* New York: Alyson Publications.

Anderson, E. (2002). Openly gay athletes: Contesting hegemonic masculinity in a homophobic environment. *Gender McCormack and Anderson 2014a,b society*, 16(6), 860–877.

Anderson, E. (2005a). *In the game: Gay athletes and the cult of masculinity.* New York: University of New York Press.

Anderson, E. (2005b). Orthodox and inclusive masculinity: Competing masculinities among heterosexual men in a feminized terrain. *Sociological Perspectives, 48*(3), 337–355.

Anderson, E. (2008a). Inclusive masculinity in a fraternal setting. *Men and Masculinities, 10*(5), 604–620.

Anderson, E. (2008b). "Being masculine is not about who you sleep with…:" Heterosexual athletes contesting masculinity and the one-time rule of homosexuality. *Sex Roles, 58*(1–2), 104–115.

Anderson, E. (2009). *Inclusive masculinity: The changing nature of masculinities*. London: Routledge.

Anderson, E. (2011). Masculinities and sexualities in sport and physical cultures: Three decades of evolving research. *Journal of Homosexuality, 58*(5), 565–578.

Anderson, E. (2012a). *The monogamy gap: Men, love, and the reality of cheating*. Oxford University Press

Anderson, E. (2012b). Inclusive masculinity in a physical education setting. *Journal of Boyhood Studies, 6*(1–2), 151–165.

Anderson, E. (2014). *21st Century Jocks: Sporting Men and Contemporary Heterosexuality*. New York: Macmillan.

Anderson, E. (2015). Assessing the sociology of sport: On changing masculinities and homophobia. *International Review for the Sociology of Sport, 50*(4–5), 363–367.

Anderson, E., & McCormack, M. (2018). Inclusive masculinity theory: Overview, reflection and refinement. *Journal of gender studies, 27*(5), 547–561.

Anderson, E., Magrath, R., and Bullingham, R. (2016). *Out in Sport: The Experiences of Openly Gay and Lesbian Athletes*. New York: Routledge.

Arxer, S. L. (2011). Hybrid masculine power: Reconceptualizing the relationship between

Baunach, D. M. (2012). Changing same-sex marriage attitudes in America from 1988 through 2010. *Public Opinion Quarterly, 76*, 364–378.

Beasley, C. (2008). Rethinking hegemonic masculinity in a globalizing world. *Men and masculinities, 11*(1), 86–103.

Berger, P. L., and Luckmann, T. (1966). The social construction of reality: A treatise in the sociology of knowledge. *Anchor*.

Borkowska, K. (2018). Approaches to Studying Masculinity: A Nonlinear Perspective of Theoretical Paradigms. *Men and Masculinities*, 1097184X18768376.

Bourdieu, P. (2001). *Masculine domination*. Stanford University Press.

Bradford, S., Hills, L., & Johnston, C. (2016). Unintended volunteers: the volunteering pathways of working class young people in community sport. *International Journal of Sport Policy and Politics*, *8*(2), 231–244.

Bridges, T., (2014). A very "gay" straight? Hybrid masculinities, sexual aesthetics, and the changing relationship between masculinity and homophobia. *Gender & Society*, *28*(1), 58–82.

Bullough, V. L. (2019). *Homosexuality: A history (From Ancient Greece to gay liberation)*. Routledge.

Burton-Nelson, M. (1994). *The stronger women get the more men love football.* New York: Avon Books.

Cancian, F. M. (1986). The feminization of love. *Signs: Journal of Women in Culture and Society*, *11*(4), 692–709.

Caruso, A., & Roberts, S. (2018). Exploring constructions of masculinity on men's body-positivity blog. *Journal of Sociology*, *54*(4), 627–646.

Cleary, A. (2012). Suicidal action, emotional expression, and the performance of masculinities. *Social Science and Medicine*, *74*(4), 498–505.

Clements, B., and Field, C. (2014). Public opinion toward homosexuality and gay rights in Great Britain. *Public Opinion Quarterly*, *78*(2), 523–547.

Coad, D. (2008). *The metrosexual: Gender, sexuality and sport*. Albany: State University of New York Press.

Connell, R. (1987). *Gender and power: Society, the person and sexual politics*. Berkeley: University of California Press.

Connell, R. (1989). Cool guys, swots and wimps: The interplay of masculinity and education. *Oxford Review of Education*, *15*(3), 291–203.

Connell, R. (1995). *Masculinities*. Berkeley: University of California Press.

Connell, R. (2000). *The men and the boys*. Berkeley: University of California Press

Connell, R. (2005). *Masculinities*. Berkeley: University of California Press

Connell, R., and Messerschmidt, J. (2005). Hegemonic masculinity: Rethinking the concept. *Gender and Society*, *19*(6), 829–859.

Demetriou, D. Z. (2001). Connell's concept of hegemonic masculinity: A critique. *Theory and Society*, *30*(3), 337–361.

Derlega, V. J., Lewis, R. J., Harrison, S., Winstead, B. A., and Costanza, R. (1989). Gender differences in the initiation and attribution of tactile intimacy. *Journal of Nonverbal Behavior*, *13*(2), 83–96.

Elliott, K., (2016). Caring masculinities theorizing an emerging concept. *Men and Masculinities*, *19*(3), 240–259.

Fairhurst, G. T., and Grant, D. (2010). The social construction of leadership: A sailing guide. *Management Communication Quarterly*, *24*(2), 171–210.

Floyd, K. (2006). *Communicating affection: Interpersonal behavior and social context*. Cambridge: Cambridge University Press.

Freud, S. (1905). *Three essays on the theory of sexuality.* Basic Books 1962.

Gaston, L., Magrath, R., and Anderson, E. (2018). From hegemonic to inclusive masculinities in English professional football: Marking a cultural shift. *Journal of Gender Studies, 27*(3), 301–312.

Gramsci, A. (1971). *Selections from the Prison Notebooks*. London: Lawrence and Wishart.

Greenberg, D. (1988). *The construction of homosexuality.* Chicago: University of Chicago Press.

Grindstaff, L., and West, E. (2011). Hegemonic masculinity on the sidelines of sport. *Sociology Compass, 5*(10), 859–881.

Hall, J. (2011). Sex differences in friendship expectations: A meta-analysis. *Journal of Social and Personal Relationships, 28*(6), 723–747.

Halperin, D. M. (2000). How to do the history of male homosexuality. *GLQ: A Journal of Lesbian and Gay Studies, 6*(1), 87–123.

Hearn, J. (2004). From hegemonic masculinity to the hegemony of me. *Feminist Theory*. London: Sage.

Hearn, J., Nordberg, M., Andersson, K., Balkmar, D., Gottzén, L., Klinth, R., Pringle, K., and Sandberg, L. (2012). Hegemonic masculinity and beyond: 40 years of research in Sweden. *Men and Masculinities, 15*(1), 31–55.

Heath, M. (2003). Soft-boiled masculinity renegotiating gender and racial ideologies in the promise keepers movement. *Gender & Society, 17*(3), 423–444.

Ibson, J. (2002). *Picturing men: A century of male relationships in everyday American photography*. Illinois: University of Chicago Press.

Jackson, C., and Dempster, S. (2009). 'I sat back on my computer… with a bottle of whisky next to me'. *Journal of Gender Studies, 18*(4), 341–356.

Johnson, H. (2003). *Sleepwalking through history: America in the Reagan years*. London: WW Norton and Company.

Keleher, A., and Smith, E. (2012). Growing support for gay and lesbian equality since 1990. *Journal of Homosexuality, 59*, 1307–1326.

Kimmel, M. S. (1998). *Manhood in America: A cultural history*. New York: Free Press.

Loftus, J. (2001). America's liberalization in attitudes toward homosexuality, 1973 to 1998. *American Sociological Review, 66*(5), 762–782.

Lugg, C. A. (1998). The religious right and public education: The paranoid politics of homophobia. *Educational Policy, 12*(3), 267–283.

Magrath, R., Anderson, E., and Roberts, S. (2015). On the door-step of equality: Attitudes toward gay athletes among academy-level footballers. *International Review for the Sociology of Sport, 50*(7), 804–821.

Magrath, R., Cleland, J., and Anderson, E. (2017). Bisexual erasure in the British print media: Representation of Tom Daley's coming out. *Journal of Bisexuality, 17*(3), 300–317.

Maloney, M., Roberts, S., & Caruso, A. (2018). 'Mmm… I love it, bro!': Performances of masculinity in YouTube gaming. *New Media & Society, 20*(5), 1697–1714.

Maloney, M., Roberts, S., and Graham, T. (2019). *Gender, masculinity and video gaming: Analysing Reddit's r/gaming community*. Springer Nature.

McCormack, M. (2011). Mapping the terrain of homosexually-themed language. *Journal of homosexuality, 58*(5), 664–679.

McCormack, M. (2012). *The declining significance of homophobia: How teenage boys are redefining masculinity and heterosexuality*. New York: Oxford University Press.

McCormack, M. (2014). The intersection of youth masculinities, decreasing homophobia and class: An ethnography. *The British Journal of Sociology, 65*(1), 130–149.

McCreary, D. R. (1994). The male role and avoiding femininity. *Sex Roles, 31*, 517–531.

McNair, B. (2002). *Striptease culture: Sex, media and the democratisation of desire*. Routledge.

Mercer, J. (2017). *Gay pornography: Representations of masculinity and sexuality*. London: I. B. Tauris.

Messerschmidt, J. W. (2012). Engendering gendered knowledge: Assessing the academic appropriation of hegemonic masculinity. *Men and Masculinities, 15*(1), 56–76.

Moller, M. (2007) Exploiting patterns: A critique of hegemonic masculinity. *Journal of Gender Studies, 16*(3), 263–276.

Morales, L., and Caffyn-Parsons, E. (2017). "I Love You, Guys": A study of inclusive masculinities among high school cross-country runners. *Boyhood Studies, 10*(1), 66–87.

Parry, K. D., Storr, R., Kavanagh, E. & Anderson, E. (2021). Conceptualising organisational cultural lag: Marriage equality and Australian sport. *Journal of Sociology, 57*(4), 986–1008.

Plummer, D. (1999). *One of the boys: Masculinity, homophobia, and modern manhood*. New York: Routledge.

Pollack, W. (1999). *Real boys: Rescuing our sons from the myths of boyhood.* New York: Macmillan.

Ripley, M. (2018). The integration of British undergraduate men's public and private masculinities. *Journal of Gender Studies, 27*(3), 288–300.

Roberts, S. (2018). *Young working-class men in transition.* Routledge.

Roberts, S., Anderson, E., & Magrath, R. (2017). Continuity, change and complexity in the performance of masculinity among elite young footballers in England. *The British Journal of Sociology, 68*(2), 336–357.

Rumens, N. (2017). Postfeminism, men, masculinities and work: A research agenda for gender and organization studies scholars. *Gender, Work and Organization, 24*(3), 245–259.

Savin-Williams, R. (2005). *The new gay teenager* (Vol. 3). Cambridge: Harvard University Press.

Sherkat, D. E., Powell-Williams, M., Maddox, G., and De Vries, K. M. (2011). Religion, politics, and support for same-sex marriage in the United States, 1988–2008. *Social Science Research, 40*(1), 167–180.

Shilts, R. (2007). *And the band played on: Politics, people, and the AIDS epidemic, 20th-anniversary edition.* Macmillan.

Smith, S., Axelton, A., and Saucier, D. (2009). The effects of contact on sexual prejudice: A meta-analysis. *Sex Roles, 61*(3–4), 178–191.

Swain, J. (2006). Reflections on patterns of masculinity in school settings. *Men and Masculinities, 8*(3), 331–349

Twenge, J. M., Sherman, R. A., and Wells, B. E. (2016). Changes in American adults' reported same-sex sexual experiences and attitudes, 1973–2014. *Archives of Sexual Behavior, 45*(7), 1713–1730.

Ward, M. (2015). The chameleonisation of masculinity: Jimmy's multiple performances of a working-class self. *Masculinities & Social Change, 4*(3), 215–240.

Weeks, J. (2007). *The world we have won: The remaking of erotic and intimate life.* New York: Routledge.

West, C., and Zimmerman, D. H. (1987). Doing gender. *Gender and Society, 1*(2), 125–151.

5

Illustrating the Bromance

The aim of this book is to examine the way in which men aged between 18 and 23 years constitute, experience, and understand bromances, within the university sports team setting. Specifically, this project observes and investigates the intimate nature of bromances over the course of a year; unpacking the meaning and significance that these relationships hold in the men's everyday lives.

Older research on same-sex male friendships shows that they have been significantly regulated in their level of physical and emotional intimacy, responding to the widespread cultural condemnation of homosexuality (Jourard 1971; Komarovsky 1974; Lewis 1978; Morin and Garfinkle 1978). Because men did not want to associate with the femininity and diseased ascription afforded to gay men, they distanced themselves from their closest friends to avoid homosexual suspicion (McKay 1993).

More recent research however draws attention to the changing nature of men's friendships in the twenty-first century. Consistently, and with frequency and rapidity, millennial-based and post-millennial based research has shown that young men have become more emotional, loving, and physical in their same-sex friendships (Adams 2011; Anderson 2014; Becht and Vingerhoets 2002; Ghaziani 2017;

Hammarén and Johansson 2014; Herlitz 2001; Magrath et al. 2013; McCormack 2012; Murray et al. 2016; Ralph and Roberts 2020; Roberts et al. 2017; Silva 2013; Way 2011); espousing much more liberal and tolerant views of sexual diversity than their parents' generation did (Anderson 2014; Herlitz 2001).

This chapter responds to Thompson's (2015) request for a further exploration into the subtext of bromances by highlighting how these university men broadly define and understand the bromance term, asking them to exemplify and explain the characteristics that constitute these relationships. Participants were also prompted to clarify what behaviors and feelings were unique to their bromances. Results are presented in four parts, based on the key characteristics the men associated with their bromance(s); shared interests, emotional intimacy, love, and physical intimacy.

We begin by providing a narrative of what a bromance looks like in popular culture.

Illustrating the Bromance in Film

One place to see the representation of ideal gendered behavior is in movies. The 1980s and early 1990s had, for example, hyper masculine characters: like Rambo and Terminator. In fact, since the dawn of cinematic representation tough men have been featured, but there seemed to be a ramping up of the power of men in films.

However, since the turn of the twenty-first century, popular culture has been less concerned with glorifying the hypermasculine characteristics of Arnold Schwarzenegger and Silvester Stallone, and instead often rejects them (McCormack 2012; Morris and Anderson 2015) or at least other images of men are equally valued by the industry.

Hollywood movies have begun to include two male characters that have an intimate friendship with tactile chemistry to play the leading role in films (Boyle and Berridge 2012). This is not to suggest that tough-guy movies are not still in theaters; but it is to suggest that there is greater diversity of characters that Hollywood desires us to relate to. This diversity includes tough women, women as super heroes, gay men, children, and others.

It's important to consider here that Hollywood may not produce films that it thinks to reflect what masculinity is for the average man today; they still produce plenty of bangs, crashes, fights, bombs, and other explosions. Yet, Hollywood is also faced with declining big screen attendance, as internet companies make films cheaper for viewing at home. Cinemas may therefore rely more on big special effects and action movies to draw people to pay for the big screen experience.

Despite this, in American films, we've begun to see the bromance as a feature of films. In defining the on-screen bromance, Davies (2014) identifies them as:

> Intimate bond(s) between two men, while ostensibly platonic, that carry greater narrative and emotional weight, perhaps even a romantic or erotic weight, than the relations either man enjoys with wives, girlfriends or other characters. (p. 109)

Gill and Hansen-Miller (2011) describe these films as the "Lad Flick" or "Lad Movies," explaining that they are a hybrid of the "buddy movie" and "romantic comedy." Critically, the romance is between the leading heterosexual male protagonists, much in the same way that Rotundo (1989) speaks of romantic friendships occurring a century ago. There has been a sharp rise in the number of on-screen bromances (Boyle and Berridge 2012; DeAngelis 2014; Gill and Hansen-Miller 2011), too.

Concerning the relationship between two men featured in the films, they tend to embody cross-characteristics from two types of relationships; the loyalty, kinship, and trust found in a brother (companionate love), and the excitement, infatuation, and intimacy found in romantic relationships (Fisher 2004). Bromantic films often carry the same narrative as traditional romantic comedies, except instead of the ending being characterized by the man and women falling in love, the films often conclude with the two male leads bearing shared hardships to achieve a stronger, more intimate, and closer friendship (DeAngelis 2014). Indeed, the word love is often used between the two leading men.

Blockbuster films such as *I Love you Man* (2009), *21 Jump Street* (2012), *Due Date* (2010), *The 40-Year-Old Virgin* (2005), *Superbad* (2007), *the Hangover* (2009), *American Pie* (1999), and *The Other Guys* (2010) have depicted a great capacity among men to constitute complex and dynamic relationships grounded in male closeness, trust, and homosociality; at least in movies. The New Statesman Magazine ran with the title: "22 Jump Street isn't just homofriendly – it's homolovely," highlighting the popular films inclusive attitude toward same-sex love.

The trends continued throughout the decade. In 2019, for example, among the highest-grossing and most talked about films revolved around a male friendship: *Once Upon a Time…in Hollywood; The Lighthouse,* and *The Irishman.* It is important to note that these films are particularly popular with young men, being that men from previous generations would most likely struggle to relate to the newer generation of characters and films. Men in these new era bromance films are not presented as heroic or unheroic, they are the everyday guys, having an ordinariness that we have not come to expect from Hollywood (Gill and Hansen-Miller 2011).

The problem of having such a media and Hollywood led concept as the bromance is that its representation and definition is created and maintained in the fictional realm and has been interpreted with significant variation and understanding. For example, there have been several media frenzies over former American President, Barack Obama, having lunch with another man, or patting them on the back, resulting in "bromance" led headlines.

These media pieces only look for the symbolic displays of bromances, through hugs or gestures, but are not able to capture the emotionality and vulnerability that operates in "real" close male friendships. Indeed, some social researchers consider the bromance in isolation as genre of film, and neglect to define them outside of this genre (Forster 2014). Indeed, scholars have not attempted to assess in detail the links between these on-screen relationships, and to what extent they exist among men. Despite the prevalence of the bromance discourse in popular culture, social science research has failed to discuss its implications, and neglected to incorporate the term into literature on close male relations.

DeAngelis (2014) problematizes the concept by noting that almost all filmic representations end in heterosexual resolution; a conclusion that confirms that whilst the men express same-sex love and intimacy, they are definitively heterosexual. This apologetic approach to same-sex touch highlights a certain cultural unease that may remain regarding homosexuality, as we leave a period of heightened homophobia.

Indeed, in discussing on-screen bromances, Pomerance (2014) suggests that "the open fakery of homosexual commitment may itself play to the detriment of gay liberation" (p. 260). Movie representations of the bromance also have implications for the marginalization of women, as the traditional romantic partner is replaced by another male character. These are the types of nuances that will be assessed as part of this research project, but in relation to the real lives of young men.

Thompson (2015) notes that there is a disagreement among scholars regarding both the benefit of having such a phenomenon as the bromance, and its definition. Nonetheless he concludes that television and film are "highlighting a subtext of male emotion within bromance[s] that warrants further exploration" (p. 3). Our research endeavored to address Thompson's (2015) proposal by engaging in, observing, and interviewing young men in a university sports team over an extensive period of time about their bromances; attempting to achieve a deeper comprehension and understanding of the way in which these bromances operate in the everyday lives of young men.

Illustrating the Bromance in Sociological Studies of Men

This ethnographic study is not the first examination of the bromance that we have conducted. Previous to this, we published an article in *Sex Roles*, entitled, The Bromance: Undergraduate Male Friendships and the Expansion of Contemporary Homosocial Boundaries (Robinson et al. 2018). That research was conducted on a different population of men, prior to this ethnographic research.

In the Robinson et al. (2018) study, over a 3-month period, between August 2014 and November 2014, we conducted semi-structured interviews into the friendship experiences of 30 undergraduate men who identified as heterosexual or mostly heterosexual and who were enrolled in one of four undergraduate sport-degree programs at one university in the United Kingdom. To be part of the research, participants needed to identify as either exclusively heterosexual or mostly heterosexual on Vrangalova and Savin-Williams's (2012) 5-point scale of sexual identity: exclusively heterosexual, mostly heterosexual, bisexual, mostly homosexual, or exclusively homosexual. Thus, sexuality was presented to participants as a continuous variable. This screening was part of the demographic information that participants filled out alongside their ethics form.

The sample comprised men aged 18–22 years (18 years, $n = 1$; 19 years, $n = 15$; 20 years, $n = 9$; 21 years, $n = 4$; 22 years, $n = 1$), and although not selected for race, the near-exclusively white student body of this British university limited our analysis to that of only white men. Our sample was also populated by participants from self-identified, middle-class backgrounds. Thus, our findings are limited to a somewhat homogeneous sample of young, largely white, heterosexual men.

Results found that, contrary to the repressive homosociality of the 1980s and 1990s, these men embraced a significantly more inclusive, tactile, and emotionally diverse approach to their homosocial relationships. All participants provided comparable definitions of what a bromance is and how it operates, and all had at least one bromantic friend. More so, all declared support for homosexuality.

And, in order to assure that the men we interviewed were not strategically presenting positive or overly exaggerated support for gay men and male homosexuality (a prerequisite for inclusive masculinities), eighteen months prior, we distributed Herek and Mclemore's (1988) Attitudes Towards Gays and Lesbians scale to these students. The survey was administered anonymously upon the students' first day of arrival at the university to all students enrolled in one of six sport-related degrees.

Results showed wide support for male homosexuality, which meant that all men espoused Pro-gay attitudes on arrival at university. We then waited 18 months for these students to have time to build bromances, before announcing that we were looking to interview students on issues related to masculinity. This meant that the students were not pre-selected for a bromance; although the nature of the population studied (athletes) suggests that they are part of homosocial environments that require a large degree of time commitment. This promotes the likelihood of these participants having time to develop a bromance. As a result, all of the 30 men had at least one bromance.

All of those in this prior study suggested that bromances had more to offer than a standard friendship. Participants described a bromance as being more emotionally intimate, physically demonstrative, and based upon unrivaled trust and cohesion compared to their other friendships. Participants used their experiences with romances and familial relations as a reference point for considering the conditions of a bromance. Results support the view that declining homophobia and its internalization has had significantly positive implications for male expression and intimacy.

We concluded from the research that the bromance had potential to improve men's mental health and social well-being because participants indicate these relationships provide a space for emotional disclosure and the discussion of potentially traumatic and sensitive issues.

A year later we published another article in *Men and Masculinities*, titled: Privileging the Bromance: A Critical Appraisal of Romantic and Bromantic Relationships (Robinson et al. 2019). In this article, we highlighted that the increasingly intimate, emotive, and trusting nature of bromances offers young men a new social space for emotional disclosure, outside of traditional heterosexual relationships.

Participants stated that the lack of boundaries and judgment in a bromance is expressed as emotionally rivaling the benefits of a heterosexual romance. Our participants mostly determined that a bromance offered them elevated emotional stability, enhanced emotional disclosure, social fulfillment, and better conflict resolution, compared to the emotional lives they shared with girlfriends. Thus, this research provided an empirically grounded conceptual framework for understanding men's view of close homosocial relationships in comparison to their romantic relationship in the twenty-first century.

There is no other, current, data-driven research on the bromance since these two articles. Whilst there are articles discussing the bromance in film, we are left with only these two articles to discuss the definition, operation, boundaries, privileges, and problems associated with the bromance. This ethnography, therefore, should provide the most comprehensive analysis of its operation.

Illustrating the Bromance in This Ethnography

In order to make salient the understandings and workings of a bromance among men we studied, we highlight what we consider to be a typical male-bonded pair, Gordon and Ronnie When asked to describe what a bromance was, Gordon said a bromance is:

> Having a best friend and it's seen like a marriage; like a relationship. I have a bromance with Ronnie and the way we are around each other, it's weird. We are so connected and so alike that we can look at each other and laugh. It's just got to that point in our relationship. Everyone says were like an old married couple and we have arguments, but we make up and get over it. I respect his friendship and he does a lot for me; he can keep secrets and always listens when I need him.

Similarly, talking about Gordon, Ronnie said:

> It is just for guys. I'm in a bromance with Gordon, definitely. It's just a guy relationship where they are really close, have each other's backs and would do anything for one another… You're not attracted to them because of a physical reason. That's why it's bro, like brotherly love. He can always set me straight if I'm pissed off, which is quite often. You love the people you care about, and they are essentially like a brother from another mother. Its cliché, but they are your best mate and you do everything together. It's nice to have something like that. Like, with me and Gordon, everyone says we are inseparable.

As Gordon and Ronnie highlight, their bromance, which they identify as a relationship as opposed to a friendship, receives recognition from "everyone." In interviews, when participants were asked to identify bromances from within the club, theirs was mentioned frequently.

Ed said, "They are a tight unit, and you know they will always be best mates." During a social evening at the local pub, having just completed an interview for this research, Ronnie promoted the interview to others as a "mind fuck eye-opener," openly (but relatively jokingly) exclaiming that he left the interview "questioning my sexuality because of the way I talked about Gordon." Indeed, Gordon said in his interview, "I've never… ever… thought about it like this before, but when I'm describing my bromance with Ronnie, I am pretty much describing a full-on romantic relationship."

These men were both final year students and had been friends since their first year at university. They were also very popular members of the club. Stefan, the lead author on this book was their roommate whilst on Tour; a weeklong holiday with 32 other members of the club (19 men and 13 women), mostly involving excessive alcohol consumption, swimming, and partying.

On the 26-hours coach journey to the destination, a game of gay chicken was initiated by the club's social secretaries. Here, two passports were drawn at random from a bag and whoever's it was, they were challenged to make out (kiss for a prolonged time) with each other, and the loser of the game was the first one to pull away. After two other sets of men had played, Gordon and Ronnie were drawn from the bag.

Before starting the kiss, both men talked hesitantly, both exclaiming, "There is no way I am backing down." In front of a full coach of people, they kissed passionately and aggressively with open mouths and tongues, wrapped in each other's arms, soon falling to the floor without breaking the seal between their lips, and eventually putting their hands down each other's trousers to further "freak" the other person into submission. The episode ended after about a minute, when Gordon hurt himself by hitting his head hard into the back of a chair.

When discussing the event later in the day Gordon said, "Because we've done it [kissed] so many times with each other before, it's nothing new. So even though they were trying to embarrass us, were so comfortable with each other that it's not an issue."

Whilst staying in their room for the week on tour, Stefan observed Gordon and Ronnie take part in some other, more novel physical behaviors. Ronnie would often walk around the room naked or lay down on his bed with his legs spread, talking to Gordon. There was no embarrassment or awkwardness in the moment. As Ronnie said before Stefan observed this behavior, "It's no big deal, being naked just shows your completely comfortable with each other." At one point on Tour, Ronnie was naked and pretended to get sexually aroused and started mimicking sex with Gordon's pillow, and Gordon would try and wrestle the pillow from his grasp.

Gordon and Ronnie's relationship provides a rich example of how the participants experience and define their bromances. Because of this, we use them as an exemplar throughout this book. However, every participant in this study said they were in a bromance like this. Some with more than one person. Using data collected primarily through interviews with participants about their involvement in bromances, and how their experiences influenced their understanding and definition of the term, their narratives highlight the importance of these relationships in their everyday lives.

Bromances Compared to Friendship

In considering the bromance and the data collected, it is appropriate here to consider how these men locate and reference their bromances in relation to their friendships. This enables us to broadly understand where bromances are situated in the men's social world and provides an overview of how important these relationships are in the men's lives. Specifically, during interviews, the men were asked to identify the differences and similarities in the way these two relationships operate, and their permitted social boundaries.

When asked about the difference between a friendship and a bromance, participants were clear to differentiate between the two, arguing that bromances were more important. Jerry said, "Bromances are a lot closer than friendships, because you can tell that person anything; stuff you would never tell your normal friends." Pete said, "For me, a bromance is someone you're always there for, and he is there for you. He's got your back and you've got his." Andy said, "Everything is more; more close, more intimate, more physical and more funny." Callum explained:

> Compared to friendships, a bromance is a lot stronger, and you see them a lot more. I speak most days to my close boyfriends, and you make the effort to do things with them like go for meals and go out together, whereas friends you will see them out and talk to them, but you don't make the same effort.

Whilst Callum draws attention to the desire to spend time together doing things, the vast majority of men suggest that one doesn't need to be doing anything to enjoy one another's company. Interestingly, he describes bromances as his close boyfriends, which some might assume means he is gay, but he identifies as the opposite. Taylor said, "If you're meeting a friend, you're doing it for a reason. But with bromances, you can literally do nothing and still have a laugh."

Taylor and Jaden, who both blindly identified one another as a bromance, lived together at university. They would always arrive at pre-drinks (the session of alcohol consumption before heading to town or the student union) together, often in the same fancy dress (costumes) having helped each other get ready. Even when being interviewed, one waited for the other for 40 minutes in order to walk 10 minutes home together.

Ed explained, "Often it can be awkward to go for dinner or the cinema with one friend, but with a bromance, you don't feel that way at all, because you're so connected." Gordon said, "You don't feel the need to invite other people if you two are doing something. It's kind of exclusive in a way." Similarly, Taylor explained "It's more exclusive. Like earlier today I went to a restaurant with just Jaden, and I didn't feel the need to invite anyone else." Andy said, "Bromances aren't regimented like friendships, they are fun. You can make fun from any situation." As Jaden explained, "When my bromances are over, we cuddle on the bed, watch a whole film sometimes without talking, but that's because we can. It's not weird." Harry's explanation encompassed many of the dominant perspectives held by the men:

> A bromance is an extra bond, and they are closer. You talk about more intimate things like sex and issues or problems in your life. But with a friend you would talk more about your interests only, like football or something. Bromances talk about more intimate stuff like your sexuality,

or things that upset you, because you can connect with them in a way you can't with normal friends.

Blake highlighted the importance of longevity in the relationship, "Friends and girlfriends can come and go, but with a bromance, you know they will be your mate for life." Similarly, Andy said, "In a true bromance, you spend all your time with each other… But at the same time, with my bromance, we can spend months away from each other, and pick up right where we left off." Rory said, "There's those one or two bros who you know will stick by your side forever" and Harry said, "I have lots of friends, but if you asked who would really be there for me if I needed them, it's a select few, and they are my bromances." Gordon said, "If you argue with friends, it can be over, but even if I argue with Ronnie, we can never properly fall out because we depend on each other."

For the participants in this study, they clearly identify bromances as having a higher social standing and importance in their lives, when compared to their normal friendships. When discussing the origins of the bromance lexis, there was a strong understanding from participants that it was a term used for the close friendships men can have, being a dyadic mix of relationship characteristics of both a brother, and a romance; hence bromance. For these men, they often said that having a bromance was like having a brother (from another mother, as many put it), because they wanted to illustrate their importance.

Lawrence said, "It's like having a brother from another mother. It's like having another family member, but one you get on with (he laughs)." Rory said, "You have always got each other's back, and you respect them like a brother. You won't let anything bad happen to them and you pick them up if they are down." Pete added, "You respect him like a family member. And my family does treat him like another son." Harry explained "you say bro because they are that important to you. You love them like a brother, unconditionally" and Danny said, "I will always see him as a brother, because were so close and I would adopt him if I could."

Distinguishing Bromances from Romance

The expression of love, physical, and emotional intimacy is something that has been traditionally associated as innate and exclusive to romantic relationships (Fisher 2006; Hruschka 2010). Accordingly, the intimate way in which these men describe their bromances solicits interest in how they understand these relationships to be different, or comparable, to their romantic relationships. Throughout the interview process, participants were asked to make comparisons between these two relationship types. This section considers the detail of those conversations, focusing on the sexual comparators of the relationships, the privileging of the bromance, and exclusivity arrangements.

The Difference is Sex

When asked of the difference between bromances and romances, one of the first things many of the participants made clear was that they differ because they only have penetrative sex in romances. Jaden explained, "If you put a bromance on a ladder, it would be one step down from a romance… the last step is sex." Danny said, "The difference is the explicitly sexual nature. I would take a bullet for a bromance, but I wouldn't be sexual with them." Blake said, "I would sleep next to a bromance, but I wouldn't shag him." Rory expressed that, "A bromance is a romance, just without the sexual stuff."

These men were certain of the sexual element that is required in their romances, but it is what they were uncertain of which raises particular interest. Gordon, discussing the differences between the two relationships, said:

> It's the sexual stuff. Like when your younger, you can have a relationship with a girl without sex because you're not interested in that then, and intercourse determines if it's a romance. If I kissed Ronnie, held his hand, messaged him and talked about my feelings, then that would be a relationship [he then paused to contemplate what he had said]. Oh my god! That's what we do, and I'm talking like I want to get with him. I've

never thought about it before, but when I'm describing our bromance, I am pretty much describing a relationship. It does show how thin that line is between a bromance and romance.

Through Gordon's narrative it is clear how he recognized, at that moment in the interview, just how similar his bromance is to a heterosexual romantic relationship. It was remarkable to watch him and others self-realize and declare through their own thought processes how similar these relationship types are. When asked, the men struggled at length to find any other reasons as to how these relationships were different, other than through having or not having sex. The men were given plenty of time and encouraged to comment and consider the differences, but the majority of the men could not initially identify any other characteristics.

Jerry said, "The difference is sexual activity. The feelings are different, but only the sexual feelings. The rest is the same. That's all I can think of. They are very similar, yes." Chris said, "The love in a romance is different to a bromance." How, I asked? "The ways you interact with each other is different… different from a boy to how I would act with a girl." Stefan, asked again, how is it different? "The sex. I was going to say kissing, but I do that with my bromances as well (he laughs)." Chris diverted back to the default answer; sex, as did others who tried to explore the differences. Andy said, "A lot of it's the same, telling secrets, but no sexual contact for bromances." He begins listing several activities, "Watching films, dinner, paintball, and training [he pauses]. Actually, I do that with both. They aren't different. I feel like I'm missing something obvious, but I can't think of anything."

This feeling of "missing something obvious" was common among the men, and no further thematic differences emerged in initial conversations. When asked if the love is different in romances and bromances, Andy said, "Nothing other than the sexual element. If you enjoy your time and forget about your problems, or work through them, then that's love, regardless of their gender." Mark said, "I guess I would love a bromance the same way as a romance. Like, its best friend love, so whether they are a guy or a girl, the love would be the same."

By deconstructing the differences in these two relationships, these comments illustrate that some men shared a progressive understanding that love can exist between two people without the need or requirement for sex with each other; they understood that love and sex can operate as two separate constructs (Diamond 2003; Fisher 1998). Indeed, whilst popular culture excessively conflates love with sex (Anderson 2012a), many of these men were able to distinguish the two. Ronnie said, "It's the same sort of love, but I guess there is that sexual element with a romance. You care for them both a lot." Danny explained:

> I've never believed in love at first sight or love as an absolute. Love and sex are completely different. But like I said earlier, physical intimacy promotes stronger relationships; whether that's with a boy or a girl. The physical embodiment of love is not sex, its embrace.

Many of the men indicated that sex is a requisite of romantic relationships, especially at university, and some said this was prone to causing tensions in those relationships. Jerry said, "If you're seeing a girl, it's expected that you're going to be banging, and that can cause tension if you're not in the mood."

Whilst these men professed that sex and sexual behavior was the primary difference between the two relationships, as earlier and later sections have and will highlight, sexual contact is not uncommon in bromances. We have established that physical intimacy is not a requisite of bromances, but it does occur frequently and is considered a benefit of the relationship. Indeed, sex in a romance is similarly regarded as a benefit but is also considered by these men to be a requisite of the relationship, stimulating certain tensions, at times.

When discussing the difference between the two relationships, Jaden said, "I think the only difference in a bromance is that you don't get off with each other, but you do everything else you do in a relationship." Stefan, asked, "everything?" And he said, "Yes." Later, Jaden would explain that he has made out with more guys than girls, and that he enjoys doing it. Just as some men earlier highlighted that an outsider might consider these men to be gay, Jaden said, "The stuff we do and say to each other, to an outsider, they would think these guys are gay." He acknowledges here that the reason someone might think the bromantic friends are gay is because they practice same-sex sexual behaviors; because they behave romantically with other men as they would with women. As Rory points out, "No one in the team is averse to sexual contact with each other, it wouldn't surprise me if people thought some of us were gay." Here, participants understand their bromances and romance to be superficially reflective of one another.

Whilst these men did not disclose that they had sex with their bromances, they were clear that physical intimacy was a vital component of romantic relationships, and similarly a frequent and enjoyable experience in bromances. However, erotic lust was not experienced between bromances. Hruschka (2010) conceptualizes relationships that are intensely devoted, but non-sexual, as intimate "romantic friendships" (p. 120), where romance is achievable without sexual lust for one another.

Through probing conversations, it emerged that these men recognized a strong resemblance in the way the two relationships operated, in terms of the physical behaviors, time shared with one another, and how that time is spent. Indeed, some other scholars conclude that the emotional and behavioral requisites of friendships and romances are more reflective of one another than people perceive (Allan 1989; Diamond et al. 1999; Pahl and Pevalin 2005), and this was certainly the case with these participants in the first instance of questioning. In the initial round of answers about the differences between the relationships, the "There's no sex in bromances" narrative was an expected finding. However, the need to make this clear meant that other important information about the differences between the two relationships was relatively absent, until asked.

Bromance and Non-exclusivity

In describing the ways in which bromances differ from romances, only two participants explicitly defined romantic relationships as exclusive to one person. From Stefan's knowledge of the men's romantic relationships, none of them were permitted by their girlfriends to share sexual and intimate experiences with other women. Equally, none of the men would want their girlfriends to engage in sexual acts with other men, as is the dominant expectation in the twenty-first century (Anderson 2012a).

Where the two relationships diverge, however, is that men are able to have multiple bromances, and share numerous emotionally and physically intimate experiences across these relationships, with little conflict or jealousy. Explicitly and unconditionally, they can be physically and emotionally polyamorous in their bromances. Conversely, their romantic relationships defined by the requirement of monogamy, are exclusive; exclusive meaning that the men are regulated by monogamous standards and boundaries that limit their emotional closeness and sexual experiences with women to one person (Anderson 2012a).

Whilst many of the men did not choose to highlight this difference as exclusivity, they articulated a clear line that men were permitted to have more than one bromance, without the social ridicule and stigma associated with non-exclusivity and cheating in romantic relationships. Ed said, "A tripod is a good analogy. You can have a three-way bromance. You can see it with Blake, Ronnie and Gordon."

Gordon, who highlighted that he was in a three-way bromance with Ronnie and Blake said, "You can have a group bromance, it doesn't have to be with just one person, as long as you are all connected on the same level." When asked how he would name that type of relationship, Ronnie called it "An org-mance or a bro orgy." Interestingly, he ascribed the sexual notion of an orgy to their relationship.

Danny said, "I had a bromance with all my housemates last year," Callum said, "Yes, I've got loads of bromances" and Lawrence said, "You maybe have that one bromance who's really close, but I have four or five that I'm completely comfortable with." In one instance, Callum explained, "Ever since that (sexual) foursome (three men and one woman), we have all been in such a close bromance and were always hanging out in our little group. It's like a bro four-way."

Chapter Summary

For the men in this study, the primary differential between bromances and romances was the requirement and desire for sex with their romantic partners, and not their bromances. The sexual tensions and pressures around early life romantic relationships were often nominated as a cause for conflict and anxiety, being a requisite that led some men to emphasize and project an orthodox manly character to their girlfriends, thus limiting their emotionality.

Without prompt, the men who are the subject of this ethnography, struggled to identify any other varying characteristics that distinguished the two relationships, bromance and romance. Statements such as, "I'm missing something obvious, but I can't think of anything" and "That's all I can think of. They are very similar, yes" were typical of how the men answered the question. These men did however engage in pseudo-sexual activities, like making out and cuddling with their bromances, but only because it was fun and emotionally meaningful, and not erotically desirable. In other words, they did not report getting an erection. In doing this, the men accepted that their bromances were marginally different to their romantic relationships, noting that onlookers might even consider their bromances to be romantic homosexual relationships—they just don't care.

Alongside pressures to maintain monogamy in their romantic relationships, the men alluded to other variables, such as better advice available in bromances and the bro code of "bros before hoes," which ultimately led to 17 of the 20 men preferring to confide, emote and disclose in their bromances.

One of the significant differences between these two relationships which was not initially obvious to the participants was the social acceptance of having multiple bromances, and group bromances, contrasting to the monogamous structure of romantic relationships. This assisted their own understanding that love and sexual desire can operate as two separate constructs (Diamond 2003; Fisher 1998), based on the knowledge that bromances exist with love, and without sexual needs and deeds.

References

Adams, A. (2011). Josh wears pink cleats: Inclusive Masculinity on the Soccer Field. *Journal of Homosexuality,* 58(5), 579–596.

Allan, G. (1989). *Friendship: Developing a sociological perspective.* Boulder: Westview Press.

Anderson, E. (2012a). *The monogamy gap: Men, love, and the reality of cheating.* Oxford University Press

Anderson, E. (2012b). Inclusive masculinity in a physical education setting. *Journal of Boyhood Studies,* 6(1–2), 151–165.

Anderson, E. (2014). *21st Century Jocks: Sporting Men and Contemporary Heterosexuality.* New York: Macmillan.

Becht, M. and Vingerhoets, A. (2002). Crying and mood change: A cross-cultural study. *Cognition and Emotion,* 16(1), 87–101.

Boyle, K., and Berridge, S. (2012). I Love You, Man: Gendered Narratives of Friendship in Contemporary Hollywood Comedies. *Feminist Media Studies,* 14(3), 353–368.

Davies, N. (2014). I love you hombre. In DeAngelis, M (Ed.), *Reading the bromance: Homosocial relationships in film and television.* Detroit: Wayne State University Press. Pp. 109–138.

Diamond, L. (2003). What does sexual orientation orient? A bio-behavioural model distinguishing romantic love and sexual desire. *Psychological Review,* 110(1), 173–192.

Diamond, L., Savin-Williams, R., and Dube, E. (1999). Intimate peer relations among lesbian, gay, and bisexual adolescents: Sex, dating, passionate friendships, and romance. In Furman, W., Brown, B., and Feiring, C. (Ed.), *The development of romantic relationships in adolescence.* Cambridge: Cambridge University Press. Pp. 45–58

Fisher, H. (1998). Lust, attraction and attachment in mammalian reproduction. *Human Nature,* 9(1), 23–52

Fisher, H. (2004). *Why we love: The nature and chemistry of romantic love.* New York: Henry Holt and Company.

Fisher, H. (2006). The drive to love: The neural mechanism for mate selection. In Steinberg, R., and Weis, K. (Ed.), *The new psychology of love.* New Haven: Yale University Press. Pp. 87–115.

Forster, P. (2014). Rad bromance (or I Love You, Man, but We Won't Be Humping on Humpday). In DeAngelis, M. (Ed.), *Reading the bromance:*

Homosocial relationships in film and television. Detroit: Wayne State University Press. Pp. 191–212.

Ghaziani, A. (2017). *Sex cultures.* Boston: Polity Press (Cultural Sociology series).

Gill, R., and Hansen-Miller, D. (2011). Lad flicks: Discursive reconstructions of masculinity in popular film: Feminism at the movies: Understanding gender in contemporary popular cinema. In *Feminism at the movies: Understanding gender in contemporary popular cinema.* Routledge. Pp. 36–50.

Hammarén, S., and Johansson, T. (2014). Homosociality in between power and intimacy. *SAGE Open, 4*(1), 1–11.

Herek, G. M., and McLemore, K. A. (1998). Attitudes toward lesbians and gay men scale. *Handbook of Sexuality-Related Measures,* 392–394.

Herlitz, C. (2001). *HIV/AIDS and society: Knowledge, attitudes and behavior 1989–2000.* Swedish National Institute of Public Health.

Hruschka, D. (2010). Friendship: Development, ecology, and evolution of a relationship (Vol. 5). Berkeley: University of California Press.

Jourard, S. (1971). *The transparent self.* New York: Van Nostrand.

Komarovsky, M. (1974). Patterns of self-disclosure of male undergraduates. *Journal of Marriage and the Family, 36*(4), 677–686.

Lewis, R. (1978). Emotional intimacy among men. *Journal of Social Research, 34*(1), 108–121.

Magrath, R., Anderson, E., and Roberts, S. (2013). On the door-step of equality: Attitudes toward gay athletes among academy level footballers. *International Review for the Sociology of Sport, 50*(7), 804–821.

McCormack, M. (2012). *The declining significance of homophobia: How teenage boys are redefining masculinity and heterosexuality.* New York: Oxford University Press.

McKay, J. (1993). Marked men and wanton women: The politics of naming sexual deviance in sport. *Journal of Men's Studies, 2*(1), 69–81.

Morin, S., and Garfinkle, E. (1978). Male homophobia. *Journal of Social Issues, 34*(1), 29–47.

Morris, M., and Anderson, E. (2015). 'Charlie is so cool like': Authenticity, popularity and inclusive masculinity on YouTube. *Sociology, 49*(6), 1200–1217.

Murray, A., White, A., Scoats, R., and Anderson, E. (2016). Constructing masculinities in the national Rugby League's Footy Show. *Sociological Research Online, 21*(3).

Pahl, R., and Pevalin, D. (2005). Between family and friends: A longitudinal study of friendship choice. *British Journal of Sociology, 56*(3), 433–450.

Pomerance, M. (2014). *Reading the bromance: Homosocial relationships in film and television*, DeAngelis, M. (Ed.). Detroit: Wayne State University Press. Pp. 255–273.

Ralph, B., and Roberts, S. (2020). One small step for man: Change and continuity in perceptions and enactments of homosocial intimacy among young Australian men. *Men and Masculinities, 23*(1), 83–103.

Roberts, S., Anderson, E., & Magrath, R. (2017). Continuity, change and complexity in the performance of masculinity among elite young footballers in England. *The British Journal of Sociology, 68*(2), 336–357.

Robinson, S., Anderson, E., and White, A. (2018). The bromance: Undergraduate male friendships and the expansion of contemporary homosocial boundaries. *Sex Roles, 78*(1–2), 94–106.

Robinson, S., White, A., and Anderson, E. (2019). Privileging the bromance: A critical appraisal of romantic and bromantic relationships. *Men and Masculinities, 22*(5), 850–871.

Rotundo, A. (1989). Romantic friendship: Male intimacy and middle-class youth in the northern United States, 1800–1900. *Journal of Social History, 23*(1), 1–25.

Silva, J. (2013). *Coming up short: Working-class adulthood in an age of uncertainty*. Oxford: Oxford University Press.

Thompson, L. (2015). Reading the bromance: Homosocial relationships in film and television. *Journal of Gender Studies, 24*(3), 368–370.

Vrangalova, Z., and Savin-Williams, R. C. (2012). Mostly heterosexual and mostly gay/lesbian: Evidence for new sexual orientation identities. *Archives of Sexual Behavior, 41*(1), 85–101.

Way, N. (2011). *Deep secrets*. Illinois: Harvard University Press.

6

Building the Bromance

Our previous research (Robinson et al. 2018; Robinson et al. 2019) showed that all of the thirty undergraduate men we interviewed had a bromance. This was not part of the selection criteria for inclusion into those studies. However, we recognize that recruiting teamsport athletes means that we are recruiting men to study who were socialized into a homosocial network that occupies a significant portion of their social time. This potentially made having a bromance more likely than choosing men who do not play sports, and as we explore below, the connection to team sports was key in our participants' accounts of bromance formation.

Rather than attempting to make claims to how widespread bromances are, this participant selection criteria from our previous research, our ethnography permits an interrogation of the *operation* of the bromance, its meanings and perceived benefits, we do not make generalizations about the frequency of bromances outside of this study. What this ethnography does, however, helps us understand how friendships are developed, and eventually how some of those friendships find or earn their way into a bromance. We highlight that it all begins with shared interests. In the case of those within this study, that shared interest mostly begins with playing dodgeball.

Shared Interests

All of the participants believed that similar to a romance, shared interests were a necessary requisite for having a bromance; "You need to be interested in the same things, because it means you have the same humor and thoughts," as Lawrence put it. Similarly, Ronnie said, "Because you're into the same things, you do everything together, and end up spending so much time with each other." Pete added, "If you're studying the same subject, playing the same sport, or listen to the same music, you've got a good chance of having a bromance."

The most obvious interest that these men shared was their interest in playing dodgeball. Indeed, a shared passion in sports has consistently been documented as a primary space for male bonding (Hruschka 2010; Benenson 2013). Gordon, a three-year veteran of the club explained, "Bromances are way more common in the dodgeball team because were enjoying something together. All of my bromances at uni have come from dodgeball." He recalled the first day he joined the club:

> Dodgeball were not that big at the start, but now it's got to be one of the best clubs. Bromance wise, everyone gets on in dodgeball… because I think it's such a unique sport to join… They are all genuinely nice people, and it was not hard to make friends. In fact, I made them instantly. There is no way I would have been friends with Andy, Harry and Taylor at school, and now I have bromances with them because playing dodgeball has opened me up to meeting new people.

Jerry said, "We are all interested in sport, even if it's not that serious." One element that is fairly unique to university sports clubs like dodgeball, and indeed ultimate frisbee and lacrosse, is that very few people had ever had the opportunity to participate before. The novel element of a new sport and a lack of experience meant that people train and progressed together, without a severe stratification of abilities being imposed, contrary to the stratification of the sporting environment and jock culture of the 1980s and 1990s (Connell 1995; Kimmel 1998, 2004; Anderson 2014).

Jerry continues, "Everything we do like birthdays and nights out are always open invitation on the Facebook page. Because you're a member, you are automatically involved in a big social network. It's easy." Callum, added, "Most of my bromances are from the dodgeball team. You're a victim of circumstance because you end up being best mates with people who you train with. It's like that in rugby, too." Indeed, several members of the dodgeball team were members of other sports clubs and suggested that a broad interest in sports was useful in developing bromances.

When Jaden was asked whether bromances were more common in sports clubs, he said, "Yes, definitely more common. Sport in general there is more bromances in my experience or any society really. It's more banterous and playful." Rob, who has been involved in sports from a young age, explained, "Sport is a space to meet people because you like the same thing. I'm sure it's the same for people who meet through religion and study. Although they probably don't have the same banter we do." In my time with the team, it was clear that issues concerning dodgeball, football, and American football were the main source of conversation.

The men were able to relate to each other deeply on these subjects and discuss details of the sport to expert levels, far beyond my understanding. One of the most popular nights out for the dodgeball team was the premiership football deadline transfer day, where many would dress up as footballers, and spend the evening drinking and discussing fantasy football teams.

Whilst many of these men played out their social life in the dodgeball setting, those who appeared to have the most, or most intimate, bromances spent time with their team mates outside of the sport. Indeed, several of the men also played in a casual six aside football tournament—not as a space to compete or make new friends—but to extend the forum in which they forged their bromances and to share other passions together.

Chris, who regularly posted on the dodgeball club's Facebook page asking for football team members said, "Sometimes dodgeball is all we talk about, so some of us play football. We're shocking, but it's good to meet outside of training." Taylor, who is not very good at football, plays with Chris. He said, "I click with Chris and Blake because we love footy, and it's as simple as that. Because we all love it, we love each other." It is not just a shared interest in sport however that helps forge bromances, on par with many of the men's interests in playing sports was also their passion for online gaming, and sharing time online with their bros.

When observed from the beginning of the academic year, when new freshers joined the team, it was salient that they were able to make social bonds and connections with senior members quickly, who shared a passion for online gaming. Specifically, insider language from games such as FIFA and Call of Duty (COD) would often dominate conversation. Blake explained:

> All my bros will message me in a second, after this interview, and ask what time were grinding tonight (playing COD). Then we will be online all night and nothing else matters other than spending time with my boys.

According to Domahidi et al. (2014), this reflects that the online gaming world is a huge social phenomenon for young men in which old, current, and new relationships are formed and maintained (see also Maloney et al. 2018, 2019). Stefan would often stay overnight at Blake's house following a team night out in town. Without fail, he would wake up early, after only a few hours' sleep, to find Blake playing his Xbox in excitement with his headset on, talking to other dodgeball members in a technical language that outsiders would not be able to make sense of. Blake said, "It's not about the game, it's just about being able to spend that extra time with your mates from the comfort of your room."

Taylor explained, "There could be 10 people on FIFA from dodgeball at one time. You can't have a bromance with someone if you don't like the same things. I guess that's quite obvious." Many of the men identified Blake and Max as having a strong bromance. Danny identified online gaming as integral to their relationships; "Whenever I log into my account, I always see Blake and Max online together, sometimes at 5am." Danny continued, "We prefer to go round each other's so were in the same room, so it's more real." For several of the men in bromances, they are interacting on headsets often for long periods of time. Clearly for some couples like Max and Blake, it's a big part of their relationship and why they are so close.

Max and Blake were identified by nine of the participants as having a bromance. Indeed, as was the way with many bromances, they were able to blindly identify each other in interviews as being in a bromance. Max and Blake share a deep interest in competition and winning and have a significant passion for online gaming. When Stefan was driving Max, Blake, and Pete to a dodgeball competition some three hours away, the depth of their bromance became clear.

Whilst Stefan and Pete were good friends with Blake and Max, and highly sociable, these two men shared in a conversation that was so animated, in depth, and connected, that they held conversation over the whole journey, with nominal interruption. The young men discussed gaming vloggers on YouTube, and how talented they are on the online video game, COD (Call of Duty). The technical speak they used regarding the game and was so advanced, there was no scope for me and Pete to join in conversation. Indeed, Morris and Anderson (2015) have documented men's increased interest in the online world of vlogging.

He asked Chris and others how important gaming was to the formation of bromances, and many iterated the same response. Chris said, "If it was not COD it would be something else because we share so much in common that we would find another thing to do together." Similarly, Danny said, "There are other things we can do, and it wouldn't mean we wouldn't have bromances, we would just spend time doing something else we like, like pissing off our housemate." Jaden said, "If Xbox Live went down, we would just go to the gym, watch the athletics or go shopping; with bromances you're interested in all the same things."

Importantly, the participants make clear that it is not the specific subject matter of their interests (although sporting interests have a specific weighting in this study because of the sample) that bring them together; it is an interest of any kind. In addition to previous research that shows men's focus on expression and socialization through labor and sporting contexts (Wright 1982; Vigil 2007), these men also maintain their same-sex platonic relationships through a closeness in online dialogue, where physicality is not needed; a trait of relationships traditionally only held between women (Morman et al. 2013; Swain 1989).

Shared interests appear to be a requisite for the establishment of bromances, and membership to the dodgeball club clearly brings people with similar interests together. For these men, the sport has facilitated the establishment of numerous close relationships.

Being a member of the club has enabled the participants to broaden their social reach, being openly invited and welcomed to a wider network of people, as illustrated through the use of Facebook. Sport itself was identified as a particular interest that helps to cement the establishment of bromances, given that it provides a space for long-term socialization and feelings of comradery. The use of sport in promoting physical intimacy and other elements of same-sex socialization is explored further throughout these results. Online gaming, in this instance, was an interest shared by many of the men who had close bromances. As we noted before (Chan and Cheng 2004), online friendships are not as deep or valuable as offline friendships; but these men were carrying over their offline friendship online. This was a world that the ethnographer did not have access too, but similarly, he and many others were invited to participate, nonetheless. No other notable interests were identified that spanned across the team. Finally, the men articulated that whilst sport and online gaming are not essential to the formation of bromances (though sport does hold certain weight), the crucial requisite component was shared interests and passions in any activity.

Emotional Intimacy

Whilst shared interests are relatively cemented in the research as a requisite for standard friendships (Hruschka 2010; Lewis et al. 2015), what distinguishes bromances, for these men, is the emotional depth and intimacy that is experienced in these relationships after they grow from friendships. Bromantic relations are described by participants as unique through the level of emotional disclosure that is permissible to one another. This includes sharing secrets and confiding exclusively with their bromantic friend(s).

This type of intimacy is not unique to teamsport athletes alone, either. Matt Ripley (2018) conducted a two-year covert insider-ethnography of undergraduate men at his British university to investigate men's private attitudes related to homosexuality and their embodied masculinities. In these contexts, Ripley was an undergraduate who had observed a great deal of tactile behaviors between men. He found that, within their private spheres, these men were found to be as emotionally open, inclusive, and homosocial tactile as they were in public. Whilst his ethnography did not include interviews about the bromance, specifically, his thick description of men in their private spheres is consistent with our findings.

Men in our study are clear that a bromance offers a deep sense of unburdened disclosure and emotionality based on trust and love. Hence, these undergraduate men inform me that they desire to develop relationships with other men premised on companionship and intimacy (Collins and Sroufe 1999), where complete emotional disclosure is possible. With the understanding that emotional disclosure and intimacy is a relatively private matter within bromances, data in this section is mostly limited to interviews.

Andy's story is one filled with a sincere appreciation for his emotional dependence on his bromance, openly recognizing that without Mark, his life may have gone in a negative direction. He explained:

In first year, I didn't like uni, and I lived opposite John, and this plays into the bromance. He rescued me when I was ready to leave. I was on the phone to my parents crying at the start of first year, but I've loved it ever since. John started uni two weeks late because of a family death, and I was so low for the first two weeks, until he arrived. John invited me to dodgeball as soon as I met him. I knocked on his door, went in and saw he was playing Grand Theft Auto, didn't even acknowledge his girlfriend, sat next to him, and he couldn't get rid of me ever since. I've always been quiet, but around him I light up. My whole 3 years at uni were defined by meeting him that day.

This vignette reiterates how some of the participant's bromances were first formed through an interest in videogames before becoming bromances. When asked what kind of things he could talk to John about, he said, "Literally anything. Like we compare bodies and talk about body image issues a lot." When asked whether concerns over body image were a unique discussion point in their relationship, he said, "It's not for me, but I know John is really conscious about it and won't talk to others about how unhappy he is. He's got me for that. I would never judge him."

Like Andy, Harry identified several issues that he could only discuss with his bromance; "We talk about more intimate things, like the serious issues in your life." He similarly went on to highlight body image issues, as well as, "Having serious conversations about whether to leave your girlfriend, as opposed to joking about it with friends." In this Harry was identifying a variance between friends (whom one jokes about their problems with) and a bromance, with who one discusses them with.

Harry's most intimate bromance was with someone from outside of the university, and he explained, "You can be more vulnerable and be your actual true self, like about your sexuality or things that really upset you because you can connect with bromances about that." Harry, who identifies as mostly heterosexual, but with occasional bi-curious thoughts, said that this was something he only discussed with his closest bromance. He said, "We talk about depression, and we can have a laugh about it as well. We have deep conversations, and I try cheer him up by calling him beautiful."

On participant said, "I rarely open up about my feelings to anyone. I'm a shut-off person. I don't even go to the doctor. I bottle everything up. But, on preference, I would always go to Gordon first." This individual had a tendency to get very aggressive, not with other people, but with furniture and the wall. If things are not going his way in dodgeball, he will punch the wall. Often, it will be Gordon, his bromance, that calms him down.

Gordon has a certain emotional tactility with this person that others cannot achieve. In one instance, he kicked a chair at a restaurant, resulting in having to pay a fine. He was furious over a derogatory comment someone made about his "girl issues." Others, as usual, were hesitant to approach him, but Gordon took him to one side and in short terms, told him to grow up. This is something that others would be potentially fearful of doing.

Gordon, who is a very socially fluid person, has an emotionally tactile bromance with Ronnie that means he can trust him to listen to him in moments of distress, without directing his anger onto him. Gordon said, "Ronnie can be a dick sometimes, but we all have those moments and I help him out, even if he doesn't want help, because I care about him."

Speaking about the extent to which he can disclose to his bromance, Danny said, "We can talk about anything and everything" and Jerry said, "You can talk about your insecurities and family issues." Andy explained, "I feel comfortable to cry in front of John because sometimes you just need to get it out." Blake said, "I don't think there is anything I couldn't tell my bromance. They know I cheat (on his girlfriend), that I've had STI's (Sexually Transmitted Infection) and am scared about dropping out of university. Only two people know all three of those things."

Rory said, "I'm so close with David, we talk about the deep stuff that doesn't seem manly, like body issues, depression and self-harm." He said, "If I'm down, it's usually because of a girl, and he has brought me out of a dark place a few times." Interestingly, Rory had only known David for 18 Months, but he spoke about him as if he was a lifelong friend. When asked to define a bromance, Harry said:

> It's romantic. Well, emotionally romantic at least. It's affectionate. It's a difficult one to define (long pause). Its emotionally romantic meaning its deeper, closer and more open. Well, like, deeper and closer than any other relationship you have.

In addition to emotional disclosure seeming to be the activity that promotes friendships into bromances, Jaden also suggested that any awkwardness and embarrassment between friends in discussing personal issues only served to limit bromances. "The less awkward you are, the stronger the bromance is. In a bromance, you need to have no embarrassment and just be you."

This was something widely reiterated by other participants. The ability to be "yourself" and express feelings and behaviors freely was noted as a crucial and unique element of bromances. Ronnie said, "I know he will never judge me. I can tell him everything." Danny equally said, "There aren't any limits in what you can discuss, because they will always keep your secrets and the more secrets you can tell, the stronger your bromance is."

Jaden said, "I think it's more expressive and people don't judge" and Jerry said, "There aren't really any limits. You need to be able to talk about the stuff that makes you sad or uneasy, so that they can support you." Jerry said, "As long as you have that bromance, you don't give a shit if others don't rate you high on the social ladder or not." Chris neatly summarized the participant's perspectives. He said, "In a bromance, there aren't any boundaries, in terms of what you say and do." I asked for an example, and he responded:

> Like, sometimes you can over-step the mark by having an argument and saying things you didn't mean. But you can always resolve it when you've both calmed down. And if you've got personal issues, like I have in the past, I talked to him and he came with me to sort it out which was nice. It's just like you're so close that no matter what you say and do you can never really fall out or feel awkward about stuff. It only works because you're both on the same wavelength and just get each other.

For these men, their bromances were important relationships that they relied upon to disclose their full feelings for emotional relief and advice. Just as the men have sourced new spaces for shared interests, they have also broadened their emotional boundaries. Whilst older research has shown men to be highly restricted in their emotionality (Morin and Garfinkle 1978; Pleck 1975), newer research broadly correlates with the finding of this study where men espouse much more freedom in their same-sex dialogues (Bullingham et al. 2014; Magrath 2016; McCormack 2012, 2014).

Some of the men highlighted that they could discuss serious issues in their lives with bromances, such as depression, self-confidence, and sexuality issues. The men used finite vocabulary in describing how their intimacy operates when interviewed; "We can talk about anything." "There aren't any boundaries." "They are deeper and closer than any other relationship." This type of language is absolute and illustrates that the men have great trust, honesty, and secrecy in their bromances. Comparable to the requirement for shared interests, emotional intimacy was expressed to be a necessary requisite in the formation of bromances, enabling a dependency on their bros for deep and cherished disclosure and advice.

They felt so relaxed with each other and free to divulge all, invoking a profound appreciation for their bromantic relationships. Evidently, the young men were confident in exploring deeper, more emotional, and meaningful friendships with other men, as recent research has alluded to (Adams 2011; Hammarén and Johansson 2014; Murray et al. 2016). Whilst discussing the emotionally intimate and elements of their bromances, many men were forthcoming enough to discuss an intense feeling traditionally reserved for their romantic relationships, love.

Love

Looking at research from only three decades ago, men were afraid to vocalize even liking their friends for fear of being thought of as gay (Williams 1985). However, in this research, many of the men were proud to publicly express that they loved their bromances, and that they loved them back. They did not suggest that this was novel, but rather a sincere element of their relationship. Illustrating this, Andy said, "Love might sound plain if someone heard me say it, but it goes deeper than that, and he knows that I mean it." Blake similarly implied that outsiders would not understand the context of their love, "People looking in might not see me saying it to them as important, but I really mean it and it's important in bromances." When Ronnie was asked about whether he loved Gordon, he confidently responded, "Yes, definitely." When asked why, he said, "Because I do! I look out for him all the time. You love the people you care about. It's nice to have something like that." Pete said a bromance was, "Two best mates who are in love" and Ed said, "Telling him I love him means he is someone I depend on and appreciate."

The men's dodgeball team was a very close friendship group and regularly said they loved each other. The ethnographer recalls an instance when he was driving the men's first team back late at night from a successful competition in a small minibus. They stopped at a corner shop to pick up some beers, before heading back to university on a long journey. Spirits were high because of our success, and shortly after setting off, with Elton John at maximum volume on the radio, Blake started massaging a teammate's shoulders and telling him that he loved him. The ethnographer noted:

> I thought he was trying to make them feel awkward as a joke, but he did it repeatedly on the way back, and without drawing attention to it. Again, at training a few weeks later, he told him he loved him, looking deep into his eyes, without indicating any reason. And again, and again; at different training sessions. This was often accompanied by a sloppy kiss on his cheek, or him grabbing his arse. Indeed, he acted this way with many of the first team members.

When Stefan (the ethnographer) asked in interview why, he responded:

> Because it's true. In the van I said it because I wanted you to know that you played well; get you pumped for a big night; cheers for driving; and that I've got your back. I love you bro. I mean it. Il always be here for you.

When Taylor was asked why he said he loved Jaden, another dodgeball player, he said "It means I care for him as a person, and if he is distressed with anything, I hope he would speak to me." Jaden said he loved Taylor back. "It's not a sexual love, obviously, but it's everything else. I love him as a best mate and care for him. I make sure he knows." Consistent with modes of digital communication interactions between young men noted by Roberts (2018), Callum said, "I would say I love you mate, put it in texts, and on Facebook. It means that I care about you a lot and get on really well with you." Ed said, "Of course. My usual sign off is, 'I love you bro.'" Gordon similarly used other forums to convey his love:

> I tell them I love them all the time because I do. I respect their friendship and they do a lot for me. Sometimes it's for an apology because love can transcend an argument. At the moment in the group chat, we do say it a

lot, calling each other best mate love you after every sentence, were saying it loads and it just seems right. Sometimes we can say it too much, but it doesn't detract from what it means.

Love for these men has a real meaning in their bromances, shown by their ability to expand what it means to them and their relationships. The men make a link between love and their bromances ability to support them emotionally and be therefore them. During discussion, it was at no point conflated with femininity or homosexuality, unlike its associations in decades previous (Fisher 2004; Cancian 1990).

It was instead named as a defining characteristic in what it means to have a bromance. The emotional stability and reassurance they receive from disclosing their vulnerabilities contribute to their feelings of love, which they openly proclaim with regularity.

Positive Mental Health Impacts of Having a Bromance

This section provides a brief case study of Stefan's observations that relates to the positive impact of having bromance for one's mental health.

After a match, the team took to a hotel bar. After music started playing loudly the team disbanded into smaller social groups. After some general small talk, one of the men decided to discuss the fact that he had autism and went on to describe how it negatively affected his life. This was something that Stefan was already aware of, but it was a relative secret to other members of the team. At this point, because they were secret sharing, they all had arms around each other, leaning in close and blocking anyone else out. Another man decided to disclose that he had battled with depression whilst at university, and said, "Its things like this, with you guys, that keep me sane." The team supported him explaining that they would always be there to talk if he wanted.

The nature of these disclosures was extensive and explicit. These results mirror what Anderson (2008) found in an American fraternity, where men performed with bravado publicly, but privately disclosed secrets for the purpose of mutual support and friendship bonding. In one instance, a man explained how he felt compelled to drink alcohol because he suffered with social anxiety, and alcohol helped to ease the stress, adding, "There's a long line of alcoholics in my family and it worries me." People were happy to express these feelings, and it appeared empowering to get these experiences in the open, at least within the group.

The fourth man spoke about once having suicidal thoughts, after breaking up with his girlfriend. The fifth man spoke at length about a historical experience of trying to commit suicide several years ago, and it appeared therapeutic for him to discuss it with others, some of whom had had similar, but milder, experiences.

These therapeutic narratives (Silva 2013) appeared to be an important way of these men coping with adverse life events, and this is just one example of the emotional disclosure that took place between bromances.

It was very distressing for Stefan to hear some of the negative experiences that these men had, but it was clear that their confidence and relations had developed to a point where the people around them, in this bromantic culture, were able to support them and maintain secrecy, all without judgment.

At that time, and ever since that day, the men have referred to that group as the circle of trust. Since then, they had several separate one-to-one conversations with these people about those experiences, and new experiences, where complete trust and support is given.

Importantly, for the people in that circle, they did not necessarily have close bromances with every other person in that group. Instead, culturally within the club, there was a depth of solidarity and support, and a lack of judgment, which reflected the emotional intimacy that was usually reserved for bromances. This is a primary example of how the social context within the club of inclusive and caring attitudes facilitated and promoted emotional disclosure. This is far from what previous research has shown to be the case, particularly in the traditionally orthodox setting of sports (Curry 2000; Harry 1995; Pronger 1990).

With consideration to the men's disclosures regarding depression and suicide, cultural restrictions on male emotionality have traditionally drastically affected men's ability to confide and discuss emotional troubles

(Fehr 1996). This has previously significantly reduced their coping strategies to deal with internal conflicts such as depression, anxiety, and suicidal thoughts (Cleary 2012; Scourfield 2005), and scholars argue that men have traditionally found it difficult to seek help with issues like depression because of cultural restrictions imposed by hegemonic masculine archetypes, based on the repression of emotion and vulnerability (Courtenay 2000; Emslie et al. 2007; O'Brien, Hunt and Hart, 2005; Scourfield 2005). The men in this study however show that their bromantic culture permits the discussion of such deep and troubling personal issues, and sincere peer support is evident among their bros.

Chapter Summary

This chapter provided an analysis of the formation of a bromance. It interrogates the operation of the bromance, its meanings, and perceived benefits. What this chapter does, is to help us understand how friendships are developed, and eventually how some of those friendships find or earn their way into a bromance. We highlight that it all begins with shared interests. In the case of those within this study, that shared interest mostly begins with playing dodgeball.

Other shared interests can bring two adolescent guys together, too. Online gaming was certainly one interest. Then, of course, there are interests of personality, matters which are much harder for us to quantify. Whatever the inception is, a bromance is not born, it is made.

Bromances, like romances, are brought together by similar interests and some form of mutual affinity for each other. They must then go through a developmental process to the point in which they develop a friendship. At this point, it might stall, remaining in the friend zone; or it might develop into a bromance. Here, the most salient signs are physical intimacy, shoulder massages, and longer hugs. As the next chapter then discusses, matters progress to include cuddling.

References

Adams, A. (2011). Josh wears pink cleats: Inclusive Masculinity on the Soccer Field. *Journal of Homosexuality, 58*(5), 579–596.

Anderson, E. (2008a). Inclusive masculinity in a fraternal setting. *Men and Masculinities, 10*(5), 604–620.

Anderson, E. (2014). *21st Century Jocks: Sporting Men and Contemporary Heterosexuality*. New York: Macmillan.

Benenson, J. (2013). The development of human female competition: allies and adversaries. *Philosophical Transactions of the Royal Society B, 368*(1631).

Bullingham, R., McGrath, R., and Anderson, E. (2014). 'Changing the game' Sport and a Cultural Shift from Homohysteria. In Hargreaves, J and Anderson, E. (Ed) Handbook of Sport Gender and Sexualities. New York: Routledge. Pp 220–231.

Cancian, F. (1990). *Love in America: Gender and self-development*. Cambridge: Cambridge University Press.

Chan, D. K. S., & Cheng, G. H. L. (2004). A comparison of offline and online friendship qualities at different stages of relationship development. *Journal of Social and Personal Relationships, 21*(3), 305–320.

Cleary, A. (2012). Suicidal action, emotional expression, and the performance of masculinities. *Social Science and Medicine, 74*(4), 498–505.

Collins, W., and Sroufe, L. (1999). Capacity for intimate relationships. In W. Furman., B. Brown., and C. Feiring (Ed.), *The development of romantic relationships in adolescence*. Cambridge: Cambridge University Press. Pp. 125–147.

Connell, R. (1995). *Masculinities*. Berkeley: University of California Press.

Courtenay, W. (2000). Constructions of masculinity and their influence on men's well-being: A theory of gender and health. *Social Science and Medicine, 50*(10), 1385–1401.

Curry, T. (2000). Booze and bar fights: A journey to the dark side of college athletics. In McKay, J., Messner, M., and Sabo, D. (Ed.), *Masculinities, gender relations and sport*. London: Sage. Pp.162–175.

Domahidi, E., Festl, R., and Quandt, T. (2014). To dwell among gamers: Investigating the relationship between social online game use and gaming-related friendships. *Computers in Human Behavior, 35*, 107–115.

Emslie, C., Ridge, D., Ziebland, S., and Hunt, K. (2007). Exploring men's and women's experiences of depression and engagement with health professionals: More similarities than differences? A qualitative interview study. *BioMed Central Family Practice, 8*(1), 43–61.

Fehr, B. (1996). *Friendship processes.* Thousand Oaks, CA: Sage.

Fisher, H. (2004). *Why we love: The nature and chemistry of romantic love.* New York: Henry Holt and Company.

Hammarén, S., and Johansson, T. (2014). Homosociality in between power and intimacy. *SAGE Open, 4*(1), 1–11.

Harry, J. (1995). Sports ideology, attitudes toward women, and anti-homosexual attitudes. *Sex Roles, 32*(1–2), 109–116.

Hruschka, D. (2010). *Friendship: Development, ecology, and evolution of a relationship* (Vol. 5). Berkeley: University of California Press.

Kimmel, M. S. (1998). *Manhood in America: A cultural history.* New York: Free Press.

Kimmel, M. (2004). Masculinity as homophobia: Fear, shame, and silence in the construction of gender identity. In Rothenberg, P (Ed.), *Race, class, and gender in the United States: An integrated study.* New York: Worth. Pp. 81–93.

Lewis, D., Al-Shawaf, L., Russell., E., and Buss, D. (2015). Friends and happiness: An evolutionary perspective on friendship. *Friendship and Happiness*, 37.

Magrath, R. (2016). *Inclusive masculinities in contemporary football: Men in the beautiful game.* Routledge.

Maloney, M., Roberts, S., & Caruso, A. (2018). 'Mmm… I love it, bro!': Performances of masculinity in YouTube gaming. *New Media & Society, 20*(5), 1697–1714.

Maloney, M., Roberts, S., and Graham, T. (2019). *Gender, masculinity and video gaming: Analysing Reddit's r/gaming community.* Springer Nature.

McCormack, M. (2012). *The declining significance of homophobia: How teenage boys are redefining masculinity and heterosexuality.* New York: Oxford University Press.

McCormack, M. (2014). The intersection of youth masculinities, decreasing homophobia and class: An ethnography. *The British Journal of Sociology, 65*(1), 130–149.

Morin, S., and Garfinkle, E. (1978). Male homophobia. *Journal of Social Issues, 34*(1), 29–47.

Morman, M, Schrodt P, Tornes, M. (2013). Self-disclosure mediates the effects of gender orientation and homophobia on the relationship quality of male same-sex friendships. *Journal of Social and Personal Relationships, 30*(5), 582–605.

Morris, M., and Anderson, E. (2015). 'Charlie is so cool like': Authenticity, popularity and inclusive masculinity on YouTube. *Sociology, 49*(6), 1200–1217.

Murray, A., White, A., Scoats, R., and Anderson, E. (2016). Constructing masculinities in the national Rugby League's Footy Show. *Sociological Research Online, 21*(3).

O'Brien, R., Hunt, K., and Hart, G. (2005). 'It's caveman stuff, but that is to a certain extent how guys still operate': MEN'S accounts of masculinity and help seeking. *Social Science and Medicine, 61*(3), 503–516.

Pleck, J. (1975). Issues for the men's movement: Summer, 1975. *Changing Men: A Newsletter for Men against Sexism,* 21–23.

Pronger, B. (1990). *The arena of masculinity: Sports, homosexuality, and the meaning of sex.* London: GMP Publishers.

Ripley, M. (2018). The integration of British undergraduate men's public and private masculinities. *Journal of Gender Studies, 27*(3), 288–300.

Roberts, S. (2018). *Young working-class men in transition.* Routledge.

Robinson, S., Anderson, E., and White, A. (2018). The bromance: Undergraduate male friendships and the expansion of contemporary homosocial boundaries. *Sex Roles, 78*(1–2), 94–106.

Robinson, S., White, A., and Anderson, E. (2019). Privileging the bromance: A critical appraisal of romantic and bromantic relationships. *Men and Masculinities, 22*(5), 850–871.

Scourfield, J. (2005). Suicidal masculinities. *Sociological Research Online,* 10(2).

Silva, J. (2013). *Coming up short: Working-class adulthood in an age of uncertainty.* Oxford: Oxford University Press.

Swain, S. (1989). Covert intimacy: Closeness in men's friendships. In Risman, B., and Schwartz, P (Ed.), *Gender in intimate relationships.* Belmont: Wadsworth Publishing. Pp. 71–86.

Vigil, J. (2007). Asymmetries in the friendship preferences and social styles of men and Women. *Human Nature, 18,* 143–161.

Williams, D. (1985). Gender, masculinity-femininity, and emotional intimacy in same-sex friendship. *Sex Roles, 12*(5–6), 587–600.

Wright, P. (1982). Men's friendships, women's friendships and the alleged inferiority of the latter. *Sex Roles, 8*(1), 1–20.

7

Cuddling and Spooning

The idea that heterosexual men cuddle and spoon together was first published in Anderson (2013). Highlighting some of these findings, Anderson interviewed Stuart, a first-year heterosexual undergraduate and asked him about sleeping in the same bed with his friends. "I do it all the time," he told him. Anderson enquired as to how often "all the time" was. "Two to three nights a week," he said. Throughout the course of the interview, Stuart told Eric who he cuddles in bed with, and why. Anderson asked him about the mechanics of what happens in bed, and the meanings associated with sleeping together. It is here that Stuart said that he even cuddles in bed with guys, immediately after "fucking a girl."

After a night of drinking and clubbing, Stuart often brings women home for sex. This is the benefit of living in a hookup culture (Bogle 2008). He has sex with these women in his bed but does not kick them out immediately after. "You don't want to send someone out drunk alone on the streets in the early hours of the morning." But that doesn't mean that Stuart wants to sleep alongside or cuddle with the woman he's had sex with, either. It is at this point that he leaves her to sleep, alone, in his bed. He then goes to sleep in the same bed with one of his male housemates.

Anderson asked Stuart if he is bisexual. He said that he is not. Anderson then asked him why he would then leave a girl in bed to be with his mate. He answered, "Just cuz I like don't wanna have to deal with them [the girls] in the morning." He added, "I would rather have time with the boys, who love me, than a girl I lusted after a few seconds ago." Eric confirmed the story with Stuart's housemate. "Yeah, he loves us, what can I say? We're like that. We all really love each other."

Interviews with undergraduate athletes both in the United States and the United Kingdom suggest that sleeping in the same bed with another male is normal throughout childhood, but somewhere around puberty, somewhere between 11 and certainly by 14, sleepovers generally end for the Americans (Anderson 2014). In interviewing older British male friends about sleepover practices, it also becomes apparent that males only began sleeping in beds together in the United Kingdom, out of choice, in the years following the new millennia.

Although it is not systematic evidence for the absence of men of older generations sleeping together in beds in the United Kingdom when they were in university, it was not the case for the five British males in their 40s that Anderson interviewed about for his book, *21st Century Jocks*. For example, one of Anderson's heterosexual British friends, born in 1970, told him that he stopped doing sleepovers at his friends when he was around 11 and that it was unthinkable to share a bed with a friend unless one was in a hotel on an away match. He said, "There was really no such thing as sleepovers in the UK in the 80s. There was no sleeping in the same bed after being drunk at university or out with mates in any capacity." He added, "There is the odd time when I have shared a bed with my brother on a family holiday or something and there might have be an odd occasion when it happened with friends, but I really can't recall any." Anderson asked him about sleeping over at other guy's places after a night of drinking. "There were occasions where a group of us have gone out, and a number of us have crashed on the floor, but not in a bed."

Another British friend, born in 1985, told Anderson that sleepovers were regular between ages 8–11 too, but that after that the boys started sleeping "tops and toes," one guy's head by the other's feet, as a way of symbolically indicating that they were not sexually interested in each other. This means that, for this male, as an undergraduate freshman in

September 2003 through his final year of university in 2007, cuddling was not happening, at least not with him or with others that he knew of. But unlike Anderson's older friend, sleeping in the same bed was occurring, there was just no cuddling.

More formally addressing the question of whether there is a history of men holding each other in bed, Anderson and Fidler (2018) interviewed 27 heterosexual men aged 65 and older in the United Kingdom, asking them about this specific question. The researchers aimed for 30 in-depth interviews about these (and other) behaviors, but they only achieved 27. Of those 27, none had ever cuddled or held another man in bed. One reported that the only time he had held another man was when he was dying in his arms, during the Second World War. The reason these researchers achieved only 27 interviews is that upon hearing the questions, three of the participants were so angry that they would even be asked such a question that they stormed out of the interview. So perhaps we can surmise that it is actually 30/30 answering no to this question.

Contrast this to January 2007, when the first episode of the British teenage drama, Skins aired. Skins is a show that featured the script of young adult writers, and the drama took place in Bristol, England, where Anderson lived at the time. We suspect that the show might have been important in reflecting a behavior that was emerging among some straight young men, and whilst we cannot say with evidence, it seems possible that the show helped spread the behavior because this critically acclaimed show regularly featured heterosexual boys sleeping in the same beds together.

Any fan of the show will recall the lead character, Tony, sleeping in bed with his mate, Sid, under sheets with a naked man and woman on them. Sleeping together was common practice not only with the hardened and economically deprived characters of skins but also with the upper-middle-class students at the highly ranked university of which Anderson was teaching at the time. Here, sleeping in a bed with another man was not only commonplace but oftentimes preferred to sleeping in bed with a female.

Desiring to know the frequency of bed-sharing, Anderson interviewed 40 heterosexual, male students in one of his sport classes in 2010 (see Anderson and McCormack 2015) as well as ten British sixth-form (high school) students and ten American high school students in 2013 (see Anderson 2014). Data from the university student-athletes indicated that 37 of the 40 had slept in bed with another male. One indicated that he wasn't sure if he had or had not, "I might have when pissed [drunk]," he said. In other words, sleeping in the same bed with another male was so normal, and so socially acceptable, that it would not be a highly memorable event: it is not marked by stigma. The same was the case for the ten British sixth-form athletes, but it was not the case for the American high school athletes. Anderson did, however, observe heterosexual men sleeping in the same beds in some of his American ethnographies of university soccer teams (Adams and Anderson 2012).

In this chapter, we address the act of sleeping in the same bed as another man as an act of homosocial, but not homosexual, physical and emotional intimacy between two (or more) ostensibly heterosexual males. We discuss the different types of sleeping/cuddling arrangements that exist and even discuss how straight men cuddle with gay men.

When Two Guys Share a Bed

Bed-sharing that occurs between young men is sometimes "relatively" without contact, particularly before boys go to university. Guys go out drinking together, or just stay over at each other's places, and sleep in the same bed as a matter of convenience of not sleeping on a hard floor. Sleeping together is also helpful, particularly in England, where it is colder. Most British people do not run their heaters at night, living in what Americans would consider very cold houses.

It is important to remember, however, that even when two men just "sleep" together in the same bed, it doesn't mean that there is no physical contact between them. British beds are much smaller than American beds. What American's call a "queen" size bed, the British call "king" size. And most all students do not have this size bed in their rooms. The standard bed in university is called a "single." Americans will recognize this size as a bunk bed. It is just 36 inches wide (less than a meter). Beds in students' homes are not much bigger, and most students also have a single bed (36 inches wide) or, if lucky, a double (54 inches wide). Rooms are small in the United Kingdom; thus, the beds are too. Accordingly, almost any bed-sharing necessitates not just some but a good degree of physical contact from one's sleeping partner.

Despite this, sleeping in bed for undergraduates is normal in the United Kingdom. This is documented in previous research on men's bed-sharing (Anderson and McCormack 2015). In that research, Tom provided an example of how one might end up doing such. "One time me and all my mates went out, and I ended up walking home to my best friends and stayed at his because I couldn't be bothered to walk the rest of the way to mine." "What did you do?" Anderson asked, "Just knock on his door and say, 'hey wanna cuddle?'" Tom laughed, "No, we have these things called phones, so I texted him and asked if I could stay at his." Tom said that his friend said, "yes," so he walked into his friend's house (who lived at home with his parents), entered his room, took his shirt and trousers (jeans) off, and that his friend (who was sleeping when he texted) opened up the covers to invite him in. Together the two men slept in their underwear until the next morning. I asked Tom if they spooned or cuddled in bed. "I'm not sure, as I was pretty out of it," he said.

Two men do not necessarily need to be close friends to share a bed, either. One participant was unable to tell Anderson how many times he has done it. "Just all the time." Others are more judicious about whom they share a bed with. There is variance in how often guys sleep together, and this variance has to do not only with how comfortable one is sleeping with lesser-than friends but that more important variables have to do with drinking and homosociality.

But for most of the British athletes Anderson interviewed, it seemed that the men have not thought systematically about the rules to who sleeps in the same bed with whom. Instead, they are loose, fluid, occurrences without norms or verbal articulation. Highlighting this, Jamie, a university undergraduate, spoke of a time he inadvertently shared a bed with a guy following a house party. "I don't remember all the details," he said. "But we were at a mate's drinking, and I just was like 'that's it. I'm going to sleep.' So, I crawled into one of the beds with some guy already in it. I knew who he was, but no, we were not friends per se." When

Jamie was asked if, perhaps the next morning, it felt odd sleeping in a single bed with a guy he barely knew. "No man," he answered. "It's just not a big deal."

Cuddling Other Men, This Study

Whilst being emotionally intimate, the dodgeball men, who are the focus of this ethnography, suggested that they valued physical intimacy and touch as an integral benefit of having a bromance. Similar to the social restrictions that had previously limited emotional intimacy and love between men, these physically intimate behaviors did not occur during the homohysteric heights of the twentieth century (McCormack and Anderson 2014a, b; McCormack 2011).

The men in this study, conversely, engaged in a great deal of physical tactility. It is hard to say if it precedes emotional intimacy, as physical gestures of touch seem to socially signal the growing affinity between people. The type of touch we refer to here is not just a handshake or a hug to someone who has previously been met. It is a more gentile way of showing inclusion to the team, and acceptance of a friendship. That touch, in both its frequency and duration, then grows as the friendship grows.

These types of behaviors have not been seen for almost a century (Ibson 2002; Rotundo 1989). Although behaviors such as kissing and cuddling were viewed as nonessential to the creation or maintenance of a bromance, all of the men highlighted the behavior as a prominent feature of the relationship. Physical intimacy was routine and enjoyed by these men. They spoke about their desire to cuddle, hug and kiss with their bromantic friends. Some agreed that this was the case when asked, whilst others offered it unsolicited as part of their definition of a bromance. Unlike emotional intimacy, physical intimacy was more easily observed among participants, enabling more observational data to be collected.

In the first week of joining the Dodgeball Club, Stefan, a graduate student at the time, was warmly welcomed. He received physical gestures of welcome, and on a night out those gestures turned into lingering hugs, arms around each other.

Within the week, Stefan could see that friendships were forming with the other players. One night a group of senior members keenly invited him to stay overnight at their house on a night out, because otherwise he would have to leave the social event early to catch the last train home. They were insistent, and he ended up staying overnight on several occasions. In Stefan's words, "They were very caring and hospitable towards me, making breakfast, making up beds and inviting me to stay for lunch."

Stefan grew to become part of this team and its culture: precisely the role of an ethnographer. He says:

> One morning, two months after meeting these men, I was sleeping on the fold out couch in their living room. I woke up to find two of the men had joined me under the covers in their underwear. They wanted to watch television, but didn't want to wake me, so they got into bed with me. We stayed there for hours talking and eating. It was an intimate setting considering I had only met these men a few times, but it did not feel strange or awkward for the most part.

A few weeks later he stayed over again. This time the men walked round completely naked in the morning in front of one another, without acknowledging it. Again, a week later, he was asleep on the couch and was woken by one of the men at 2 am. He came down the stairs and said to the ethnographer/teammate, "This is the first night I haven't pulled (met a woman and had sex), come spoon with me. I feel bad you're down here on your own." It was presented as a question, but rather an assumption that he would join him upstairs. Stefan says:

> For me, it was an odd request, but I felt the need to make an effort with these men because I liked them, and I knew it was something they and others in the team did. I was nervous and awkward because I had never actively spooned another man in his underwear before.

Stefan said that they got into a small single bed in the early hours of the morning in a cold room, and the teammate said, "I'm always little spoon." I was squeezed against the wall man, and it was rather surreal. I was awake for over an hour whereas he fell straight asleep. There was no element of convenience in this situation. As opposed to having a bed each, two 6-foot-tall men were squeezed into a small bed with little breathing space. A housemate came into the room in the morning and made no comment about our situation—there was no awkwardness.

Stefan's teammate's comment about "not pulling" (not getting sex), and his insinuation that my spooning might alleviate and mitigate the sadness of that situation, was reiterated by others during the research interviews.

Jerry said, "On tour, if you don't pull, there is that sadness you get, and you go back to spoon with a mate for the night. I did that with Ed." Similarly, Blake said, "If I don't pull, I will end up coming onto my mates … I've made out with loads of my bromances, and we end up cuddling." When asked why he chooses to spoon his bromances if he doesn't "pull" women, he said, "Well, it's sad to go back on your own after a night out. You do it with a mate who hasn't pulled as well. It sounds gay but sometimes you need it." When asked if kissing and cuddling was important to bromances, Blake said:

> Yes definitely. They symbolize unity, togetherness and how comfortable you are with someone. In the first team, the only person I couldn't do it with is David, because I'm not comfortable enough with him, and I wouldn't call him a bromance.

Blake had a picture of him cuddling with another player posted on the dodgeball Facebook page, with the caption "snuggle buddies," which was seen by 176 people at the time of writing. Stefan asked him how that situation came about and how it made him feel that it was on Facebook. He said:

> Well 176 people know I've got big arms now. Na, I don't give a fuck what people think. But because it's on the dodgeball page, the boys wouldn't see it as gay or anything because it's normal to them. Fuck, I've spooned with most of the boys…That night I left my girlfriends bed and went upstairs to check if my mate was alright, and I fell asleep with him and spooned … It was because I was cold.

His attitude indicates, in line with research produced by Scoats (2017), that physical affection pictured between two men on social media is not embarrassing. Blake was again shown the picture, in which he was shirtless, and questioned whether he was really cold as he expressed. He said, "That's us just being hungover, and having and nap, and being gay; I'm gay. I'm gay aren't I? All this evidence proves I'm gay. Na, he hurt his leg that night and I was just looking after him."

Blake was not the only person to have their intimate bromantic moments posted on Facebook. On a weekly basis, photos of team members making out and spooning were uploaded. When discussing his cuddling picture on the Facebook page, Callum said, "If anyone thinks it's gay, and about your sexuality, then they would probably be someone outside of the club. I'm proud that I have bros that I'm that close with. Better that than no cuddles."

Another study participant said:

> If my parents caught me cuddling in bed with another guy, it would be really embarrassing. My dad hates gay people, and he has tried to engrain that into my head, however bad that sounds. I would hide in my room for a few years (he laughs). But in front of the team, its fine, because everyone does it and it's not something to shy away from. I cuddle with (bromance) a lot because it's nice for company. He's a definite bromance, but I would cuddle most people on the team.

This participant's view draws attention to a recurring narrative, in which members of the team were unsure or skeptical of how people outside of the team would react to their behavior. Rory said, "I'm Catholic, and I know they (the church) wouldn't like me being all physical with other guys" and Ed said, "Outside of the sport, it might seem weird to people." Similarly, Danny said, "I love a good spoon … It's kind of a male bonding thing but it's cool."

Importantly for these men, what people from outside of the club think of them does not bother them or make them embarrassed. It is altogether a normal experience (Anderson and McCormack 2015). This is consistent with other recent research by Scoats (2017), in which 44 young men and a total of 1100 of their Facebook photos were analyzed for their same-sex tactility, finding that they "overwhelmingly adopted inclusive behaviors (including homosocial tactility, dancing, and kissing each other" (p. 1).

In describing why he cuddles his bromance, Jaden said, "It's playful banter. It's just playing around and like, let's have a little spoon mate, cuddle up and be like ahh love you." Andy said, "Well because you love them and your so close, sometimes a cuddle just feels right" and Lawrence said, "In my bromances, cuddles are one of the most important things, everyone needs that intimacy in their lives. It's sad if people don't."

Harry said, "Especially if you don't have a girlfriend, cuddling and hugging with a bromance fills that gap and shows that you care about them."

Affirming what Anderson and McCormack's (2015) found among 40 men, in which 37 had cuddled with a male friend (39 had slept in the same bed overnight), this research finds that 20 out of 20 men had cuddled a male friend, and this occurred with regularity in many bromances.

The participants were asked on how many occasions they had cuddled with a man in the past year. Like kissing, this was highlighted as a regular experience in bromances. Danny said, "I can literally say in the past five days I've slept with five guys on three separate occasions. That's sharing a bed. Four of us squeezed in for cuddles at one point." Jaden said, "I cuddled 20 times plus on tour" and Ronnie said, "I normally cuddle on nights out, maybe 6 times in the past year. Maybe more!" Callum and Blake both said, "Me and my bromance cuddle all the time."

Chapter Summary

Whereas there is no history of heterosexual men cuddling and spooning in bed in British culture (Anderson and Fidler 2018), recent research suggests that matters have changed for adolescents and young adults. Anderson first started observing and describing the behavior of college men doing this around the year 2007. Given that it was observed in a youth TV program, Skins, during this time, it may have emerged into certain youth cultures prior to this.

Previous research on athletes since the beginning of the new millennium has shown this to be a standard practice for heterosexual British boys (Anderson 2014; Anderson and McCormack 2015; McCormack 2012). Cuddling and spooning were frequently experienced in this ethnographic study, too. All 20 men interviewed had cuddled in bed with another male at least once.

Cuddling and spooning emerge for several reasons, including structural reasons. Beds in the United Kingdom are small, and student rooms tend to be cold. Sharing a bed is commonplace after nights out to keep warm. But cuddling also exists for emotional reasons. When two men who have bromantic affection for each other they often cuddle or spoon each other because it feels good. Thus, cuddling exists for these men not as a homoerotic activity, but as a homosocial act of love and nurturance between two friends.

References

Adams, A., and Anderson, E. (2012). Exploring the relationship between homosexuality and sport among the teammates of a small, Midwestern Catholic college soccer team. Sport, Education and Society, 17(3), 347–363.
Anderson, E. (2013). Adolescent masculinity in an age of decreased homohysteria. *Boyhood Studies, 7*(1), 79–93.
Anderson, E. (2014). *21st Century Jocks: Sporting Men and Contemporary Heterosexuality*. New York: Macmillan.
Anderson, E., and Fidler, C. (2018). Elderly British men: Homohysteria and orthodox masculinities. *Journal of Gender Studies, 27*(3), 248–259.
Anderson, E., and McCormack, M. (2015). Cuddling and Spooning Heteromasculinity and Homosocial Tactility among Student-athletes. *Men and Masculinities, 18*(2), 214–230.
Bogle, K. (2008). *Hooking up: Sex, dating, and relationships on campus*. New York: New York University Press.

Ibson, J. (2002). *Picturing men: A century of male relationships in everyday American photography*. Illinois: University of Chicago Press.
McCormack, M. (2011). Mapping the terrain of homosexually-themed language. *Journal of homosexuality*, 58(5), 664–679.
McCormack, M. (2012). *The declining significance of homophobia: How teenage boys are redefining masculinity and heterosexuality*. New York: Oxford University Press.
McCormack, M., and Anderson, E. (2014a). The influence of declining homophobia on men's gender in the United States: An argument for the study of homohysteria. *Sex Roles*, 71(3–4), 109–120.
McCormack, M., and Anderson, E. (2014b). Homohysteria: Definitions, context and intersectionality. *Sex Roles*, 71(3–4), 152–158.
Rotundo, A. (1989). Romantic friendship: Male intimacy and middle-class youth in the northern United States, 1800–1900. *Journal of Social History*, 23(1), 1–25.
Scoats, R. (2017). Inclusive masculinity and Facebook photographs among early emerging adults at a British university. *Journal of Adolescent Research*, 32(3), 323–345.

8

Kissing

The act of heterosexual men kissing on the lips and cheeks is something not found in Ibson's (2002) pictorial evidence. Whilst the practice has certainly existed, sporadically and perhaps within a limited age-range, between father and son; there is no recorded history of heterosexual male friends engaging in this behavior.

However, after taking a post at his first British University in 2005, Eric Anderson saturated himself into youth culture for his studies. This included attending the university dances. Here, he noticed a phenomenal number of men kissing, including his own students—some of which he knew had girlfriends. This began a research agenda of examining the rates, frequencies, and types of heterosexual men kissing across three continents.

This chapter examines the significance of this new phenomena. It accounts for varying levels of homohysteria, the permissiveness of alcohol, and cultural variance in examining kissing behaviors among English, Australian, and American college-attending, heterosexual men before turning its attention to the prevalence and meaning of kissing among men in this study.

The First Study of Straight-Men Kissing, England

Anderson et al. (2012) published the first-ever account of straight men kissing a year later. The primary method they used to collect the data was to approach every third male student that emerged from a common area during the day. They gave each volunteer a short questionnaire, orally.

They combined this form of data with three ethnographic investigations of heterosexual male students in the United Kingdom from multiple educational settings. In total, they interviewed 145 young men in England. Their results indicate that 89% have at some point kissed another male on the lips which they reported as being non-sexual: a means of expressing platonic affection among heterosexual friends. Moreover, 37% reported also engaging in sustained same-sex kissing, something they construed as non-sexual.

Although the students in their study understood that this type of kissing remains somewhat culturally symbolized as a taboo sexual behavior, they nonetheless reconstructed it, making it compatible with heteromasculinity by recoding it as homosocial. The researchers hypothesized that both these types of kissing behaviors are increasingly permissible due to rapidly decreasing levels of cultural homophobia. Furthermore, they argued that there has been a loosening of the restricted physical and emotional boundaries of traditional heteromasculinity in these educational settings, something which may also gradually assist in the erosion of prevailing heterosexual hegemony.

No other research, to date, has examined rates of heterosexual men kissing in this country. This research does not, either. Instead of using a straited (every third male) approach to randomly sampling a student population, it uses a convenience sample of those on the dodgeball team. Still, kissing was prolific, as will be detailed in this chapter. This same research method of interviewing every third student was, however, performed at another university, this time in Australia, the following year.

The Second Study of Straight-Men Kissing, Australia

The Australian university study was mirrored on the work of Anderson et al. (2012). Authors of this study, Drummond et al. (2014), sought to examine whether this cultural shift and corresponding homosocial intimacy, evidenced in the United Kingdom, was also evident among Australian undergraduate men. Accordingly, they conducted interviews with 90 heterosexual men who match the demographic sample of the Anderson et al. (2012) study.

Among the men interviewed at this university, 29% reported having engaged in at least one same-sex kiss with another heterosexual male. Because this was a new behavior among Australian undergraduate men, these results were theorized to be indicative of a changing relationship between the construction of masculinity and heterosexuality in the same way that Anderson theorized was occurring in the United Kingdom (2009).

The Third Study of Straight-Men Kissing, America

In order to further examine the impact of decreasing cultural homohysteria, Anderson took a group of researchers (Anderson et al. 2019) to the United States. Using the same methods of approaching every third male that walked through a common area of a university, they gave short interview to 486 men across eleven American universities, representing small and large institutions in urban areas.

Overall, 40% of the self-identified heterosexual undergraduate men in that sample reported kissing or being kissed by a male friend on the cheek, whilst 10% reported kissing or being kissed by a male friend on the lips. This compares with 89% of men in the United Kingdom who report having kissed another man on the lip (Anderson et al. 2012). Despite overall kissing rates varying across universities, statistical models accounted for the fact that observations were nested within universities.

Thus, estimates refer to the sample at large, demonstrating that this form of kissing occurs across these 11 universities that positioned in different areas of the country and hold diverse student populations.

Whilst same-sex kisses could be viewed as sexual exploration, the narratives of these American participants is consistent with the British men, who suggest that kissing does not have sexual connotations. They described it as a form of social bonding and a way of demonstrating close friendship. Corroborating international scholarship on men's kissing behaviors (Anderson et al. 2012; Drummond et al. 2014), same-sex kissing among heterosexual undergraduate men appears to be an act of emotional expression and not sexual fluidity.

In addition to the short interviews, the research team also conducted 75 long-form interviews on men who were approached using the same 1/3 system. Of these men, five participants said that same-sex kissing would connote a gay identity—7% of that sample. Thus, whilst heterosexual men kissing one another may not be as widespread as in the United Kingdom or Australia, it is similarly a socially acceptable behavior among participants in this study.

The emergence of heterosexual men kissing documented in this study has important implications for theoretical understandings of masculinity. Whilst limited in prevalence, these behaviors provide a challenge to orthodox forms of masculinity that marginalize behaviors associated with femininity or gay. Whereas articulations of masculinity during periods of homohysteria do not permit heterosexual men to engage in intimate behaviors with other men (Kimmel 1998; Plummer 1999), a great deal more behavioral flexibility is afforded to participants in this study who do not see kissing another man as a threat to their heterosexual social identity.

With participants espousing positive attitudes toward gay people (see also Ghaziani 2011, 2017; Twenge et al. 2016), and engaging in feminized behaviors such as kissing without censure, this study supports the growing body of literature that discusses the emergence of inclusive masculinities (e.g., Anderson 2014; McCormack 2012). Expanding recent research showing that some men engage in same-sex sex whilst maintaining heterosexual identities (McCormack 2018; Vrangalova and

Savin-Williams 2012), this study highlights that kissing is not necessarily sexual and can be coded as an emotional, bonding experience.

The data does not enable an understanding of other men's perceptions of kissing behaviors—as such, it is possible that these men are perceived as gay by others and that the onetime rule of homosexuality still exists more generally. This is an important factor in guarding against too broad interpretations from these results. The researchers also highlight, participants had the opportunity in these semi-structured interviews to discuss impediments to same-sex kissing and social issues around it: only five of the participants discussed maintenance of a heterosexual identity as a reason for avoiding kissing. Thus, even if others still perceive participants to be gay for kissing, it seems that such perception has lost its ability to police other men's behaviors and expressions of emotional intimacy for me in our sample (Anderson et al. 2012).

This American study develops the growing body of research on inclusive masculinities in several ways. Firstly, by providing quantitative evidence of the emergence of same-sex kissing among undergraduate heterosexual men, it demonstrates the extent to which a once-censured form of tactility is present among men in the United States. It also corresponds with research demonstrating the increasing range of homosocial behaviors that inclusive straight men engage in (e.g., Anderson and McCormack 2015; Scoats 2017). Whilst not the main focus of the study, the positive attitudes toward homosexuality and gay men found among almost three-quarters of the sample population is further evidence of the social trend of decreasing homophobia, particularly given the random sampling procedure at 11 different universities across the United States As such, this research supports the argument that dominant forms of masculinities in US university cultures are transitioning away from a homophobic jock figure, where homosexuality was exceedingly stigmatized to a set of masculinities that are inclusive both of same-sex sexual desires and non-sexual displays of intimacy between male friends (Anderson 2014; Scoats et al. 2018).

This study also enables comparison of levels of kissing in the United Kingdom (Anderson et al. 2012) and Australia (Drummond et al. 2014). The authors contend that it is the differences in attitudes toward gay people in these cultures that are the primary reason for the cross-cultural differences in kissing (see Anderson 2014). However, structural variance in access to alcohol is also likely a contributing factor. Given that alcohol has a disinhibitory effect that escalates emotional expression, the more liberal drinking laws in the United Kingdom and Australia (where drinking is permitted at 18) and on university campuses, may result in more tactile gendered behaviors in these contexts. Importantly, whilst Peralta (2007) showed how alcohol consumption led men to engage in a number of damaging masculine behaviors, this research found that alcohol may facilitate less harmful masculine behaviors in particular social contexts.

Age and social context are likely to be important factors in this finding. In contemporary research, kissing has only been demonstrated among younger men, and it is argued that youth culture is an important context in which these behaviors occur (Anderson 2014). The developmental stage of "emerging adulthood" (Arnett 2004), in which these young men are currently situated, likely provides the space to explore same-sex kissing with heterosexual friends. In addition to being a period in life where it is possible to bond closely with other young men (Kimmel 1998), the social context of decreased homophobia means that men are less likely to be regulated if they engage in such behaviors (Anderson et al. 2012).

Another interesting American finding was that association with a fraternity or sports team saw elevated rates of same-sex kissing. This may be attributed to the heteromasculine capital afforded to men in these organizations (Anderson 2005). When masculine capital is elevated, men are afforded more space for gender transgression without being labeled as gay. However, given that fear of being socially perceived as gay was only the third stated reason for not wanting to kiss other men, the link with fraternal organizations is likely more attributable to the way these institutions' structure men to spend increased time socializing together and where close friendships can form. It is in these contexts that "bromances" between friends are more likely to occur and in which homosocial friendships are often privileged (Robinson et al. 2018), and that homosocial spaces such as fraternities may facilitate exploration of such intimacy.

Comparing these findings with women's same-sex kisses in university contexts is a useful endeavor. Rupp et al. (2014) argue that the college hook up scene is a gendered and heteronormative sexual field that fosters the practice of women kissing other women in public for the benefit of male onlookers, rather than because of same-sex sexual desire—even though women's sexual desires have been shown to be quite fluid (Diamond 2008). Whilst they contend that these kisses are primarily for men's benefits, they also provide new perspectives on how kisses are perceived socially, arguing that as their participants "act in ways that uncouple desire, behavior, and identity from heteronormativity, they are participating in the process of undoing gender" (Rupp et al. 2014: 229). They discuss how these same-sex kisses serve to undo gender and act in ways that subvert dominant binary categorizations of sex and sexuality. In a similar manner, whilst further research will need to interrogate how men's kissing behaviors are determined by institutional context and masculine capital, they can also be interpreted as a mechanism by which norms of orthodox masculinities are subverted and the onetime rule of homosexuality undermined.

The Fourth Study of Straight-Men Kissing, This Study

We have seen that varying rates of cultural antipathy toward homosexuality, along with the presence of the legality of drinking from age 18, compared to 21, influences the rates of heterosexual men kissing each other. Notably, it appears that the practice is most common in the United Kingdom, and less in Australia and then America. These figures, we caution, are now quite dated—at least in terms of youth data. So, whilst we cannot make generalizations about whether kissing rates in America or Australia would have increased or not—we hypothesize that there will be more kissing because homohysteria continues to erode—we can "test" what is occurring in the United Kingdom.

Unlike Anderson et al. first examination (2012) of the phenomena in England, which found 89% of men had kissed, we found that 100% of the men had kissed another man on the lips, and many regarded this as an important embrace in their bromances.

More interestingly, 100% of the men had also engaged in prolonged kissing (making out) with their bromances. Ronnie explained, "I've kissed most guys in dodgeball, and any that I haven't, other people have. And anyone who says they haven't, then they are lying."

When asked who they engaged in these kissing behaviors with, many of the men identified this as a behavior exclusive to their bromances, whilst some extended this to their friends. Gordon said, "It would only ever be close friends … I do it when I'm with my best mates and having a laugh, or if were emotional, because it's generally quite fun." Taylor said, "It's a symbol for how close your bromance is," and Jerry, who was identified by others as a prolific same-sex kisser said, "It's a way of showing your love, just like cuddling." When defining what a bromance is, Rory said, "It's like a girlfriend, but with a guy. Someone you can kiss and appreciate for their friendship." Lawrence said, "I've kissed a fair few guys in my time, but it's a way of saying, hey, I'm comfortable with you." Chris highlighted the fluid nature of same-sex kissing, explaining:

> I couldn't actually tell you why I do it. It's like a mutual thing where both guys in the bromance instigate it. You don't go up to them and say 'Let's make out;' it's more organic than that. You don't have to say anything before or after, especially if there's loud music around, and sometimes it's easier to socialize through kissing and physical stuff if you can't hear each other.

Indeed, Chris was someone who would make out with his bromances in public regularly. When on a night out in a club or pub, he would often walk past and make out with his friends, then continue to the dancefloor or bar. One time, he was dancing with Gordon, with a girl in the middle of them, and they started making out over the top of her, and she eventually left them to it. In another scenario, he would pair up with his bromance and pretend to be gay. He would confidently approach girls on a night out, saying, "Do you want a threesome with me and my boyfriend?" Inevitably, the girls asked him to prove that he was gay, resulting in a passionate and prolonged tongue kiss.

In one of these scenarios, Chris gave his bromance two large love bites on his neck, in an attempt to have a foursome with two women in a same-sex relationship. This behavior accords with what Anderson (2008) describes as the good cause scenario, where men are permitted a level of homosexuality when it is done to access heterosexual sex. However, in interview, he did not use this as a defense for his behavior. When asked about this situation it was observed that Chris was laughing intensely at the detail in which the researcher recorded his behavior. When asked why he gave love bites to another male member of the team, he said, "I made out with lots of the boys that night. It's not just me you know. But I do it because it's fun and it just shows how strong your friendship is."

When Stefan asked Ronnie what he thought of the love biting, he said, "It's not gay. Who cares? Let boys be boys." Ronnie was also a fairly prolific kisser of men in the dodgeball club, and he implied that same-sex behaviors as this were the norm and natural; just part of "boys being boys."

A minority of the men said that who they kissed depended on how good-looking and attractive they were, as well as how close a friend they were. Whilst at training, Pete walked up to Ed without saying anything and kissed him on each cheek and on the lips sensually. When Stefan asked about why he did that, he said:

> Ed is a good-looking guy. I find him very attractive. I'm very open in my sexuality in that I know what I find attractive and what I don't, and I couldn't care what people thought about it. It was like "ahh, good to see you mate," and give him a little French kiss.

The man he kissed, Ed, described the first time he made out with his bromance; "We were all in the car and (bromance) asked if I ever kissed a guy. I said no, and he asked me to make out with him, in front of the guys. So, I did. He's a decent looking bloke actually." Later, he explained when talking about Jerry in the team, "Quite often on a night out, he loves a good kiss on the lips. He leans in straight away and goes for it. I think he's a good kisser and not bad looking." Callum said, "Some boys I wouldn't kiss because I don't find them very attractive. I think most of my mates are good looking … Obviously you can say a boy is good looking, like, you can find them attractive."

Lawrence added, "I would prefer to make out with good looking guys like Chris, because he's got a good body, long hair and soft features." Jaden explained, "When I get off with guys, I enjoy it, not sexually, but the banter and people laughing and because I can't say I'm entirely straight."

The number of men that expressed a physical attraction to other men was a minority, but it represents an interesting perspective from men who identify toward the heterosexual end of the scale.

Just as these men did not regard their cuddling behaviors as private or embarrassing, Callum explained how this is no different for kissing:

> I've made out with my bros quite a few times. I've been filmed doing it. It's normal for the dodgeball team and in all sorts of sports where you need to bond. Like nowadays, there's not much stigma about it and you wouldn't be called gay or anything like that. It's funny, isn't it?

Rob said, "Where I'm from, its tradition to make out with a guy on New Year's Eve, just in the street."

When Eric Anderson asked Stefan how many times he saw men kissing each other in the course of his research, his answer was: "I observed hundreds of kissing instances between friends and bromances, and as many when they made out."

Discussing same-sex kissing in public, Harry said, "No one cares," and that was exactly what was observed. The men did not care who saw, where they were, and how often they made out. Ed said, "I don't think the girls in the team care either. Like my girlfriend knows I get off with my mates. Sounds weird right?"

James said, "With a bromance, you are comfortable flirting with them and you would kiss and wouldn't mind seeing each other naked …We snog and kiss on nights out and we both have girlfriends but it never goes further than that."

Jaden said, "Because more people today embrace gay behaviors, that's why less people care. I think it's fine for a cheeky kiss. I think today society is more expressive and people don't judge." This articulate perspective broadly aligns with recent research that documents a rapid decline in cultural homophobia (McCormack 2012; McCormack and Anderson 2014a, b).

Another participant, Blake, was shown a picture that was taken professionally at a local night club and was posted on Facebook. In this picture, Blake was passionately kissing another member of the team, wrapped in his arms. When asked about it, he said, "Fuck. My hair looks bad." In other words, he cared more about how his hair looked than the fact he was pictured kissing a guy. Stefan asked why he was kissing him, and Blake responded, "Purely for the photo. Love the camera. It's not embarrassing, just my fucking hair is shit."

Danny explained that people did not feel embarrassment in same-sex behaviors, "Because of the internet, you are exposed to liberality." Danny went on to articulate how the physical realm of bromances connected with the emotional:

> Basically, a physical embrace backs up an emotional embrace. If you have no physical contact with someone then you struggle to bond on an emotional level. If you want to have a bromance with someone that you can physically and emotionally depend on, there's got to be a level of emotion expressed through acts like cuddling and kissing.

Three-Way Kissing

Results have thus far highlighted that men, particularly in bromances, enjoy kissing one another on a regular basis. However, these men did not just limit their kissing behaviors to one-on-one. Twelve of the 20 men had also engaged in three-way kissing with at least two other men. Indeed, some of the men had made out with four other men at the same time.

There is a lot of cultural meaning to unpack in this section. We highlight that when a group of guys engage in a kiss, it is funny to them. It is also intimate because they don't just kiss any male. It thus represents a fusion of humor and intimacy. One could theorize that it is the humor which makes the intimacy acceptable in a homophobic culture, but we see no supporting evidence of that. Instead, we think the humor make the intimacy acceptable as a behavior that is associated with sexual desires, that do not manifest for the guys we study. We see these types of behaviors as signaling to other men that they want to progress their bromance. These types of behaviors are often an important aspect of relationship building.

Stefan first noticed the prevalence of this behavior during a game of "never have I ever" at a pre-drinks social (the alcohol drinking session that is usually held between 7 and 10 pm before heading out to a pub or club). Never have I ever is a game where one person says a statement, prefixed by the phrase never have I ever, and if any participant has done what the statement suggests, they have to finish their drink.

In this case Ronnie said, "Never have I ever had a five-way kiss with just guys." Without hesitation, Ronnie and four other men in the room drank: all of them good friends. Considering that Ronnie proposed the question, it appeared that he was proud of kissing his friends, and it was funny to most people. This again represents a fusion of humor with intimacy. We argue that attempts to theorize this behavior with either of those two variables alone are not academically valid.

Stefan observed this kissing behavior very early on in the year, and he soon began to see it with frequency. In one instance, it was challenge night, which meant that each person was given a list of challenges written on their t-shirt that they needed to complete by the end of the night. Gordon wrote on Max's top to have a five-way kiss. Max asked, "Does it matter if its boys or girls" and Gordon responded, "I don't care mate, just make sure I see it." Soon, Max was making out with three men and one woman. As part of their interviews, Stefan asked participants if they had engaged in this behavior and why they thought it occurred. Gordon said:

> Gender isn't important. It's sometimes a way of getting guys and girls together, and then you can all kiss and leave two to get on with it. I do it a lot, it's my matchmaker technique. I just lend a helping hand.

Talking about Gordon's matchmaker technique, Andy said, "I did it on tour. Quite a few actually. Gordon comes in and does it to be a wingman. It worked for me." From what Stefan observed, Gordon was very good at breaking the ice between two people who were flirting, and he would arrange these three-way kisses and slowly pull away leaving the couple to continue kissing. On one specific night, Gordon shared a non-penetrative threesome with Andy and a girl they had a three-way kiss with earlier that night.

When asked about his three-way kissing experiences Jerry said, "One of your mates can be getting off with a girl and you think, I want to join in. It's not pushy or anything, people love it." Blake simply said, "I do it because it's funny as fuck." Ed said, "I remember it was a guy and a girl, and she was like let's have a three-way kiss. I think there is sexual enjoyment if a girl is involved."

Chris said, "It's just something we do. It's just showing you're comfortable with your mates. Weird right?" Compared to one-on-one kissing, there was less consistency in the answers the men gave in regard to their reasons for kissing. They broadly identified that three-way kissing was a useful tool for matchmaking and that it was funny to do. Some could not specifically identify a reason for their behaviors.

All of the men in this study engaged in public kissing behaviors and were relatively unmindful of what others thought, largely because others in the team did not judge it, and they did not care about what outsiders thought. Alcohol plays a role, too.

Kissing was recognized as a benefit of a bromance and a physically demonstrative way of showing affection for each other. It was not made clear by the participants, and it was not observed that kissing and cuddling were essential in the formation of bromances. Instead, these behaviors served to reinforce the strength and comfortability of the relationship. As Danny articulately put it, "A physical embrace backs up an emotional embrace."

Frequency of Kissing

This section is specifically concerned with presenting observational and interview data on the frequency in which these men kiss and cuddle each other; a variable that has not been empirically considered before. Importantly, this is the first long-term study that considers both observational and interview data on the frequency of same-sex kissing behaviors.

All of the participants were asked on how many occasions they had kissed another man on the lips in the past year. It was most common for the men to state that they had kissed or made out with another man between 10 and 30 times in the past year, most of which were fellow club members. This may not seem as many as the research notes indicate occurred, however.

When counting kisses, it is important to remember that these men mostly kiss their university bromances and that university is only in session 24 weeks a year. If each man kissed another 20 times during that year, and with 30 men studied that's 500 kisses. Given that not every night is a night out in a club, it means that there is a lot of kissing happening during the ethnographic fieldwork.

Chris confidently said, "Well, on Tour (a one-week holiday), I reckon I made out with guys at least 50 times, more than I did girls." This was not a novel exaggeration of Chris's behaviors. Indeed, Stefan observed Chris's statement of 50 in a week to be a fairly accurate description, with most of those involving prolonged open-mouth kissing. Stefan asked for an estimate of his same-sex kissing frequency over the year, to which he replied, "Over 100 I recon. Others do it more."

Stefan observed Chris kiss approximately 15 kisses of different men in one night. This one-night count was estimated to be Jaden's yearly count. Jaden answered, "15 people in the past year. It's funny and you get caught up in a situation and you just need to go with it." With enthusiasm, Ronnie said "20 guys on lips, if not more, purely because it's fun." Callum said, "Ah mate. Loads! Maybe 10 or 15 times. Maybe more. There are videos on Facebook of me doing it."

Whilst these men engaged enthusiastically and confidently in answering the question, consciously or subconsciously, they consistently indicated that their given number was likely fewer than the reality; they were reserved to increase the amount.

In early interviews, it became clear that given more time to consider the question, the men progressively increased their number. They would sometimes try to add up in their head how many times they had kissed another man in the past year. Furthermore, after the first few interviews, Stefan decided it would be useful to prompt the men on some occasions where he felt their estimations were unrepresentative of the behavior observed. For example, his conversation with Andy went like this:

Interviewer: How many times have you kissed a guy on the lips in the past year?
Andy: Maybe 2.
Interviewer: Are you sure?
Andy: Well, it's more like 4 probably.
Interviewer: Is that including on tour?
Andy: Oh god, quite a few then. At least 8 and lot with Gordon.
Interviewer: How many times with Gordon in the past year do you think?
Andy: Well, maybe 6.
Interviewer: And are you including gay chicken in any of this, and when you made out with me, and Jerry at pre-drinks, and with that guy on the Tour bus?
Andy: Na, it's a fair bit more isn't it?
Interviewer: Ha, you tell me. What's your best estimate in the past year?
Andy: Honestly, maybe 12 or 15 times then.

With the observational knowledge he had prior to interviewing these men, Stefan was able to attain greater accuracy of the men's kissing rates and behaviors than was likely possible in other interview only studies (Anderson 2008; Anderson et al. 2012). With a little exploration, Andy was quick to raise his estimate from 2 same-sex kisses in the past year, to potentially 15.

Similarly, Harry said, "Oh I reckon I've made out with at least six." After revealing approximately how many specific instances Stefan had observed kissing among teammates, Harry soon explaining that he kissed, "20 times or maybe 30, and probably made out with a fair few of those too." Blake said, "Around the 20 mark. It could be higher." Stefan asked how much higher? Blake said, "Maybe more like 25." Later in the conversation he said, "Thinking about it, it's probably over 30." Stefan jokingly remarked, "Why say 20 then"? To which he said, "I don't know, I don't keep a fucking tally."

When Mark was asked about his kissing frequency, he said, "I only ever make out with my bromances. A peck on the lips is just weak if you ask me." When asked to elaborate, Mark said, "If you're going to kiss a bro, you might as well go whole hog and snog them. That's how most of the boys do it."

For those asked to explain why they were underestimating their kissing frequency, they were not able to say why they did it. On one hand, they were not embarrassed about their behaviors, but they were still limiting their answers. They did not indicate that it was because it was a gay behavior, or that they were embarrassed, just that they struggled to recall it.

We do not think that a valid explanation for this underestimation comes from a belief that these kisses are still stigmatized; instead, it seems to us that kissing has become routinized and thus forgettable.

Exemplifying this perspective: we ask readers to recall how many times they shook hands with another person in the last week or year? You might recall some of those times, particularly the awkward ones, but could you accurately give a number as to how many? Likely not. The same principle might hold true of estimating making out with males, too. This might be the equivalent of asking people to consider how many times they hugged others.

Before we leave this section, we wish to highlight that we regret not having asked the men how many times they have kissed another male who they knew to be gay or bi. There was evidence that this, too, was an acceptable practice. For example, Jerry seemed to have a propensity to kiss gay men. He said, "I have made out with loads of guys including ten gay guys in the past year." We wish we had asked all the men this question.

Chapter Summary

Anderson first began charting the emergence of heterosexual men kissing one another around the year 2005, in England. His observations of his own students in clubs and pubs lead him to more formal research.

Throughout a series of studies on heterosexual undergraduate men, Anderson and his colleagues examined multiple groups of heterosexual men in England, Australia, and the United Kingdom (Anderson 2014). Here, evidence was found of the existence of men kissing at varying rates, but no more than 89% that which was found in England.

The international emergence of heterosexual men kissing each other is attributed to decreasing cultural homohysteria, alcohol, affection, and perhaps for the attention of heterosexual women in certain situations, too. Throughout his many studies of the topic Anderson has found that there are a great variety of types of kisses, on the lips, and cheeks, as well as deep kissing: all with varying meanings and purposes. None of this is meant to degrade gay men, however.

This study picks upon the history of study of men kissing. Although not using a random sample like some of Anderson's other work, it uses ethnographic investigation of the dodgeball team for which this book is focused to find that kissing is prolific among all of the men in the study (Table 8.1). More so, this study adds to the literature on heterosexual men kissing with an expose of three-way kisses between men. It shows that men kissing each other on the dodgeball team was a highly regular activity, including making out with other men.

Collectively, results of this study show that kissing exists in some regards for strangers, and in other regards for bromantic friends. It is a behavior that occurs less in private spaces than cuddling but more often appears as a performance, in public spaces, and often occurs under the influence of alcohol. Still, the location of these kisses should not be taken as an assumption that they do not reflect genuine reflection. When asked why men kiss, it was common to hear them say, "Because I love him."

Table 8.1 Frequency of self-identified and recalled kissing

Name	Number of times kissed another man on the lips in the past year	Number of times made out with another man in the past year
Ronnie	20	4
Lawrence	15	3
Harry	33	6
Andy	15	5
James	15	5
Chris	100	30
Jerry	60	15
Pete	10	4
Rory	2	1
Danny	20	1
Taylor	3	1
Jaden	15	15
Ed	5	2
Callum	15	10
Gordon	20	5
Blake	30	15
Tim	12	8
John	16	3
Mark	10	10
Max	22	12
Mean average	22	8

References

Anderson, E. (2005). *In the game: Gay athletes and the cult of masculinity*. New York: University of New York Press.

Anderson, E. (2009). *Inclusive masculinity: The changing nature of masculinities*. New York: Routledge

Anderson, E. (2014). *21st Century Jocks: Sporting Men and Contemporary Heterosexuality*. New York: Macmillan.

Anderson, E., and McCormack, M. (2015). Cuddling and Spooning Heteromasculinity and Homosocial Tactility among Student-athletes. *Men and Masculinities, 18*(2), 214–230.

Anderson, E., Adams, A., and Rivers, I. (2012). "I kiss them because I love them": The emergence of heterosexual men kissing in British institutes of education. *Archives of Sexual Behaviour, 41*(2), 421–430.

Anderson, E., Ripley, M., and McCormack, M. (2019). A mixed-method study of same-sex kissing among college-attending heterosexual men in the US. *Sexuality and Culture, 23*(1), 26–44.

Anderson, E. (2008). "Being masculine is not about who you sleep with…:" Heterosexual athletes contesting masculinity and the one-time rule of homosexuality. *Sex Roles, 58*(1–2), 104–115.

Arnett, J. (2004). *A longer road to adulthood*. New York: Oxford University Press.

Diamond, L. M. (2008). Female bisexuality from adolescence to adulthood: Results from a 10-year longitudinal study. *Developmental Psychology, 44*(1), 5.

Drummond, M., Filiault, S., Anderson, E., and Jeffries, D. (2014). Homosocial intimacy among Australian undergraduate men. *Journal of Sociology, 51*(3), 643–656.

Ghaziani, A. (2011). Post-gay collective identity construction. *Social Problems, 58*(1), 99–125.

Ghaziani, A. (2017). *Sex cultures*. Boston: Polity Press (Cultural Sociology series).

Ibson, J. (2002). *Picturing men: A century of male relationships in everyday American photography*. Illinois: University of Chicago Press.

Kimmel, M. S. (1998). *Manhood in America: A cultural history*. New York: Free Press.

McCormack, M. (2012). *The declining significance of homophobia: How teenage boys are redefining masculinity and heterosexuality*. New York: Oxford University Press.

McCormack, M. (2018). Mostly straights and the study of sexualities: An introduction to the special issue. *Sexualities, 21*(1–2), 3–15.

McCormack, M., and Anderson, E. (2014b). Homohysteria: Definitions, context and intersectionality. *Sex Roles, 71*(3–4), 152–158.

McCormack, M., and Anderson, E. (2014a). The influence of declining homophobia on men's gender in the United States: An argument for the study of homohysteria. *Sex Roles, 71*(3–4), 109–120.

Peralta, R. (2007). College alcohol use and the embodiment of hegemonic masculinity among European American men. *Sex Roles, 56*(11), 741–756.

Plummer, D. (1999). *One of the boys: Masculinity, homophobia, and modern manhood*. New York: Routledge.

Robinson, S., Anderson, E., and White, A. (2018). The bromance: Undergraduate male friendships and the expansion of contemporary homosocial boundaries. *Sex Roles, 78*(1–2), 94–106.

Rupp, L., Taylor, V., Regev-Messalem, S., Fogarty, A., and England, P. (2014). Queer women in the hookup scene: Beyond the closet. *Gender and Society, 28*(2), 212–235.

Scoats, R. (2017). Inclusive masculinity and Facebook photographs among early emerging adults at a British university. *Journal of Adolescent Research, 32*(3), 323–345.

Scoats, R., Joseph, L. J., and Anderson, E. (2018). 'I don't mind watching him cum': Heterosexual men, threesomes, and the erosion of the one-time rule of homosexuality. *Sexualities, 21*(1–2), 30–48.

Twenge, J. M., Sherman, R. A., and Wells, B. E. (2016). Changes in American adults' reported same-sex sexual experiences and attitudes, 1973–2014. *Archives of Sexual Behavior, 45*(7), 1713–1730.

Vrangalova, Z., and Savin-Williams, R. C. (2012). Mostly heterosexual and mostly gay/lesbian: Evidence for new sexual orientation identities. *Archives of Sexual Behavior, 41*(1), 85–101.

9

Popularity and Banter in a Bromantic Culture

This chapter examines how men become popular within a bromantic culture. It highlights that a bawdy type of humor is the chief mechanism for gaining status. This serves alongside banter to promote social cohesion among the players on the team. We show that the concept of banter is the idea of making fun of one another in order to promote, not demote, a sense of cohesion. We then highlight how banter varies from bullying in order to help nuance this social practice.

Humor

What makes someone popular is clearly a complex array of factors. However, in asking the players what they thought was most important variable in making someone popular on the team, the answer came through one's ability to be perceived as funny to others. Thus, where previously popularity has been conflated with the masculine hierarchy (Jocks) (Anderson 2014), these men idolized humor over athletic performance—similar to the charisma that McCormack (2012) highlighted as important in his work on 16–18-year-old boys in English schools.

Blake was reported by most as being the most popular on the team. Ronnie said, "Everyone loves Blake, he's a funny character. People are attracted to that. He's such a funny guy and he can usually make me laugh just from staring into my eyes." Ed agreed, "He's the most popular because he's really funny. When we walk around campus, everyone says hello to him." When asked who was popular, Rory said, "Without doubt Blake is, because he always makes everyone laugh, without needing to insult people."

Humor is of course a complex social phenomenon. Yet there is a particularly, bawdy, form of humor that the men on this team appreciated. In order to exemplify this type of humor, Stefan describes an instance where the whole tour team posed for a memorable group photo, before disbanding after the sport tour holiday. Whilst humor is contingent on taste, the picture revealed that one team member had hung his testicles out of the bottom of his shorts. In another example of what type of performance, the players enjoyed, in a hotel room, Blake had flaccid sex with his roommate's pillows and his sheets. These events are illustrative of the laddish humor that they enjoy—outlandish behaviors.

We have had some disagreement with analyzing this type of humor. In reading a draft of this work, Professor Mark McCormack, who studies popularity among adolescents (2012) looked critically upon this type of humor as being funny. To him, it just is not funny. Conversely, Professor Eric Anderson, who studies adolescent masculinity among athletes and has coached adolescent athletes for decades, sees it as being funny. We thus think that in analyzing this type of behavior we need to highlight that the nature of this humor is perhaps funny not simply because of what or how men act in this outrageous, pseudo-sexual, or as some would call, laddish, behaviors, but because these behaviors are in fact breaching exercises.

Sociologist, Harold Garfinkel (1917–2011), studied people's customs in order to find out how societal rules and norms not only influenced behavior but also shaped social order. He postulated that social order was a result of a combination of overt and covert social norms (1967). One of Garfinkel's research methods was known as a "breaching experiment," in which the researcher behaves in a socially awkward manner in order to test the sociological concepts of social norms and conformity.

If the breach is successful bystanders will find amusement or curiosity about what they see. Standing in an elevator backwards, talking, playing tic-tac-toe with a stranger at lunch, or a businessman skipping on the Manhattan sidewalk in suit and tie, serve as examples of behaviors that are not offensive, but breach social etiquette for the environment. The point is to deviate from a specific social norm in a small way, to subtly break some form of social etiquette, and see what happens.

In the case of these athletes, what happens is laughter. The breaching of the norm (i.e., to keep one's genitals out of sight of others) in an environment of friends, elicits an illicit form of humor.

But humor may, in fact, not fully capture alone what we portray here. What makes Blake popular is that his humor (extraversion and a bawdiness) breaches social norms, and sometimes because his humor is used as a form of mild denigration of his own self.

When humor is generated by the demise of another, it deserves a different label and social analysis. We call this banter.

Banter

Blake's humor worked at many levels, irony, perversion, parody, and most of all, physical comedy. But another form of humor is that of banter. It was also readily identifiable as another characteristic of popularity. Banter, or being banterous, is a practice of playful, teasing remarks between friends in a way that requires reciprocation and a mutual understanding. It is this which differs from bullying. At first glance, it seems paradoxical, but the participants in this study seemed to enjoy it as a passage, a symbolic marker, of friendship. In this way, banter seems to operate in the same way as hazing.

Hazing is a more formalized practice of ritually degrading a friend or potential friend. In this case, those looking to join a social group, like a fraternity or sports team. Here, members are required to engage in a number of degrading activities before being accepted onto a team. Hazing is more complex than banter, because it normally involves more than just verbally "abusing" others, but often involves physical acts that are sometimes dangerous. Hazing also works only one way. Traditionally, those being hazed do not get to speak up against, banter with, or otherwise get to defend themselves against those doing the hazing.

Hazing and banter are something that is both found within male sports culture. In the United Kingdom, hazing is often referred to as an initiation and aligns itself with a long history of initiation rituals. Examining why athletes themselves engage in initiations is an interesting question for which the simplest answer is that athletes who were hazed in order to join a program feel that they need to "get back" by hazing new recruits. Yet the practice is more complex than that.

The actual effect of hazing is that it exists as a key means of creating team cohesion (Bryshun 1997). Recruits often describe the experience of hazing initiations as a positive bonding experience between friends (Feist et al. 2004). Furthermore, athletes assume that the more extreme a hazing initiation is, the greater the level of commitment and interdependency will be produced (Anderson et al. 2012). Essentially, surviving a brutal event at the hands of one's future friends/teammates has the perverse effect of bonding them closer to those friends and teammates. In studies of those who are hazed, they show more affection for those who hazed them after the event (Groves et al. 2012). It is also the same fact that leads to hazing deaths and the prohibition of hazing at many American universities.

Banter seems to have the same cohesion-building effect as hazing. It is a paradoxical way of tearing someone down as a way to say, 'I love you' and is something that is only done with friends. It links in with humor because the banter must be humorous. Few people find bullying of another humorous unless of course one also dislikes the person being bullied.

This is to suggest that there is a delineation between banter and bullying. In helping to describe what that line is, we highlight that banter is something that you do between friends. One does not banter with someone they do not like. Conversely, one does not bully someone they do like. To an outsider, it may be difficult to spot the difference.

Ronnie explained:

> Banter is picking something that someone has joked about themselves, and then using that, like a funny story, such as being shit in bed and not getting a hard on. We give abuse for that because it's funny and it's just a joke. Bullying is where someone says it's not funny, but people carry on joking anyway, repeating it and clearly trying to make someone feel bad. It's a fine line, and it depends on who it's coming from and how it's said, not necessarily what is said. It's best you know that person's personal circumstances before you give someone banter.

Understanding the use of banter, its difference from hazing, as a masculinizing tool at the same time as performing inclusion is difficult. Language is difficult to analyze, as it involves both intent of the giver, perception of the receiver, and cultural context for the observer. Previous work has shown that athletes can use language in compartmentalized ways.

Adams, Anderson, and McCormack (2010) examined, for example, how coaches and players constructed and regulated masculinity in organized sport. Using participant observation, they examined the role of discourses in the construction and regulation of sporting masculinity within a semi-professional British football (soccer) team. Two predominant discourses were present: (a) masculinity establishing discourse and (b) masculinity challenging discourse; heuristic tools to understand the use of toxic language in the construction and maintenance of masculinity. Coaches frequently used discourses that drew on narratives of war, gender, and sexuality in order to facilitate aggressive and violent responses for enhancing athletic performance. However, the researchers also found that these discourses have limited influence beyond the playing field, highlighting the segmentation of the sporting and social identities of these players, and a loosening of the traditional and empirically evidenced ability of sports to socialize men into narrow forms of masculinity.

This compartmentalization of how the same language can have different uses helps make sense of the second part of Ronnie's explanation about banter, which clearly aligns with McCormack's (2011) conclusions on how homosexually themed language should be interpreted. Both scholar and participant highlight how something is said, to whom, and the relationship between those two people is crucial as to whether there is pernicious intent (bullying) or banter.

For example, Blake was regularly identified as being popular in the club. One of his leading characteristics was his obsession with hurling insults and abuse at other team members in a banterous way. If someone was bad at dodgeball, he would identify their inability and label them "can't dodge" if they frequently got hit. If they were overweight, he would call them fat. Stefan, who was older than most of the team members, would be called dad, and an old man.

On the surface, these behaviors may be interpreted as offensive and misguided, and they would be to people outside of the club. However, he was regularly mentioned as the most popular member of the club and people enjoyed his company. The men explain a clear reason why they find this behavior acceptable. Danny said:

> The guys love Blake because he keeps everyone entertained. He spreads the banter across everyone and will only get harsh with his closest mates. Like when he calls Ed fat. He is his bromance and he's not going to get upset about that.

Rob said:

> In sport, there are always people like Blake. He would never intentionally hurt anyone's feelings. He's like Frankie Boyle. His jokes are so crude but you enjoy his company, he makes you laugh and brings people together. People don't take anything he says seriously.

And Ed said:

> Saying something horrible isn't banter, that's people using banter as an excuse. But banter needs everyone to be having a good time. If that person (the subject of the banter) says its fine, then great. Blake is able to gauge it right and knows when to stop. But there is a line. I know he

doesn't make jokes about my weight because he knows it gets to me, but it doesn't to others.

One of Blake's most common approaches to banter would be to tell people why they were so ugly, and why he was so attractive. In Stefan's experience, and as described by participants, the men in this study found this funny. What made this possible was that Blake was friends with everyone and had several bromances in the team. As the men explain, he did not victimize specific people, and he was emotionally intelligent enough to know when his jokes could go "too far."

On the other hand, some people were said to be less popular because they tried to emulate Blake's behavior, but without the same social tactility. In other words, they were not able to traverse the "fine line" that Ed speaks of. All of this points to the complexity of personal politics and humor that any seasoned comedian will be aware of. As our culture grows more civil, with the accompanying policing of discourse, humor is increasingly a more tricky, and risky business. Perhaps this is one reason that this type of breaching humor was so well enjoyed by the team: it is increasingly rarer. Perhaps this is why, as a result, research has identified that humor is increasingly being recognized as a more weighted characteristic when gauging people's popularity (Closson 2009; McCormack 2012).

The Precarious Nature of Humor

In McCormack's (2012) work on adolescent males and popularity, he found that there was no genuine hierarchy of masculinity among the various types, or groups, of boys that he studies in an English sixth form (where students are aged 16–18). The jocks were not praised compared to the geeks.

Exemplifying the social composition of this hierarchy in this setting, Callum and Max were suggested by several participants to copy Blake's behaviors, without the same social success as Blake. They were ranked the least popular on several occasions. When asked why he thought they were less popular, Rory said, "They are loud, confident, brash, outspoken and arrogant." Stefan responded, "That's the same characteristics that you have used to describe the most popular people though?" He responded:

> It's weird isn't it? They fall outside of being popular, but they behave similar to Blake. But they fall different sides of the line. The difference is in the ability to give shit and take shit, and to have the humility to say, "Fair enough, I dish it out, so I'm not going to get upset about people taking the piss out of me." That's the difference between Callum and Max, and Blake.

It was clear for these men that in order to be popular, one had to be able "To give shit and take shit;" to give banter, and receive it, without hostility or taking offense. For example, Danny said, "I would take any banter because I can give as good as I get, and I think there is a good number of people who are the same. That's why we all get on." Similarly, Lawrence said, "If you're willing to give banter, you need to take it, too. That interaction makes up a big part of team life, and we are pretty good at it as a team." Indeed, Blake was always open to insult, challenge, and banter. He had his floors, and his friends could exploit them humorously without upsetting him.

There is thus a contradiction here: to be popular, one has to give banter; but that then means that one has to also be able to take banter. So, it seems that you can either choose to be unpopular or receive banter. In this group of men, this makes the production of banter a socially compelled activity.

Pete, a man who said that he was "Not very popular in the team" said, "Me and Callum are not loved by everyone. Like, we're funny to some people, but not to everyone." He similarly adopted Blake's approach to banter. Talking about Pete, Jerry explained, "He is a fresher and not well established enough in the group to be making those kinds of remarks, whereas Blake has been here for four years." This illustrates the pre-existing effect of a dodgeball network of trust which is then made synergistic with his social charisma. Danny similarly said, "Less popular people aren't genuine, and copy Blake. They may do it for the popularity to get the most laughs out of it, but it can backfire." Blake, speaking about those who copy him said, "They will copy my behavior and people won't think it's genuine." Consequently, it may very well be that this combination of talents Blake had, made him socially dominant in this environment.

Once someone has dominance, it is easier to transgress lines that are not socially acceptable, without social repercussion. There are several examples of how other teammates tried to emulate Blake's behaviors in form and content, but it instead made people feel uneasy. Often, they would target quieter and more socially anxious team members with insulting banter, but with a sense of aggression, whereas Blake would rather take on the social heavyweights in the club, without pernicious intent. For example, Blake would say statements like, "You're a complete fucking loser at sport," and everyone would laugh, including the subject of the insult.

On the contrary, less popular emulators have said, "Your shit, why don't you leave dodgeball?" Here, no one would laugh; the atmosphere would be tense, and the person would feel insulted. This highlights both that with social dominance someone can say something inappropriate and not be judged, compared to those who had less popularity.

Connoisseurs of discourse will note that part of the variance between the popular and unpopular insult will depend on tonality, who it comes from, and what their history is with the person receiving the insult. But another part comes in what was said. In Blake's example, he just proclaimed one shit at dodgeball with no other directives. In the later example, the player added "why don't you leave?" This changes the possibility of banter into a direct insult. More so, Blake is not on the first team. He is not an accomplished player, so his calling another player shit at dodgeball has an air of paradoxical humor to it because, he too, is not that good at dodgeball.

For some, the differences in these insults may not appear obvious, but to see the execution of the comments would show a vastly different approach. Blake would target popular and resilient members of the club with his insults, whereas the two least popular members of the club would target the more vulnerable. Taylor said, "Honestly, if any of the guys do say stuff that's out of line, they realize it, and say sorry. Max and Callum won't. In fact, they probably don't understand that they are being out of line." Fortunately, this was not the esteemed culture of the club, and it was consequently why these men were ranked as less popular. As Danny explained, "For individuals to be popular, it needs to be founded on humor, as long as it doesn't offend people."

The most prominent example noted is where banter from two individuals was misguided and pernicious during a rap battle on a coach. In front of a full coach of 50 students, members of the dodgeball team took it in turns to rap battle against each other, to the entertainment of everyone else. Part of the elevated mood was that the banter was lighthearted. When it was one person's turn, however, he and another decided to rap against one of the quieter and shyer members of the club. Banterous insults quickly turned to insults, and whereas each rap battle had been spontaneous and unprepared, each side took an increasing amount of time to prepare their raps, and it went on far longer than other battles. Soon, few people were laughing, and everyone was supporting the quiet person. Eventually, someone told the two aggravators to stop because they were being "out of order." This is a good example of where the ability to "give shit and take shit, to have the humility to say fair enough," as Rory put it, did not register in some people's behavior.

Codifying Banter

Reviewing the ways in which these men define, express, and limit their banter, we have distinguished seven rules that guide the team's behaviors and rules of banter:

Behavioral

- Rule 1: You must tolerate banter on the same level that you apply it, and not take offense as a response, as this will appear hypocritical.
- Rule 2: You must understand someone's personal situation and emotional insecurities, and they must know you understand them, before applying banter. A state of friendship thus helps mitigate the risk of misunderstanding in this area.

- Rule 3: You must take account of the emotional harm that banter may cause to an individual, recognizing that all individuals have varying levels of capacity for banter.
- Rule 4: You must rotate and vary your banter between friends; otherwise, this could be interpreted as targeted bullying.
- Rule 5: You must stop giving banter when asked to stop.

Cultural

- Rule 6: How something is said is equally as important as what is said.
- Rule 7: How one uses banter has a fundamental impact on their popularity and likability.

"No One is Unpopular"

More dated research has shown that masculine environments operate on stratified parameters, whereby those who are popular are idolized, and those who are unpopular are marked out (Bishop 1999; Curry 2000; McGuffey and Rich 1999). Whilst results have thus far described some individuals as less popular, these men never described anyone as unpopular.

All the men that were interviewed explained that whilst some people were more popular than others, no member of the club was unpopular. Harry said, "No one is unpopular. Dodgeball is good and I know people make jokes about each other, but it's how everyone gets included. It's a way of starting a conversation." Blake said, "I can't think of anyone who's unpopular, but John is less popular because he's a lying fuck. He has a long history of talking shit, but we all like him." Lawrence thought, "Being a dick to the opposite sex would make you unpopular, but the guys are protective of the girls, so that doesn't happen."

Jaden said, "A range of things can make someone unpopular, but I don't think anyone is unpopular in the club." He went on to say, "Like, Tim embraces being quiet and that's who he is, and that makes him popular. I think everyone's popular in their own way" (see McCormack

2012). Tim was a regular member of the club but rarely spoke to the other men in the team. Speaking about Tim, Jaden said, "He is really likable but maybe least popular, because he doesn't talk much." As Chris said, "Someone who is popular needs to be sociable. You can't make lots of friends if you don't talk. But that wouldn't mean you were unpopular."

Taylor said, in that, "If you speak to Tim on his own, he has good chat, but I don't think he likes speaking up in front of a big group." Ed said, "Tim is cool. Keeps to himself but he's always up for a night out and a laugh. Like, that makes him popular."

Indeed, there were several members of the team who were not as confident or loud as others, but they were long-term committed to the club and were good friends to many. Here, the men's relaxation of the social hierarchy permitted a wider apperception for alternative social types, and the recognition that no one person is unpopular in a diverse team. Whereas under hegemonic masculinity in the 1980s, men would seek to replicate the same identical jock behaviors and attitudes to reach the top of the masculine hierarchy (Connell 1995), these men were not esteeming the same negative values. Instead, as found in other recent research (White and Hobson 2015; McCormack 2012), these men valued alternative masculinities and social identities.

Athletic Ability

One of the traditional archetypes associated with popularity in orthodox environments is one's athletic ability (Anderson 2009; Connell 2005; Curry 2000). Participants in this study were asked whether they believed athletic ability had an impact on popularity within the club. When asked, Blake responded:

> No not at all. Not every first team player is popular. You find that some of them don't make the effort with the freshers. They are nice guys though. Those in the second team, like me and Chris, are very well known. Third team; Taylor and Ronnie are popular because they make the effort with everyone. Ability lets you show off, but if you don't make the effort then

you're not going to be liked. If Christian Ronaldo walked in, great, but if he doesn't make the effort with everyone, then he won't be liked.

Danny was equally adamant that one's athletic ability did not correlate with their popularity. Responding to the same question he said, "Absolutely fucking not. Blake and Ed are up there in popularity. You can't have a bad word to say about them, yet they are completely physically inept at dodgeball, but they are friendly, committed and so funny." Taylor said, "You might get mugged off more in banter if your crap at sport, but you're still popular. I wouldn't not speak to someone because they were crap at sport."

Accordingly, this esteemed view was reflected in earlier responses when asked what makes someone popular. At that point, no participants said that being in the first team or being good at dodgeball contributed to one's popularity. Callum reflected on his own social standing:

> I play in the second team, but I've also played in the first and third team. At no point over the years have I felt like people have treated me differently because of what team I'm in, or how good I am.

As noted by the participants, and in Stefan's observations, it appeared that athletic ability did not correlate with one's popularity among their peers. In response to questions around who was most popular in the club, there was a relatively even distribution of names from the first, second, and third teams (including social members). The two most popular men both came from the second team, and they did not compete at a higher level in any other sports. This contrasts significantly to the jock archetype that traditionally assumed the most popular social status in college and universities, both in the United States and the United Kingdom, throughout the late twentieth century (Anderson 2014).

Sociability

Another characteristic that was mentioned several times in relation to one's popularity was whether individuals made the effort to involve and speak to teammates. This is consistent with McCormack's (2012) findings on English adolescents. Blake, the man recognized as the most popular person in the club, recalls his experience of joining the dodgeball team:

> Bromances are more common in the dodgeball team because were quite an open society and it's always been that way and ever since I joined three years ago. When I started, straight away I was made to feel at home, and I was going out with everyone. I was speaking to people who were not in societies, and they were not having the same experience. Dodgeball were not that big at the start, but now it's one of the biggest clubs. Bromance wise, everyone gets on in dodgeball, were like a family, whereas in other societies you can get bitchiness, because I think it's such a unique sport to join.
>
> I did Football trials and joined tennis and frisbee, but it was not the sport, it was the people that made me feel the most welcome at dodgeball and made the effort with me. They were all genuinely nice people, and it was not hard to make friends. I made them instantly. I hate to say it, but because it's not a typical sport and maybe seen as an outcast sport, you have different social and sporting abilities. Like if you asked me if I would have been friends with Tim or Taylor, Andy and James at school, I would have said no. But these are people who are actually my closest mates and bromances now.

Blake's statement is relatively all-encompassing of the data that was collected in this area. Indeed, Stefan recalls his warm welcome into the club, too. Blake's appreciation for inclusivity is replicated in his own popular behavior. He was the social secretary for the club and made an active effort to involve all of the men in the social activities. Following Tour, several men thanked him for making the holiday such an enjoyable experience. This kind of behavior, coming from the most popular people in the club, reproduced and reflected similar perspectives among other members of the club.

Danny explained, "Popularity is about making the effort and giving an impression that others should put the effort in as you do. You will get an amount of admiration from the team for that." For example, knowing how well I was treated upon joining the club made me want to make a very proactive effort to include others.

In one instance, Harry, who was not very good at dodgeball, recalled how one of the elite athletes gave him a one-to-one training session at his house. "I don't really connect with the sporty types, but he took the time to come over, and show me and my housemate how to properly grip the ball and throw, and that was really nice."

In relation to bromances, Callum explained how "making the effort" supports bromantic development; "I speak most days to my close boyfriends, and you make the effort to do things with them like go for meals and go out together, whereas friends, you don't make the same effort."

One of Blake's earlier comments was replicated by several others, who also suggested that dodgeball was more inclusive and welcoming than other sports. Jaden said, "No one's excluded. Everyone's welcome for lunch and stuff. I know in football the fourth team are treated like a third world country and are not allowed to the pre-drinks with the firsts and seconds."

Among all of the men, none said that anyone was socially excluded in the dodgeball club. Taylor also mentioned the university football team, "It's a thing in football to split the firsts and seconds from the other teams at pre-drinks, maybe because they can't fit everyone into one house. But then again, dodgeball is a bigger club, and we manage." Danny said, "At dodgeball, if you're up for a laugh it doesn't matter how good you are or what team you're in, or if you're a social member, we do everything as a society." Ed said, "Unlike some of the other sports at uni, dodgeball is brilliant because it fine to be part of a club and socialize, and get kit, and at the same time you don't have to commit your life." Callum, who is also part of the university's rugby team, said:

Rugby's a bit more do whatever. They do crazy things whereas dodgeballers; only a few boys are like that. Rugby's more like lad culture, where people get arrested and houses get trashed. But with dodgeball, if it gets out of hand, someone will pipe up and say chill out, and people will respect that. It's not much of a segregated society, like everyone likes to mingle and its mixed gender as well, unlike rugby. In rugby, it's definitely like, the first team captain everyone ass licks him. Ability is a much more important factor in rugby for being popular. There is more of a hierarchy in rugby. Nobody really gets the piss taken out of them in dodgeball because it's such an inclusive sport.

Highlighting what these dodgeballers thought, Jackson and Sundaram (2015) highlight that there is a lack of inclusivity in some rugby and football settings which are recognized as operating a "lad culture." As participants highlight here and elsewhere in these results, these sports are not viewed as positively as dodgeball, and people recognize a more stratified hierarchy within them. However, more broadly, this view should be tempered alongside extensive research that shows a wealth of inclusive masculine behaviors in Rugby and Football (Anderson 2009; Magrath 2016; Jarvis 2015; Murray et al. 2016; Muir et al. 2021). Nonetheless, the men view dodgeball as having a *more* inclusive and bromantic culture than other sports.

All these men highlight that the dodgeball club had a good social offer in terms of its welcoming and inclusive approach to new members. Indeed, unlike the lad culture that Callum describes as occurring in the rugby team, someone would always speak up if things were getting out of hand at pre-drinks, and they were not victimized for doing so. For example, Stefan recalls when Blake pushed over a table at pre-drinks in a fresher's flat for comedic effect. All were quick to condemn his behavior. It had gone too far. Similarly, at pre-drinks, the social secretaries would ensure, as far as was possible, that everyone would tidy up the host's accommodation to return it to a decent state, before heading into town. This was an impressive social herding of sorts, where even though a large group of thirty people were drunk and excited for a night out, with taxis waiting, most committed to tidying.

Aggression

We have previously shown that emulating another is not a way to raise one's social popularity. In this section, we highlight another unacceptable behavior that will lower one's popularity—aggression.

In overall observations, there was very little aggression expressed by the men in the club. Highlighting one aspect of this, Stefan did not observe or hear of any acts of physical altercation between any of the dodgeball team whatsoever throughout the course of the year he studied the team. Yet, and contrary to traditional typecasts (Cancian 1986; Dunning et al. 2014), it was dodgeball women who were several times banned from the student union for physical fighting.

Whilst dodgeball is a contact sport, it is relatively passive, and Stefan witnessed no injuries from direct contact with other players, either; only sprained ankles and knee problems caused by people's rapid movement across the court.

Given the sport does not require aggression and given the sport might appear to symbolize hurting another (through throwing a ball at them), there is no culture of harmful desire within the sport. Thus, acts of aggression are likely less than other sports like rugby and football. Still, aggression can occur in the sport. In this study, the two men that were specifically identified as being less popular were also regarded to be aggressive at times, more so than any other members of the club. Andy explained:

> Callum is excluded in a way because people pick on his faults. He has a huge ego and can't manage his anger well. He's such a bad looser and really arrogant. Blake is popular because he's not aggressive on court and he is approachable and fair. The ones who aren't liked are Max and Callum because they can be aggressive and that's not cool.

Danny said, "Max doesn't want to show he cares, wants to be alpha male, and always has his guard up. You will never hear him talk himself down or take any banter. He doesn't seem like he could be emotional."

James reflected on his own behaviors, explaining, "I would say I'm mid-level popular, because sometimes I'm quite loud and aggressive on court, and people don't respond well to that." He described an example of the aggression that one of the less popular individuals was prone to; "Calling the ref a name is a bad idea. If people do that it looks bad on us and the uni and shows, we can't keep our cool."

Indeed, this type of behavior was observed among a small minority throughout the year when some became highly agitated at questionable referee decisions, as did even Stefan in some circumstances. However, regardless of who was right in the situation, the team as a whole condemned conflict with the referees.

Stefan recalls an incident when the men's first team, which he played on, lost to the second team in an important competition. Throughout the match, the first team was leading comfortably, and one person said, "Get off my court" to the second team, and shoulder barged one of them on his way off the court. This was abnormally aggressive and unfair to the second team. In a quick turn of events, in front of a small crowd, the second team won the match in a sudden death scenario, leaving the first team beaten and out of the competition.

Tensions were high. Stefan asked a teammate to calm down when he was irately lecturing the first team about their failure. The entire journey home was awkward and quiet. It was later revealed that all of the first team members individually approached the second team to congratulate them on their win, apart from the aggravator. Lawrence, a member of the second team, explained:

> When seconds beat firsts, that's the only time I've ever seen a competitive nature in dodgeball. I never saw it before, but I don't know if its personal rivalries. Seconds are the underdog. Everyone said well-done except Tim, who called me lucky.

We have thus shown that fighting is not acceptable within male dodgeball culture. We then showed that aggression on the court does occur (anger and pushing). This second type of aggression is perhaps typical within sport. However, dodgeball is a mixed-sex sport and for this reason it posed a third category of aggression: that between males and females.

For the male and female players in the club, one of the most controversial elements of mixed gender training was whether the men should, rightly or wrongly, adjust their throwing speed for the women when they were in competitions (i.e., they were trying to win for their team).

At training, the majority of people threw balls at a speed that matched the ability of the target, in an inclusive approach to the sport. In other words, most men threw the ball softer toward women than men. However, some would always throw full power, regardless of the gender of the target. This brings disagreement as to what equality within the sport is.

Lawrence said, "The guys who go full whack at the girls are out of line. They don't need to throw like that at training." In Stefan's observations, it was the same people who were rated as less popular, that were the people who would intimidate less athletic players (regardless of gender). Ogilvie (2019) highlighted similar tensions in elite volleyball, where men valued training with women but several still believed that they had a natural physical dominance because of their sex, even though several women were on national teams.

The questions about what to do about gender-integrated sports are out of scope for this particular research project. However, it does pose interesting questions about what might count as aggression in the sport.

Chapter Summary

This chapter highlights the mechanisms of social popularity among the group of men studied. We highlight that, before the twenty-first century, athletic ability was hailed as a defining characteristic of one's popularity and social status (Mangan 2000; Spring 1974; Sabo and Runfola 1980). However, this was not the case in this study.

Instead, a particular form of bawdy humor that breaches social norms was the most esteemed popularity building agent among participants in this highly energetic group of young men. That humor is complex, particularly given that the type of humor that is most valued relied on extreme personalities, and banter. The complexity of this humor also meant that when it went poorly, it could lower one's popularity among the men.

The same is true of the other agent of popularity building, sociability. Socializing with others, and being inclusive, raised one's popularity and the opposite reduced popularity. Conversely, physical aggression between men was not acceptable. This only lowered men's popularity.

Whilst the participants recognized that people could be more and less popular, none of the men were ultimately able to conclude that any one person in the club was unpopular. Indeed, the men adopted an inclusive culture that recognized and appreciated a variety of personalities and masculinities within the club.

References

Anderson, E. (2009). *Inclusive masculinity: The changing nature of masculinities.* New York: Routledge

Adams, A., Anderson, E., and McCormack, M. (2010). Establishing and challenging masculinity: The influence of gendered discourses in organized sport. *Journal of Language and Social Psychology, 29*(3), 278–300.

Anderson, E. (2014). *21st Century Jocks: Sporting Men and Contemporary Heterosexuality.* New York: Macmillan.

Anderson, E., Adams, A., and Rivers, I. (2012). "I kiss them because I love them": The emergence of heterosexual men kissing in British institutes of education. *Archives of Sexual Behaviour, 41*(2), 421–430.

Bishop, J. (1999). Nerd harassment, incentives, school priorities and learning. In Mayer, S., and Peterson, P. (Ed.), *Earning and learning: How schools matter.* Washington: Brookings Institution Press. Pp 231–281.

Cancian, F. M. (1986). The feminization of love. *Signs: Journal of Women in Culture and Society, 11*(4), 692–709.

Closson, L. (2009). Status and gender differences in early adolescents' descriptions of popularity. *Social Development, 18*(2), 412–426.

Connell, R. (1995). *Masculinities.* Berkeley: University of California Press.

Connell, R. (2005). *Masculinities.* Berkeley: University of California Press

Curry, T. (2000). Booze and bar fights: A journey to the dark side of college athletics. In McKay, J., Messner, M., and Sabo, D. (Ed.), *Masculinities, gender relations and sport*. London: Sage. Pp.162–175.

Dunning, E., Murphy, P., and Williams, J. (2014). *The roots of football hooliganism (RLE sports studies): An historical and sociological study* (Vol. 2). New York: Routledge.

Feist, D., Shenton, B., and de Souza, T. (2004). Induction ceremonies in university sport in the UK. Unpublished communication to Athletic Union presidents. *British Universities Sports Association*. London.

Garfinkel, H. (1967). *Ethnomethodology*. Englewood Cliffs.

Groves, M., Griggs, G., and Leflay, K. (2012). Hazing and initiation ceremonies in university sport: Setting the scene for further research in the United Kingdom. *Sport in Society*, 15(1), 117–131.

Jackson, C., and Sundaram, V. (2015). *Is 'lad culture' a problem in higher education? Exploring the perspectives of staff working in UK universities.* In International Conference on Research into Higher Education. Pp. 1–8.

Jarvis, N. (2015). The inclusive masculinities of heterosexual men within UK gay sport clubs. *International Review for the Sociology of Sport*, 50(3), 283–300.

Magrath, R. (2016). *Inclusive masculinities in contemporary football: Men in the beautiful game*. Routledge.

Mangan, J. (2000). *Athleticism in the Victorian and Edwardian public school: The emergence and consolidation of an educational ideology*. New York: Psychology Press.

McCormack, M. (2011). Mapping the terrain of homosexually-themed language. *Journal of homosexuality*, 58(5), 664–679.

McCormack, M. (2012). *The declining significance of homophobia: How teenage boys are redefining masculinity and heterosexuality*. New York: Oxford University Press.

McGuffey, C. S., and Rich, B. L. (1999). "Playing in the gender transgression zone": Race, class, and hegemonic masculinity in middle childhood. *Gender and Society*, 13(5), 608–627.

Muir, K., Anderson, E., Parry, K. D., & Letts, D. (2021). The changing nature of gay rugby clubs in the United Kingdom. *Sociology of Sport Journal* (published online ahead of print 2021).

Murray, A., White, A., Scoats, R., and Anderson, E. (2016). Constructing masculinities in the national Rugby League's Footy Show. *Sociological Research Online*, 21(3).

Ogilvie, M. E. (2019). *Masculinities and sexualities of elite male team sport athletes. An ethnographic examination.* Unpublished PhD Thesis. Durham University.

Sabo, D., and Runfola, R. (1980). *Jock: Sports and male identity.* New Jersey: Prentice Hall.

Spring, G. (1974). Mass culture and school sports. *History of Education Quarterly, 14*(4), 483–499.

White, A., and Hobson, M. (2015). Teachers' stories: physical education teachers' constructions and experiences of masculinity within secondary school physical education. *Sport, Education and Society*, 1–14.

10

Bromances and Gay Men

Anderson (2002) and Anderson et al. (2016) suggest that prior to the twenty-first-century male team sport athletes were characterized, above all, by antipathy toward homosexuality. Homophobia was theorized to be used as a tool to maintain orthodox prescriptions of masculinity, in order that boys did not become homosexual themselves. Anderson suggests (2005b) that this belief, that homosexuality is socially constructed, dates back to the works of Freud at the turn of the twentieth century. Sport was understood to be a masculine preserve to ward against the social construction of homosexual desire.

However, as cultural attitudes toward homosexuality improved in the last decade of the twentieth century (Ghaziani 2011, 2017; Loftus 2001), it became apparent that new ways of thinking about homosexuality would emerge. Particularly the widely held view that homosexuality is at least partially and most likely a heavily influenced product of biology. This is theorized to have helped further reduce cultural homophobia. As previously referred to, it was this cultural change in which Anderson first developed his theory of Inclusive Masculinity (2009). Since then, there have been over a hundred studies showing that masculinity has changed.

This chapter examines what is now a well-trodden academic trope: investigating for, homophobia among men, and instead finding inclusivity.

Inclusivity

Similar to Magrath's (2016) interviews with young British sportsmen, Stefan asked hypothetical questions around the reaction that one would likely receive from the dodgeball club if they or a teammate came out as gay. Responses were overall very positive and inclusive towards homosexuality.

This perspective is contrary to a vast body of research conducted in the sporting environment throughout the twentieth century (Anderson 2000; Curry 2000; Pronger 1990). However, this finding of inclusion does correlate with a growing, and increasingly prominent, set of literature published in the twenty-first century that highlights the declining significance of homophobia (Anderson 2014; Drummond et al. 2014; Magrath et al. 2013).

When asked whether he thought there was any homophobia in the club, Andy responded:

> People who discriminate are just uneducated. I see gay people holding hands at uni and think they are brave, and I respect that, because it's fine. Uni is a lot more liberal, and you have the LGBT society. Were really lucky in the society were brought up in and in the team. When I was 15, I realized I was straight, but I wouldn't think any differently when sharing a bed with a gay person. It would be sad if people thought that way or didn't want to disclose their homosexuality. I hope for their sake, if there are any gay people in the club, they just say "I'm gay this is who I am." But then again straight people don't need to do that, so maybe they don't need to.

Andy picks up several interesting points. He recognizes that sexuality is not a choice, supports gay people coming out in the club, and said that society is more supportive of diverse sexualities than before. Like Andy, many others offered their support for homosexuality. Ed said:

I think some churches not doing gay marriages is weird, and the condemning of homosexuality has been massively reduced in society. Like, I know this doesn't mean someone's gay but in the team people put their dicks in their mate's mouths and stuff which is fine. Society is more gay generally. You will always get people who frown on it but most people don't think twice about it.

Here, Ed describes homophobic behaviors as "weird," and recognizes that young men in the club are permitted to engage in homosexual behaviors, regardless of their sexuality, without stigma (Anderson 2008; Branfman and Stiritz 2012; Branfman et al. 2017).

Ronnie similarly suggested that the gay behaviors that occur between men in the club serve as a symbol of homosexual inclusion, and gay friendliness. He said, "I don't think anyone's homophobic in dodgeball. Like, I've kissed most guys in dodgeball, and any that I haven't, other people have. I don't think it's an issue, everyone gets naked together and that's fine."

Jaden is another person that suggested same-sex physical behaviors were a sign of inclusivity saying, "Everyone has a good little grind on each other. It's because more people embrace gay behaviors, I think it's fine for a cheeky kiss. I think it's more expressive than in the past and people don't judge anymore." Gordon said, "In dodgeball were getting off with each other left, right and center. People definitely wouldn't give a shit if you were gay straight or bi or whatever."

When asked about the hypothetical situation of a teammate coming out as gay, Jerry said:

I think being in a sport would help people, and him being friends with us. If someone came out he would be welcomed. Not one person is going to bat an eyelid. He would still get same chat and maybe a nickname as before, but nothing's going to change. No one cares. When I was at school, one of the lads came out and it didn't bother me. It wouldn't affect me, he's still the same person as when he started off in dodgeball and that doesn't change if he starts seeing guys.

Echoing the words of Jerry, many more men expressed gay-friendly attitudes towards the hypothetical situation of a teammate coming out as gay. James said, "I think if there was an openly gay couple in the team it would be ok. I don't think people would treat them any different" and Rory said, "If there is a gay guy in dodgeball it wouldn't be an issue."

For the first semester, Pete thought there was already an openly gay man in the club. He said, "I thought Harry was gay, and thought it was good that no one gave a shit about it. But then I met his fit girlfriend, and I was like oh, didn't see that coming." When asked how the club would react to someone coming out as gay, Danny said:

> Objectively fine. If it's sensitive for someone I think people would be caring. I don't think it would matter at all in a country and university like this. If I came out as gay, which I think I would be pretty good at, I would happily take any banter and I think there is a good amount of people who are the same.

Again, Danny, like Andy and Ed, recognized that contemporary society and their social context espouses more liberal and inclusive attitudes towards gay men than previously experienced (Cullen and Johnston 2018).

Taylor, who came from an all-boys school, highlighted a transition in attitudes that he experienced:

> In dodgeball, at the very first tournament, every guy got naked in the showers and had a laugh and I had never seen that before. I came from an all-boys school, and it was quite homophobic there actually. I remember at school, a guy was getting changed in the changing room, and they asked someone why they were looking at them and they were being proper homophobic and aggressive, and ready to fight that person. It was not banter. From school to university, it was a big jump. At uni you see lots of gay and transgender people and promotional material. Not a bad thing of course. The team wouldn't care about anyone being gay or not.

These men presented positive attitudes toward the hypothetical situation of a gay man coming out in the team. Stefan recalls two instances when men were asked if they would have sex with another man. In one case, the men were on their way to a tournament and playing the game, "If you could fuck a footballer, who would it be?" Interestingly, the word "could" instead of "had to" was used. Ronnie, who identifies as heterosexual said, "I would bend Thierry Henry over big time." He was then asked without any jest, "Have you ever had sex with a guy before?" To which he responded, "No, but who wouldn't fuck Thierry Henry." Stefan also observed the same game being played, but this time, it was "If you could fuck any guy on the team, who would it be?".

Kissing Gay Men

The descriptions of inclusivity of homosexuality are supported by behaviors of men on this team, too. Some of the men said that they had bromances with gay men, which involved all the same physical characteristics. Among the sample, 25% (four men) identified as having a bromance with gay men. They suggested that their sexuality had no impact on the ability to form and engage in bromances. Reflective of the views expressed by these participants, Barrett (2016) recently found that bodily touching has become common in friendships between straight and gay men, also.

Danny did not feel that being gay would limit someone's ability to have a bromance. He said, "That's not to say you can't have a bromance with a gay guy, like a mate I have. Like, I would take a bullet for him. We do cuddle and kiss, but not out of sexual desire."

Ronnie added, "I have a mate at home who is openly gay and we've kissed a few times … I'd say he was my bromance, yes." Jerry said, "I do drama. It's a stereotype, but there are loads of gay guys on my course. I have loads of gay bromances and I get with them, too. It's no different."

James, who identified as between mostly heterosexual, and bisexual said, "I've had thoughts about what it would be like to suck someone's cock, but that doesn't get in the way of me having physical bromances like everyone else, because they aren't sexually driven, but for fun and friendship."

Harry explained more detailed elements of his bromances with gay *and* transgender men:

I have a transgender friend who I'm in a bromance with (transitioning from a man to a woman) who I cuddle with quite often. Every time we meet, we always hug. They are really masculine though. I've cuddled and spooned with my gay mate overnight as well. We have a bromance and he hasn't had sex in a while and suffers with depression and I like to comfort him by having a little cuddle in the bed. If I was gay though, I would definitely go for one of my close mates, like (bromance), because I would get on well with them and they would treat me well.

Curious but not Concerned

During interviews, several of the men freely voiced their perceptions about people in the club being gay. However, there was no direct correlation between the people that they selected. Some suggested the more effeminate types, whilst others suggested that the more traditionally masculine types were overcompensating. At no point were anyone's views based on the level of same-sex behaviors that those men had been involved in. Furthermore, the two men that self-identified as between mostly heterosexual and bisexual (the furthest away from heterosexual in the club) were never mentioned, suggesting that these men were not particularly accurate in their suspicions. The next chapter considers the men's self-identified sexualities, and what factors they base their sexual identity on.

In his time with the dodgeball club, Stefan only ever witnessed one situation that could be considered homophobic. At a service station, on the way home from a tournament, there was a group of about ten male club members sitting around a table having dinner. It emerged that one of the men had a gay housemate. An individual asked, "Mate, why do you live with a gay man?" It was asked in a way that suggested it was unusual, or strange. Before that person had a chance to respond, John, one of the senior members of the club said, "Why did you ask that? What's wrong with living with a gay guy? Do you have an issue with that?" the person responded, "I was just wondering mate."

It was an awkward and confrontational moment because John was clearly not happy about the way that this person presented the question.

Another person followed up with the comment, "Nothing wrong with being gay mate" and several others agreed at that moment. Importantly, people were willing to challenge a friend on an occasion that presented the potential for homophobia. Unsurprisingly, the person who raised this comment was rated as one of the less popular, more aggressive members of the team.

Gay Discourse

There seems to be a paradoxical relationship between these men and their attitudes toward homosexuality. Their attitudes and behaviors are, without doubt, social proof of their desire to have a kinship with gay men. However, perhaps as a vestige of cultural lag, there was sometimes used discourse that was once considered homophobic. Specifically, the term "gay" has multiple meanings, one of which means "less than."

Several of the men were clear to distinguish that the word "gay" had lost its pure associations and meanings with homosexuality alone; that it was a complex word. Andy said, "People can still say stuff like gay boy, but it's harmless. It's a thing you learn when you're really young, but you don't know the meaning, and it sticks." Danny said, "'That's gay' used to be homophobic in nature, but now it's kind of a translucent insult, not having any relation to someone's sexuality." Rory similarly suggested that it had lost its meaning, saying "The gay word is slung around and just used day to day, and it's lost any meaning."

When asked why he frequently called people gay boy as an operation of banter, Blake said, "I say it to my mates, and if one of them came out as gay, I would still call them gay boy. I'll say, 'alright gay boy' when I meet my mates, not because they are gay, but it's just my greeting." Chris said, "I get called gay boy when I ditch the guys to bang a girl, which is quite weird, it doesn't seem right, does it? They aren't being harsh though. It goes to show how gay boy doesn't mean gay boy."

In Stefan's experience, several of the men did use phrases like, "Aright gay boy" and "You're bent" regularly, but the majority of men did not speak like this. It was usually the loudest and most brash people in the club that would use these phrases. As Rory explained, "Blake and Max are the main culprits. They don't do it to offend people though; they just use the word loosely, like society generally."

The operation of homosexually themed language is complex and mediated by several important variables (McCormack 2011, 2012; McCormack and Anderson 2014a, b; McCormack et al. 2016). These scholars highlight how homophobic language tended to require two components: (1) that it was said with homophobic intent and (2) that it was said in a homophobic context. This is not to say that intent is all that matters because context is also paramount.

In this context, the pro-gay views of these men (discussed below) suggest that the language is not simply homophobic; however, the language use is complicated by the absence of gay people in these teams. In this way, it sounds like the use of language by rugby players in an ethnography conducted a decade earlier (McCormack and Anderson 2010). Here, the language use is problematic because whilst the group does not intend it to be homophobic, they cannot control how it is perceived. Unlike the use of words like "gay" by gay youth (McCormack et al. 2016), these men perhaps lack critical reflection on their language which can be exaggerated in the competitive and masculinized style of the banter and sport in which they are situated (see also Adams et al. 2010).

In short, it appears that cultural lag is in effect: the men's attitudes are decidedly pro-gay, but some (not all) of the men still use vestiges of language from a time in which cultural attitudes toward gay men were not good. This gap between intent and usage is impacted by the dual meaning of the word gay, which is often removed from homosexual content. Whilst this is still problematic, it highlights that social movements take time.

Chapter Summary

As with recent research on gay athletes' experiences (Anderson et al. 2016), homophobia was not a prevalent or espoused behavior in this team. Instead, the men welcomed the notion of a man in the team coming out as gay, suggesting that he would be welcomed and treated no differently to other team members. This was not to say that they would not be called gay boy, or another nickname, but that this should be expected as part of the club environment, with no pernicious intent.

Many suggested that being gay was a non-issue. The men recognized that attitudes had changed from previous generations (Ghaziani 2011, 2017; McCormack 2012; Savin-Williams 2005) and that contemporary society and particularly university students alike were far less concerned with homosexuality. The men suggested that their own same-sex behaviors were characteristic of their inclusivity and acceptance of homosexuality. In this regard, the men provided some thought-provoking insights into their own sexuality and their recognition of other and more diverse sexualities. Some had bromances with gay men, and many of the men had kissed other gay men, too. It was for these reasons that, despite some cultural usage of the term "that's so gay" we describe this as an inclusive culture of male homosexuality.

References

Adams, A., Anderson, E., and McCormack, M. (2010). Establishing and challenging masculinity: The influence of gendered discourses in organized sport. *Journal of Language and Social Psychology, 29*(3), 278–300.

Anderson, E. (2000). *Trailblazing: The true story of America's first openly gay track coach*. New York: Alyson Publications.

Anderson, E. (2002). Openly gay athletes: Contesting hegemonic masculinity in a homophobic environment. *Gender McCormack and Anderson 2014a, b society, 16*(6), 860–877.

Anderson, E. (2005a). *In the game: Gay athletes and the cult of masculinity*. New York: University of New York Press.

Anderson, E. (2005b). Orthodox and inclusive masculinity: Competing masculinities among heterosexual men in a feminized terrain. *Sociological Perspectives, 48*(3), 337–355.

Anderson, E. (2008). "Being masculine is not about who you sleep with...:" Heterosexual athletes contesting masculinity and the one-time rule of homosexuality. *Sex Roles, 58*(1–2), 104–115.

Anderson, E. (2009). *Inclusive masculinity: The changing nature of masculinities*. New York: Routledge

Anderson, E. (2014). *21st Century Jocks: Sporting Men and Contemporary Heterosexuality*. New York: Macmillan.

Anderson, E., Magrath, R., and Bullingham, R. (2016). *Out in Sport: The Experiences of Openly Gay and Lesbian Athletes*. New York: Routledge.

Barrett, T. (2016). Friendships between men across sexual orientation: The management of sexual difference through humour. *Journal of Sociology*, 52(2), 355–370.

Branfman, J., and Ekberg Stiritz, S. (2012). Teaching Men's Anal Pleasure: Challenging Gender Norms with "Prostage" Education. *American Journal of Sexuality Education*, 7(4), 404–428.

Branfman, J., Stiritz, S. and Anderson, E. (2017) Relaxing the Straight-Male Anus: Decreasing Homohysteria around Anal Eroticism. *Sexualities*. https://doi.org/10.1177/1363460716678560

Cullen, F., & Johnston, C. (2018). Playwork goes to school: Professional (mis) recognition and playwork practice in primary school. *Pedagogy, Culture & Society*, 26(3), 467–484.

Curry, T. (2000). Booze and bar fights: A journey to the dark side of college athletics. In McKay, J., Messner, M., and Sabo, D. (Ed.), *Masculinities, gender relations and sport*. London: Sage. Pp.162–175.

Drummond, M., Filiault, S., Anderson, E., and Jeffries, D. (2014). Homosocial intimacy among Australian undergraduate men. *Journal of Sociology*, 51(3), 643–656.

Ghaziani, A. (2011). Post-gay collective identity construction. *Social Problems*, 58(1), 99–125.

Ghaziani, A. (2017). *Sex cultures*. Boston: Polity Press (Cultural Sociology series).

Loftus, J. (2001). America's liberalization in attitudes toward homosexuality, 1973 to 1998. *American Sociological Review*, 66(5), 762–782.

Magrath, R. (2016). *Inclusive masculinities in contemporary football: Men in the beautiful game*. Routledge.

Magrath, R., Anderson, E., and Roberts, S. (2013). On the door-step of equality: Attitudes toward gay athletes among academy level footballers. *International Review for the Sociology of Sport*, 50(7), 804–821.

McCormack, M. (2011). Mapping the terrain of homosexually-themed language. *Journal of homosexuality*, 58(5), 664–679.

McCormack, M. (2012). *The declining significance of homophobia: How teenage boys are redefining masculinity and heterosexuality.* New York: Oxford University Press.

McCormack, M., and Anderson, E. (2010). The re-production of homosexually-themed discourse in educationally-based organised sport. *Culture, Health and Sexuality, 12*(8), 913–927.

McCormack, M., and Anderson, E. (2014a). The influence of declining homophobia on men's gender in the United States: An argument for the study of homohysteria. *Sex Roles, 71*(3–4), 109–120.

McCormack, M., and Anderson, E. (2014b). Homohysteria: Definitions, context and intersectionality. *Sex Roles, 71*(3–4), 152–158.

McCormack, M., Wignall, L., and Morris, M. (2016). Gay guys using gay discourse: Friendship, shared values and the intent-context-effect matrix. *British Journal of Sociology, 67*(4), 747–767.

Pronger, B. (1990). *The arena of masculinity: Sports, homosexuality, and the meaning of sex.* London: GMP Publishers.

Savin-Williams, R. (2005). *The new gay teenager* (Vol. 3). Cambridge: Harvard University Press.

11

Sexuality

This chapter examines how heterosexuality is performed among the men in this study, and crucially the impact that declining homohysteria has on expanding the boundaries of acceptable heterosexual behavior for them. Specifically, and corresponding to the decrease in cultural homophobia, there has been a change in the manner in which young men behave in regard to other men in recent decades. For example, we highlight that these men have all kissed one or more other men. However, there is also a redefining of the labels upon which men identify: on a scale, as opposed to a binary.

Whilst this approach dates back to the work of biologist Alfred Kinsey, who argued for a seven-point scale of sexuality, it has recently found renewed interest—not least through the scholarship of Ritch Savin-Williams (e.g., 2017). The social aspect is not that sexuality was categorical and became a continuum as homophobia decreased, but rather that decreased homophobia provided space for men to explore desires and behaviors more complex than gay, straight, or bi (Ghaziani 2017).

In this chapter we report upon the data that was collected in asking participants to define their sexuality based on Vrangalova and Savin-Williams's (2012) scale of sexuality ranging from heterosexual, mostly heterosexual, bisexual, mostly homosexual, and homosexual. This was set out as a scale, and participants were asked to point to where they felt their sexuality was located.

Sexual Identity

Unlike other studies that have used pre-set definitions of sexuality types (Ferguson 2001; Lindley et al. 2012), these men were asked to identify their position on the scale, without a pre-set definition of what each category meant. This was done in order to understand how the men perceived the meaning of each category (e.g., Brim and Ghaziani 2016; Ghaziani and Brim 2019). This fits with McCormack and Savin-Williams' (2018) typology of rationales for non-exclusive sexualities—which documented four distinct rationales: sexual rationales, where it is the presence of sexual desire for non-preferred sex that determines the use of label; emotional rationales, where men had emotional crushes for their non-preferred sex; intellectual rationales, where men did not want to shut off possibilities or be exclusive; and cultural rationales, which mostly related to homophobia stopping them adopting an exclusively gay identity. Wignall and Driscoll (2020) have found similar rationales for women.

Of the 20 men that we asked:

- 10 Identified as Heterosexual
- 8 Identified as Mostly Heterosexual
- 2 identified as between Mostly Heterosexual and Bisexual.

None of the men identified as bisexual, Mostly Homosexual, or Homosexual (see McCormack and Savin-Williams 2018), perhaps for the combination of this accurately reflected their sexual identity and also because of the decreased prevalence of discussion around the gay-side of the sexuality spectrum—supporting the notion that the mostly label can be a level of heteronormative (Galupo 2020). Interestingly, the further that one positioned themselves towards bisexuality, the more open and comprehensive their answers were. This trend only became clear during coding. Accordingly, the responses from the 10 heterosexual men were short and succinct.

Andy said, "I'm heterosexual because I don't have sexual feelings towards guys. Only girls." Similarly, Blake explained, "I can't see myself having sexual relations with a boy." Danny said, "I'm heterosexual because I'm comfortable enough that on a lads' night out, I can kiss a guy because I have no problem with it." Stefan asked him to elaborate why he defined himself as heterosexual, and he said, "I don't know. I just am." Lawrence said, "I've always been straight. It's how I am, and I would never have sex with a guy." Ed, said, "I've never done anything with a man, so I can't say I've tried, but I don't find men attractive" (see McCormack and Wignall 2017; Wignall and McCormack 2017; Wignall 2019).

Among the 8 mostly heterosexual men, their responses were more detailed and appreciative of same-sex attraction, same-sex contact, and male femininity (see Adams and Anderson 2012). This is best evidenced by one participant, who said:

> You sometimes look at a guy and think, not bad looking. I've looked at a guy and thought he's kind of hot, but the thought of anything more than kissing isn't something I would be attracted to. I've wanked over a good-looking guy before and my male to female transgender friend before, well, when she does herself up. There was also a guy who had feminine features who I was really interested in, and I wanked over him. I don't think that makes me gay because it was a one-off. Sometimes I watch films, think a guy's attractive, and then think, why am I thinking these things? Obviously, my girlfriend doesn't know about this though. But honestly, I am way more into girls. But for that reason, I can't say I'm 100% straight. Mostly heterosexual fits me best.

Callum also had some attraction to men:

> I would say I'm mostly heterosexual because I find some boys that are quite good looking, and I think, ah, he's really good looking. Like, I was

offered a threesome with a guy and a girl, and I was like nah, I would rather do my hair. Like, I take care of my appearance and that's feminine. I can be attracted to guys. Some boys I wouldn't make out with because I don't find them very attractive. I think most of my mates are quite good looking. Obviously, you can say a boy is good looking, like, you can find them attractive.

These two men said that they could be attracted to men in some circumstances, and Callum suggested that (whilst he is a very muscular, athletic, and traditionally masculine man) adopting a feminine fashion sense and taking care of his appearance also illustrated his sexuality. The men in the club did seem to obsess over their hair, tan, and fashion sense.

The remaining five men who identified as mostly heterosexual broadly suggested that because of their same-sex behaviors, like kissing and cuddling, they could not realistically identify as heterosexual (see McCormack and Savin-Williams 2018). Their responses all suggested that they based their self-identified sexuality on the behaviors that they had been involved in, as opposed to the feelings of desire they had towards each sex. For example, Gordon said, "I would be lying to myself if I said I was completely straight, just because of the stuff I've done with guys." Chris said, "I would say I'm mostly heterosexual because I've done a lot of homosexual things. I'm not physically attracted to the male form but I'm emotionally attracted."

In conversation with Chris, following Tour, Stefan noted that he said, "Everyone on tour is bisexual" and Jerry, a mostly heterosexual teammate, interrupted to say, "That's so fair. Everyone's bisexual on Tour. I pulled more guys than girls and everyone's up for it." Gordon said something similar; "I pulled three people on Tour, and two of them were guys." Describing his sexuality, Rory said, "I'm mostly heterosexual because I kiss other guys, and I would take part in a threesome with a dude and a girl. If I couldn't bare that situation, then I would say heterosexual."

The two remaining men identified as somewhere between mostly heterosexual and bisexual. Jaden was very publicly open about his feelings in this regard. In one instance, at pre-drinks, he enjoyed joking about his interest in receiving anal pleasure. He said to a room full of people, "I don't think there's a girl I've been with who hasn't slipped a cheeky finger in my ass. It feels good. I've been dildo fucked by a girl before as well, actually." There were no social repercussions to this and it was funny for everyone, whilst accepted as a novelty of his sexuality (see Branfman et al. 2017; Wignall et al. 2020). During interview, Jaden said:

> I don't know why I like it. I think because it's kinky, I've always liked someone having a little play with my ass. I don't think the dodgeball guys care. I wouldn't have a problem with anyone knowing. I would be like yes, and? I like it. I think a lot of guys think, "Oh that's kinky, I will give it a go one day."

In the same way as the other mostly heterosexual men defined their sexuality, Jaden based his identity on previous behaviors. He said, "Like, the stuff I've done, I couldn't say I was completely straight. Obviously, I've done things that people would think is gay, like cuddling and kissing and being naked with men." He went on, "When I get off with guys I enjoy it, not sexually. I can't say I'm entirely straight. I wouldn't have sex with a man, but I would do a lot of other things with them."

Jaden was very open about his thoughts and experiences of sexuality and had no embarrassment in the interview or in the club. Indeed, shortly after the interview, he told me that he went and spoke to his bromance, another member of the team, about how he defined his sexuality in the interview.

James, the second man to identify as between mostly heterosexual and bisexual, had a stronger sexual attraction towards men than Jaden. He said, "Since I've grown up, I've liked girls and I'm sexually attracted to girls. As I've grown up, I've had thoughts about what it would be like to suck someone's cock and what it would be like to be homosexual." Unlike most other men in this study, James based his sexuality primarily on his intentions and curiosity of homosexual behavior, as opposed to considering how his past actions defined his current sexuality. He explained:

> I've decided it's (sex with another man) something I would try when I'm older, or really drunk. I see it as only a sexual thing. I could never have a

full relationship with a guy. For me, maybe when I'm older and maybe in an orgy, I might try it. But it's purely sexual attraction. One time when I was drunk, I said I would have a threesome with my mate and a girl. And I said to him I wouldn't mind sucking his cock and the next day I was like, "Oh I didn't mean it." But the week before I thought about doing that, and I think the alcohol allowed me to say it. I think I knew there was guy down the road who wants a blow job, I would try it but it's not something I'm ready for yet.

James was not open about these feelings with other club members. He said, "I would only want sexual stuff with a guy and still a romantic relationship with a girl. I don't think people would understand that, and I'm still exploring it myself."

James complicates his own situation here. Whilst the men broadly recognize that their bromances possess romantic characteristics, James is saying that he needs to distinguish his sexual desires from any romantic feelings, as to limit his own perceptions of being bisexual or homosexual. By explaining that he could never be involved with another man romantically he makes a reflection of heteronormativity, and potentially his own heterosexism. However, James recognized that his own feelings and desires needed exploring and that he was not overly certain of how he felt at that time.

Pushing Heterosexual Boundaries

In their research on same-sex kissing behaviors, Esterline and Galupo (2013) define gay chicken as a game in which:

> The objective is to come as close as possible to kissing without any actual physical contact. Although an actual kiss is socially unacceptable, the first person to pull away is named the "loser," a rule that creates as much tension as possible. The tension associated with almost kissing another male and the final act of pulling away serves to reinforce and preserve the heterosexuality of the players. (p. 117)

In addition, Anderson et al. (2012) recognized gay chicken as a game that would traditionally embarrass and degrade new recruits in university sports clubs, though they highlight this is no longer effective due to a declining homophobic environment. For the men in the dodgeball club, however, this game was played and understood very differently from Esterline and Galupo's (2013) perceptions. In Stefan's observations, and through discussion with the participants, it emerged that the game could be played between anyone in the club, at their own request or the request of others, and always with their lips touching.

Whilst gay chicken is a relatively new behavior for young men, the traditional assumption has been that the men who pull away from the prospect of a same-sex kiss are unable to engage in homosexual behaviors because they will feel humiliated in a homophobic environment. Anderson et al. (2012) suggest that in a declining homophobic environment, gay chicken loses its associated deviance and degradation, and this is accurately illustrated in the data. They found that the homophobic sentiment was present in the first year of their hazing study, but by the 7th year gay chicken no longer worked because participants would kiss each other—the idea of sportsmen kissing each other was no longer stigmatizing, so the hazing turned to excessive and dangerous consumption of alcohol instead.

When asked to describe what gay chicken was, Jaden said, "It's where you make out and it's the first one to pull away that loses" and Taylor, the only person Stefan interviewed not to have played the game, said it was, "Where two guys get off until there is a winner. Well, till someone pulls away."

Stefan observed more than forty instances of gay chicken, and he never saw an instance where someone declined to kiss another member of the team. At the first social event of the year, when numerous freshers had joined the club, there were some games of gay chicken taking place among the seniors. Stefan recalls a moment when Tim, a fresher, said, "That's sick!" and started laughing. In response Jaden, a senior in the club said, "Why? Are you scared of getting with a guy?" Tim then proceeded to make out with Jaden for about ten seconds. In this instance, the game was self-instigated, and not put on them by an external source as commonly understood (Esterline and Galupo 2013). Indeed, it was not uncommon for these men to instigate their own gay chicken games, without any pressure or influence from other team members.

Stefan describes the operation of kissing in his field notes:

> After a long day traveling and competing, it was common for everyone to go out the same evening. Our first stop one evening was at a busy local pub in the center of town. There was about ten of us on a small table, talking and having our first pint of beer. People were sat back quite far from the table to allow enough space for everyone to fit in a circle. I looked over at Blake and for a reason unbeknownst to me, or anyone else at the time, he was confidently making out with Chris.
>
> These two popular men were pressed up against each other upright in their chairs, kissing for about twenty seconds. They were getting really passionate and into it. Then, Chris leaned back in his chair onto the back two legs, and slowly moved up against the wall whilst Blake mounted him, continuing to make out. For this thirty second period, none of the men at the table gave any recognition or comment on their behavior, and after they stopped, no one asked why they did it.
>
> At that moment, I asked why they did it, and Blake said, "Because he bet me I wouldn't do it. There was no embarrassment expressed from these men, given that they were just very physically intimate in a public space early in the day.

Stefan interviewed both of these men about this situation. To seek more clarity, he asked again why that situation occurred. Blake, the man who instigated the challenge to make out, said:

> Because I bet Chris that he couldn't do it. I've done it with Gordon and Ronnie, too. Ronnie is the worst. He reckons he's a bit wild, a bit cool and a bit London, and he says he will do most things. I will do most things. In every year I wanted to prove myself. Making-out with a guy is always a go-to thing for me. It's an easy win, because I don't care. I wouldn't do an arm wrestle because I lose them (he laughs). Chris is a masculine guy, he shags loads of girls and it doesn't dawn on him that he could lose against me. I said to him, "You couldn't pull me." He said, "Yes I could." And I said, "Go on then, see who backs off first."
>
> Easy win. Its macho isn't it, winning? I wanted to be the alpha male. I love winning. If someone bets me something, and the stakes are right.

I will do it. I think sometimes I'm very gay. Now that I think about it, ultra-gay! I don't think I'm gay. Chris is stubborn like me, so he wouldn't stop, and it got to the point where we were pulling each other and it went weird, and he pulled away. When I say pulling, I mean mouths go open, tongues go in, and you're grabbing each other's nuts. I'm fucking squirming thinking about it though.

From the same perspective, when asked, Chris said:

I've done stuff like that with a few guys haven't I? With Gordon, I've done something similar, and I've given Ed a hickey on the neck. It's funny, isn't it? I guess the difference to traditional gay chicken is that Blake called me out in a one-to-one challenge. In gay chicken you can say no, but to back down form a one-on-one challenge wouldn't be something I would do. It is pretty gay. The thing is when everyone is watching you, you want to win, and you go the full mile to do it.

Simply, these men demonstrate that it is more important to them that they are suspected of being a homosexual winner, than a heterosexual loser. Of course, the men in their immediate friendship circle are aware of their self-identified sexualities, and only outsiders may suspect them of homosexuality. It should be noted that both the participants found the recollection of this moment to be hilarious, and much of the discussion was conducted through laughter.

Emerging from their statements, they highlight that variants of gay chicken can be self-instigated, out of a need to beat the other person, in a less traditionally masculine way than previous generations. In addition to Jaden and Max, Blake and Chris, many of the other man shared the same perspective.

In another observation, two men made it clear to each other that they were not going to back out before a game of gay chicken had started. One of them said, "You know I'm not backing out of this. I go the whole hog." Shortly after that, they were on the floor making out and grinding against each other. When asked if he had ever played gay chicken, Pete, who worked at a local nightclub, said:

Yes. Twice with someone when I was at work. Like, my job is to sell shots and one of the guys challenged me to make out with them. I tried selling them a drink and they were like, "Play gay chicken with me" and I was not going to pussy out and we ended up making out.

From their statements, and Stefan's observations, it was clear that gay chicken had evolved to be more self-instigating and many of the men took pride in their ability to win a game.

Describing their willingness to play, Danny said, "Guys jump up wanting to play. I will commit because I'm going to kiss a guy like I have a million times before and you can have a laugh and joke and boost your happiness." Ed said, "When people play chicken, they don't think twice about it. You don't go out saying, 'I'm going to get with Jaden,' but it happens."

During observations, Andy was picked from a hat to make out with a man from a different sports team. He was half the size of the other man who mounted him and made out with him for about two minutes. Andy pulled away and all of the dodgeball team booed him for loosing. When I interviewed him about it, he said, "I wanted to win, and everyone was cheering me, but I felt uncomfortable in front of 50 people with a stranger, and he was huge." Critically, the whole dodgeball team was disappointed that Andy lost, rather than being concerned with the homosexual nature of the game. The culture of the male environment had evolved to be stoic in the face of homosexual challenges.

Moreover, many of the men strongly desired to win these games, which meant that their behaviors often extended beyond the traditional limits of just kissing (see also Ogilvie 2019). Recalling one instance James said, "Two of the guys were on the floor trying to poke bums and they were being egged on, and they were trying to preserve their manhood by not backing down and being the dominant man." Rob, speaking about two different teammates said, "They ended up on the floor and his hands were in his pants both back and front groping and everyone's just cheering, you know how it is?" Taylor said, "Some freshers went down each other's trousers in the first few weeks" and Harry said, "We did gay chicken, and James grabbed my dick and put his tongue right down my throat." Ronnie's perspective reflected the mainstream of thought among the men, drawing attention to their competitive nature and lack of boundaries:

> At the pre-drinks last week, we played chicken again. There were two guys kissing and then someone went, "Gordon and Ronnie do it," and things got weird. We went full on kissing, getting off, tongues, I put my finger... well I tried to put it up his arse and he grabbed my dick. Chicken to the next level. We didn't get aroused, but I was like, "I'm making you back-out of this first, because I want to win." I wanted to prove I'm not the chicken. That's a good example, like the length's boys are willing to go to win, it's like "look, I'm gayer than you are." It actually means I'm gayer than you, but guys can go to extremes to prove a point and be the alpha male, and it doesn't matter what people think.

Ronnie's view and experience condenses and recaps how these men interact with one another through gay chicken. Firstly, they have redefined the traditional game. Or rather, the game of gay chicken has become obsolete, and they have invented their own new way of having fun, that importantly does not degrade the participants. Secondly, the game is sometimes self-instigated as a way of competing to be the "Alpha male." Discussions on this highlighted that the men give more weight to the importance of winning, than they do to the maintenance of a heterosexual image. This is highly convoluted when compared to older research, as the men are appropriating homosexuality to being the alpha male, in this particular game. Esterline and Galupo's (2013) said that the game features tension associated with almost kissing another man, and pulling away to reinforce heterosexuality, but these men operated on the contrary with some distinction. Their competitive spirit pushed some of them to more extreme versions of the game. All of these evolved elements of the game, accompanied by the men's unanimous perspective that the game is not embarrassing, show that they are unconcerned with the homosexual connotations of the game.

Group Sex

The lack of stigma for same-sex interactions has also reconstructed the cultural significance of having a threesome, foursome, or more. There is a relatively little data on young men's openness to and engagement in threesomes; primarily because of the taboo that has surrounded non-monogamous sexual interactions (Scoats 2019a, 2019b; Scoats et al. 2018). Whilst observing and interacting with these young men, however, it became clear that having a threesome was on many of their sexual agendas.

During interviews, the men were asked if they had ever been involved in a threesome; if they would want one; and what their preference would be in terms of male–male–female (MMF) or male–female–female (MFF). Out of the 20 men interviewed, 19 said that they desired to have a threesome. The one man who did not want to have a threesome was also the same and only person who had never played gay chicken.

Nine of the 20 men had been involved in threesomes, seven of which had experienced an MMF whilst four men experienced a FFM threesome. Five of the men had also been involved in either foursomes or fivesomes. When compared to Scoats et al. (2018) study on young men, where 30% of participants had engaged in a threesome, the men in this study elicited a 45% participation rate.

Whilst all of these men identified nearer to heterosexual than they did to homosexual, all of those wanting to have a threesome would readily take part in both a FFM and an MMF. This it to say that 19 out of the 20 men would willingly engage in a shared sexual experience with one other man and a woman at the same time, though most specified restrictions on interaction with the man.

In addition, four of the men said that their preference would be to have a MMF and 15 would prefer MFF. Among the men, two suggested that their desire to engage in an MMF was based on the experience being more sexually appealing, and the remaining 17 broadly said that they would have a MMF because of the humor and comfortability of the situation (Scoats 2019a). For example, many of them suggested that they would feel more comfortable in a threesome situation if one of their close male friends or bromances was involved. Lawrence, who had never had a threesome, explained:

> I wouldn't do it with a stranger, it would have to be with my bromance. It's because you feel comfortable naked around them because you've seen each other like that so many times before. That stuff doesn't bother me in the slightest.

James said, "We are all good friends, but compared between who you would say hello to and who you would have a threesome with, it is completely different. I would do it with my best mate and another girl." Harry said, "If I did a MMF with a bromance, they wouldn't be a dick about it, and I could learn from them and feel more comfortable." Pete, who had three MMF threesomes that year said, "My preference is with a mate because it is fun and there is less pressure on you because between you, it's easier to get the job done." Callum said, "Yes I would want a MMF because I think it could be quite funny." Andy said, "FFM is my preference, but I would with a mate for a laugh and if a girl asks you to get with the guy for her pleasure, I would." When asked for his preference, Ed said, "The immediate answer from what you see on TV is two girls. But my preference would be MMF with a bromance because I would feel more relaxed."

One person recalls their experience of a fivesome:

> It is a bit gay with a guy there just watching you and it's a bit off-putting, but I had no trouble getting a hard on. It's obviously a bit gay because everyone had their dicks out and its very weird and surreal experience, but I don't regret it. It's a funny experience and I was completely comfortable with it and my sexuality. It was chilled.

Rory said, "It would be a laugh with a mate, and I do see the attraction of two guys having sex with one girl." In one instance on Tour, many of the men were openly declaring that they wanted to have a threesome with Max, because they perceived him to be "a complete shagger" as one man put it; they thought he was the most likely to have sex. At one moment, a teammate revealed to the club that he followed Max around for most of the night, explaining, "I thought if I stuck near him, I would end up getting a threesome."

Gordon, who shared a threesome with Blake said, "I would have a threesome with a guy if I was really good mates with him. I was in a threesome recently when you look at each other and laugh." The man he was in that threesome with, Blake, said:

> I've had about six MMF threesomes. It's all about accessibility. It is more about the girl wanting it than the guys. That's where the limitation comes from. But sometimes there is a girl that just wants to. For example (names girl) a lot of my friends have slept with her.

During interviews, the men were asked whether having a MMF would mean that anyone would think that they were gay or bisexual. None of the men said that this would be the case, and the broad consensus was that two men could preserve their heterosexuality by "Staying at opposite ends" and "Not doing any one-on-one stuff between the guys" as Gordon and Danny put it, respectively.

However, similar to the results shown in the gay chicken section of this study, some same-sex sexual behavior would be permissible if it was at the request of the woman involved. This is described by Anderson (2008b) as the good cause scenario, where men are permitted a level of homosexuality when in the pursuit of heterosexual sex. Scoats (2019a) describes this sort of threesome as a "sexual compromise" (p. 61); engaging in a threesome as to have sex with one of the others present, rather than specifically wanting a threesome.

James explained, "Like, if the girl wants us to do stuff, I would if it meant we both got with her after." Talking about his experience of a MMFF, he said, "The girls asked me and my best mate to get off, and we were both naked in the bed. So, we masturbated aside each other for them and kissed each other whilst doing some of it. That's as far as I would go though." Blake said, "All the boys know it's like *American Pie* (the movie), where it's you go we go kind of thing" and Rory said, "If the girl asked them to get off, it would be fine and it would be a lad story." Research also suggests that MMF threesomes where men interact together sexually may also reduce some of the perceived objectification and anxiety some women have around these threesomes (Scoats 2019b).

Suspicion of homosexuality was not something that these men were concerned with when engaging in MMF threesomes. In interviews, they were clear on this, and in observations they were proud to publicly disclose these experiences. Callum said, "I don't think anyone would think it was gay unless you were doing stuff to the boy." Rory said, "No, people wouldn't think they were gay. They would just think they were confident in their own sexuality." Taylor said, "People would just see it as laddish, even though it might not be" and Jaden said, "No. I don't think it would be seen as gay at all." Callum, who shared an MMMMF with Chris said, "I didn't get any gay comments about it."

Whilst all of the men suggested that they could maintain their heterosexuality in a MMF threesome, under certain parameters, two of the men suggested that women were more likely to receive homosexual suspicion in an MFF situation. Jerry said, "People wouldn't think the two guys in the MMF were gay, but if it was two women, I would think they were curious." Similarly, Blake said:

> Bromances make threesomes easier because boys will always do it but girls wont because then their lesbians aren't they? It's not gay for us. There's not even any doubt over it, guys are still straight when they do it.

The prevailing logic here is that males are up for sex most of the time with women. Thus, if a woman is attracted to men, she can have as many as she wants. So, if she chooses to have a woman and another man, it's likely because she's attracted to the woman, too.

For the men in this study, whilst the majority of them preferred the idea of having a MFF, as opposed to MMF, all of the 19 men that wanted a threesome were broadly open to the idea of having a MMF, with 7 having done so already. Homosexual suspicion was not anticipated as a result of having a MMF, and those who already had a MMF did not experience any homophobic taunts or comments.

The men articulated that they were able to maintain their heterosexual identities, despite sharing, and wanting to share, sexual experiences with one another (Scoats 2019a). The participants highlighted that they were more likely to be comfortable and relaxed in an MMF, than a FFM, particularly if they were accompanied by a bromance.

Evidently the development of the bromance has lessened social stigma for same-sex sexual interactions. As Scoats (2019a) has suggested, men may view MMF threesomes with their male friends as a novel and exciting experience, rather than an erotic one. What happens once this novelty wears off, however, remains unclear.

Nudity

Nudity was commonplace within the team, especially when getting ready for a night out or when changing clothes after a tournament or training. Ronnie explained that, "Being naked just shows you're completely comfortable with each other," the men regularly got naked in relatively random situations to make people laugh.

Andy said, "In my bromance, I have no issue being naked around him." Talking about his bromance, Chris said, "There was one incident where we were both naked at the house and we jumped on our housemate's bed for a laugh and ended up staying naked in his bed for a while." Danny said, "Mate, we walk around naked all the time. It's the done thing" and Jaden said, "I think I naked spooned with Taylor just last night. It's a bit fuzzy because of my hangover, but that's how we woke."

Stefan noted a moment when he arrived at Jerry's house, before heading out into town. His male housemate answered the door and called for him. Jerry shouted down the stairs, "I'm having a wank, give me a few minutes." He called Stefan up after, where he was showering with the door wide open. Ronnie was also in the bathroom brushing his teeth. Jerry proceeded to have a long conversation with Ronnie about whether he should join them on the night out. At no point was it acknowledged that Jerry was showering. Stefan asked Jerry about that situation in interview. He said:

> That's not odd to me. I do it all the time. I started showering with the boys when I was 16. I could name anyone in the team just by looking at their cock. I see it as a working tool for laying a seed and pissing. Ronnie

showers when I shit and brush my teeth. That's what it's like this day and age, maybe not for everyone, but guys at uni, I think. Mate, honestly, I've done shots of vodka out of someone's foreskin, as if I could have an issue with being naked?

Sexual Bravado

This section briefly highlights some other same-sex behaviors that were observed and discussed among participants, where the embodiment of yet more hetero-rebellious behaviors was prevalent. The activities described in this section belie heterosexual orthodoxy, but they do so through a performance of masculinity. They are thus still heteromasculinity, but they represent a broader perspective on heteromasculinity. Critically, many of these examples have not been identified elsewhere in existing contemporary research.

The boner game was a common activity that the men engaged in, particularly on long bus journeys. The aim of this game, as Danny explained, is, "The first one to get a boner wins, and you can't touch it or look at pictures. It's a competition common in sports teams and you have to power up for it." In several instances, the winner would have to show their naked erection to prove that they had one.

In another instance, on a journey back from a competition on the all-male members' team minibus, there was an episode of "cock fighting." There were about twenty people on the minibus who were mostly men. Stefan's notes recall that Blake stood up in the middle of the aisle and declared, "I am the undefeated cock fighting champion. Three wins, no losses! Who's the challenger going to be?" He then got his penis out and waved it around. Two of the men agreed to challenge him. In an interview after the event, Blake explained the background and premise of the game:

> In first year, we would go to competitions every week on really long bus rides and we were bored and the girls had shit music. I spy gets boring. I came up with who can get a hard cock first (the boner game). Who has the willpower and you can't touch yourself. Very gay and its funny. It

evolved into who can keep a hard dick whilst hitting it against another guy's dick, and it happened every time at pre-drinks and you would stand there till one of you limped out and went soft.

Blake then went on to describe the specific details of his three cock fighting victories. Returning to the instance Stefan observed, there were two challengers to Blake's proposal. The three men then proceeded to masturbate in daylight on the motorway in order to achieve an erection. There was an attempt between two men to fight and their penises rubbed up against each other, but neither man achieved a full erection meaning there was intermittent masturbation, followed by more attempts to fight. Danny, the man next to the researcher declared, "I'm going to wank to see if I can get a boner, just out of interest." In interview, Stefan asked him if he remembered what he did when the men were cock fighting. He recalled:

> Yes, I was having a bit of a bash out and they got to the point where they were having a cock fight. I thought it was hilarious. That is homosexual behavior but I'm sure they are not gay. I know gay porn stars are often not gay, and I get that they do it for the money incentive. The incentive on the bus was winning.

Similar to the men's perspectives on gay chicken, Danny highlights that the incentive of winning in this homosexually themed game far outweighed any fear of homosexual stigma, and the competitive element again took priority. This then can be understood as competitive heterosexual boundary pushing.

The boner game and cock fighting were not the only forms of sexual bravado engaged in. Five of the men indicated that they had put another man's penis in their mouth, though always as a result of a dare or forfeit. Ed said, "The condemning of homosexuality has been significantly reduced in society, and you can see that in the team where people have put their dicks in mates' mouths and stuff."

Gordon told Stefan about a forfeit he was involved within a drinking game. "I had to lick his dick because I lost at downing my pint." And, in a game of "never have I ever," the issue of having a penis in their own mouth was raised, Stefan counted four men that drank, indicating that four men in the room had put another man's penis in their mouth. Surprisingly, no questions of those situations were asked, and the game proceeded to the next person. As Harry described that moment, he said, "We were playing never have I ever and I said, "had a dick in my mouth," and some of my mates drank. It's weird right."

This data is a complete contrast to the way in which men behaved three decades ago, where simple same-sex touch, of any description, was suspected of homosexuality and thus fearfully avoided (Morin and Garfinkle 1978; Williams 1985). Lots of hypermacho behaviors occurred among men in sports in decades past, but the types of behaviors accounted for here are not described in that literature set. These men thus show that they can be hypermasculine (in this capacity) without being homophobic.

Chapter Summary

Whilst this data has been collected from a small sample, the men's interpretation of the categories proposed by Vrangalova and Savin-Williams (2012) showed a varied response. Whilst all of the men identified as closer to heterosexuality than homosexuality, half of them did not identify as explicitly as heterosexual, instead opting for a non-exclusive, inexact, and partial heterosexuality.

This illustrates that the men understand their sexualities to be more subjective, complicated, and less culture-bound than earlier generations have considered (Ghaziani 2010, 2017; Summers 2004; Savin-Williams 2005). For those who did not identify as heterosexual, they used a portfolio of past same-sex experiences to justify their unwillingness to identify as explicitly heterosexual.

This chapter has also identified and complicated where these men's physical same-sex boundaries lay. In this bromantic culture, gay chicken has evolved into a more intimate and less embarrassing game that holds little shock factor for participants and onlookers. Indeed, some men willingly instigated the game themselves in order to challenge teammates, as a way of demonstrating their alpha male status. This highlights that the incentive of winning in homosexually themed games outweighs any fear of homosexual stigma.

There is also a great deal of pseudo-sexual activities that occur with these men: activities that challenge traditional notions of what sexual activity is. Threesomes are hard to clarify in terms of sexual desire because sexual and social desire are not separate with these men. They are in a sense, homosocial. Further evidence of their homosociality comes from their comfort in being nude around each other, showing each other their erections, and even licking or placing their friends' cocks into their mouth.

This data is vastly contradictory to the behaviors espoused among the men's fathers' generation (Connell 1995). It is not particularly easy to classify, but it is easy to theorize. If, as Inclusive Masculinity (Anderson 2009) suggests, men are no longer afraid to be thought homosexual, they are essentially no social limitations placed on their voluntary, adult, consensual sexual, semi-sexual, or pseudo-sexual practices. The question then becomes, why not engage in these behaviors if they make one feel closer to their friends?

This is not to suggest that there is no masculinity in these behaviors: there is. What it is to suggest, however, is that these men redefine heterosexual masculinity to exist in ways that press the boundaries of heterosexuality and that they do this without being homophobic.

References

Adams, A., and Anderson, E. (2012). Exploring the relationship between homosexuality and sport among the teammates of a small, Midwestern Catholic college soccer team. Sport, Education and Society, *17*(3), 347–363.

Anderson, E. (2008). "Being masculine is not about who you sleep with...:" Heterosexual athletes contesting masculinity and the one-time rule of homosexuality. Sex Roles, *58*(1–2), 104–115.

Anderson, E. (2009). *Inclusive masculinity: The changing nature of masculinities.* New York: Routledge

Anderson, E., McCormack., and Lee, H. (2012). Male Team Sport Hazing Initiations in a Culture of Decreasing Homohysteria. *Journal of Adolescent Research, 27*(4), 427–448.

Branfman, J., Stiritz, S. and Anderson, E. (2017) Relaxing the Straight-Male Anus: Decreasing Homohysteria around Anal Eroticism. *Sexualities.* https://doi.org/10.1177/1363460716678560

Brim, M., and Ghaziani, A. (2016). Introduction: Queer methods. *WSQ: Women's Studies Quarterly, 44*(3–4), 14–27.

Connell, R. (1995). *Masculinities.* Berkeley: University of California Press.

Esterline, K., and Galupo, M. (2013). "Drunken curiosity" and "gay chicken": Gender differences in same-sex performativity. *Journal of Bisexuality, 13*(1), 106–121.

Ferguson, A. (2001). *Bad boys: Public schools in the making of masculinity.* Ann Arbor: University of Michigan Press.

Galupo, M. P. (2020). Mental health for individuals with pansexual and queer identities. *The Oxford Handbook of Sexual and Gender Minority Mental Health,* 331.

Ghaziani, A. (2010). The reinvention of heterosexuality. *Gay and Lesbian Review, 17*(3): 27–29.

Ghaziani, A. (2017). *Sex cultures.* Boston: Polity Press (Cultural Sociology series).

Ghaziani, Amin, and Brim, M. (2019). Queer methods: Four provocations for an emerging field. In Ghaziani, A. and Brim, M. (Ed.), *Imagining queer methods.* New York: NYU Press. Pp. 3–27.

Lindley, L., Walsemann, K., and Carter, J. (2012). The association of sexual orientation measures with young adults' health related outcomes. *American Journal of Public Health, 102*(6), 1177–1185.

McCormack, M., and Savin-Williams, R. (2018). Young men's rationales for non-exclusive gay sexualities. *Culture, Health and Sexuality, 20*(8), 929–944.

McCormack, M., and Wignall, L. (2017). Enjoyment, exploration and education: Understanding the consumption of pornography among young men with non-exclusive sexual orientations. *Sociology, 51*(5), 975–991.

Morin, S., and Garfinkle, E. (1978). Male homophobia. *Journal of Social Issues, 34*(1), 29–47.

Ogilvie, M. E. (2019). *Masculinities and sexualities of elite male team sport athletes. An ethnographic examination.* Unpublished PhD Thesis. Durham University.

Savin-Williams, R. (2005). *The new gay teenager* (Vol. 3). Cambridge: Harvard University Press.

Savin-Williams, R. C. (2017). *Mostly straight: Sexual fluidity among men*. Harvard University Press.

Scoats, R. (2019a). *Understanding threesomes: Gender, sex, and consensual non-monogamy*. Oxford: Routledge.

Scoats, R. (2019b). 'If there is no homo, there is no trio': Women's experiences and expectations of MMF threesomes. *Psychology and Sexuality, 10*(1), 45–55.

Scoats, R., Joseph, L. J., and Anderson, E. (2018). 'I don't mind watching him cum': Heterosexual men, threesomes, and the erosion of the one-time rule of homosexuality. *Sexualities, 21*(1–2), 30–48.

Summers, C. (2004). *The queer encyclopaedia of music, dance, and musical theatre*. New Jersey: Cleis Press.

Vrangalova, Z., and Savin-Williams, R. C. (2012). Mostly heterosexual and mostly gay/lesbian: Evidence for new sexual orientation identities. *Archives of sexual behavior, 41*(1), 85–101.

Wignall, L. (2019). Pornography use by kinky gay men–A qualitative approach. *Journal of Positive Sexuality, 15*(1), 7–13.

Wignall, L., and Driscoll, H. (2020). Women's rationales and perspectives on "mostly" as a nonexclusive sexual identity label. *Psychology of Sexual Orientation and Gender Diversity*.

Wignall, L., and McCormack, M. (2017). An exploratory study of a new kink activity: "Pup play". *Archives of Sexual Behavior, 46*(3), 801–811.

Wignall, L., Scoats, R., Anderson, E., and Morales, L. (2020). A qualitative study of heterosexual men's attitudes toward and practices of receiving anal stimulation. *Culture, Health and Sexuality, 22*(6), 675–689.

Williams, D. (1985). Gender, masculinity-femininity, and emotional intimacy in same-sex friendship. *Sex Roles, 12*(5–6), 587–600.

12

Privileging the Bromance

Thus far, the data has drawn attention to many progressive, endearing, and appealing characteristics of bromantic relationships, particularly in relation to the physical and emotional freedoms and comforts that are permissible. However, this chapter considers one of the main detriments and challenges in managing bromantic relationships; that is, how these young men are seemingly unable to maintain long-term romantic relationships alongside their bromances.

Benenson (2013) suggests that men have a higher threshold for intolerance and conflict in their same-sex friendships, than they do with women, leaving romantic relationships more likely to fail where structural necessity does not bind the dyad. This section draws on the wider context of men's relationships and their social environment, recognizing that bromantic friendships do not operate in isolation from other relationships. The participants highlight that their closest and most loyal friends rarely support their involvement in romantic relationships, beyond casual sex. Some of the men even blame their bromances from the demise of their romantic lives. Demands on time between the two relationships are discussed, and abusive and jealous behaviors are documented and explored.

Romance as Problematic

One of the most detrimental things observed in this study is how some of the men would look poorly upon their friends for being in a romantic relationship with a female. This is because their friends viewed romance as a threat to their bromance. Observations of men not in romantic relationships showed them frequently using banter toward those who were in a relationship, sometimes to the extent of abuse.

For example, James is a relatively popular member of the club. He is funny, confident, and sociable with everyone, and has several visible bromances with his teammates. James, like others on the team, was in a long-term relationship with a girl in the club. Talking about his experiences, he said, "People have a front and that can be against you having a girlfriend. And because you want to be one of the boys, or girls, you sort of have to put on a front yourself." James' public relationship suffered immensely from external pressure, and from what Stefan observed, this came mostly from his closest friends and bromances. He explained:

> My best mates can put restrictions on my relationship sometimes. It limits your relationship because the way I am with my girlfriend outside of the club is much more romantic and I show her off. But if I was romantic with her in the club, I would be seen as a pussy or not being a man basically. I would say we partly broke up because she couldn't handle the abuse we got. Like, if I cry when my dog dies, then the guys are there for me when I need them, and that's fine. But if I'm upset about breaking up with my girlfriend, they put up edited photos on Facebook making fun of us. Me crying was frowned on because I was not supposed to be getting upset over a girl.

Following this break up, there were endless public taunts on the dodgeball Facebook page and elsewhere online. His closest friends would tag him in all of his ex-girlfriend's new pictures, photos of her with other men, and leave comments on his new photos saying, "Don't cry mate. Your ugly" and, "She's got new meat now." Furthermore, even months after they had broken up, his bromances would still post pictures of them both together on the group page, with comments like "It's all over now."

To the men making the comments, they felt that they were close enough to James to make these comments without the perception of bullying. They were not however necessarily cognizant of the upset they were causing. Reviewing the rules on banter, these men were in breach of three rules. First, they did not fully understand James' personal situation. Second, they did not take account of the potential for emotional harm. Third, they were overly persistent in their insults.

Accordingly, interviews with James and others repeatedly highlighted the upsetting and distressing feelings caused by this "banter." As Ronnie said on this subject, "Problems have come up on social media because people read things differently and don't think sometimes."

Taylor, who had a relationship with a girl in the dodgeball team said, "If I'm with a girl, I get mugged off for it and some other guys do, too. It happens on Xbox, and they upload old pictures on me and her in the Facebook chat."

Ronnie was another man who was in a long-term romantic relationship, this time with a girl outside of the club, but still at the university. He was clearly happy in his relationship when the teasing began. After about two months, when the novelty of Ronnie being sexually involved with a new girl had faded, his bromances were quick to push him to break up with her. I overheard statements like, "Break up with her mate. She's a fucking pig and we want you back … Mate she makes me sick just looking at her [and] why are you wasting your time with her."

This kind of pressure would come at a time when Ronnie was not seeking advice, or discussing his relationship; seemingly, it would start randomly but often. Ronnie would laugh it off or say, "At least I'm getting laid."

Indeed, the, "I'm getting sex and you're not" phrase was used by several men when defending their relationships. As Jerry said, "My good mates would give me shit for spending time with her, but then I would always say, well it's a shag, isn't it? And they would say fair enough, fair play."

Interviews with these men highlight that the reality is that they cared for their girlfriends on a much deeper level than represented here. However, even their closest bromances could not appreciate the legitimacy of their romantic relationships, and thus, those men with girlfriends would only use sex to justify their relationships. Anderson

(2009) explains that men's sexual storytelling is highly important to male homosociality, both gay and straight. In the case of these men, they valued hearing about sex, but not romance.

Harry said, "The guys say nasty stuff because they are jealous that you have a hot girlfriend in a good relationship. They will joke about her cheating on me and it can upset me." Ed raised this in his interview, he said, "When people were saying Harry's girlfriend was cheating on him, and they were lying, that was unfair. I wouldn't say that to anyone."

Stefan remembers this being said to Harry during a banterous exchange, but it clearly caused him upset, for which there was no comfort given. Ed went on to explain how many of the men championed cheating behaviors:

> Cheating is celebrated and promoted, definitely. I remember it was a game of never have I ever and it was about cheating, and basically everyone drank apart from me. If someone cheats on a night out, they will get a text the next morning saying well done from the guys.

Other men were told that their girlfriends were cheating on them also. It was often said in a way that was joking but also sincere. Taylor said, "People cheat all the time" and Gordon said, "A lot of the guys promote cheating." For the men in relationships, they would regularly be asked, "Are you going to cheat tonight then mate?" The men would usually say no, to which they received significant criticism from their friends. They would say that the man was too young to be in a relationship, that their girlfriend was ugly, and/or their relationship would not last.

Danny had not had a relationship with any girls at the university, but he was still very popular with women, boasting to have had sex with forty women. When asked if there were any barriers in maintaining bromances and romances alongside one another, he said:

> Every time there has been a relationship between two club members, it always gets pushed. Some people take it too far and lack emotional empathy. Some people can put a lot of pressure on couples in the club, which can be unfair. People need to remember that there's a difference between humorous grief and emotional bullying. If your friends with a girl and the guys are mean about her, and she is a genuine friend, it

becomes difficult. But you don't want to put yourself out of the pack by not presenting as one of the boys.

Blake, one of the culprits in these pressuring behaviors said, "I'll say to the boys that I am spending the night with the mises, and they will get shitty with me. Some of the guys go shag girls whilst were gaming and we give them shit, too." Chris said, "The simple fact that I'm going to see a girl, I'll get ripped for that" and Taylor said, "They mug me off, but I know I would probably do the same if I was them." In discussing these issues, many of the men did not recognize their own contributing behaviors to this environment.

Competing Priorities

A possible reason for the contempt for their bromantic partners having girlfriends may come from a sense of competition for attention. The vast majority held their bromance in a higher regard than their romances. It is thus clear that there are certain social pressures to prioritize their bromances, as indicated by the "bros before hoes" rhetoric. The men explained that it can be difficult to manage their time between the two relationships, which often caused tensions. As Harry said, "It feels like they are both trying to pull me away from each other sometimes." Lawrence explained:

> She doesn't care about the physical contact with other guys, but she does get annoyed about the amount of time I spend with them. She can be quite clingy, but I like to be with my mates for an extended period of time. And they take the piss if I've spent a long time with her, and they will be like, "What have you been doing? You're always with her?" It's definitely jealousy, one hundred percent, and they bring it up a lot.

Lawrence identifies that both of these relationship types are competing with one another for time, which can cause criticism from both parties. Jerry said, "My last girlfriend was annoyed that I was spending too much time with my bro's, and I said, "I can't spend every waking minute with you!" She didn't take that well." Chris said, "If you're seeing a girl, you're naturally not going to be on the chat (Facebook) as much, and then you will get booted from the group for it." Taylor said, "My flat mate is missing nights out now because he has a girlfriend. Last year I was not out as much because I had a girlfriend. It's hard to keep social and have a girlfriend." Harry similarly said, "It's annoying because I want to spend time with both of them, but there's not enough time." Ed said, "Last year you barely noticed some people, because they were always with their girlfriends. Now their single, they are big social figures."

Gordon said, "Like, as soon as someone gets a girlfriend, they are under the thumb. They won't have time for the boys and won't be at socials." Stefan asked Gordon if there was a solution to the issue. He responded, "I've always tried to do it evenly; I always put bromances first but have tried to balance it. If I made plans with her before, then I wouldn't go out with the guys."

Blake spoke about how his romance did not understand how much he valued his bromances:

> She gets annoyed because I'm on the boys group chat messaging all the time. She doesn't understand how I can talk to them all day every day, and it literally is like that. My phone dies in an hour because I'm furiously typing. When I'm on the phone to them, she's recently started saying 'bloody hell, how can you talk for that long?' I definitely can't talk to her for that long.

Many bomantic couples keep in touch with smartphones (McCormack and Ogilvie 2020), supporting the notion that these bromances are loving relationships. Anecdotally, it has historically been women who have been stereotyped as spending too much time on the telephone (Rakow 1988) and not men. Danny spoke about how his previous girlfriend was concerned with how much time her was spending with his bromances, explaining, "She got frustrated, saying I neglect her for my bromances. In future, I will always look for a girl who is really laid back and understands how important my bromances are to me." Jaden reiterated this point, saying, "I think if you're in a romance, in my experience, a bromance can become the topic of an argument because she doesn't get that you want to spend time with them." An example of this conflict is explained by Harry:

> Last week she wanted me to come back to hers, which is a long drive. But I had already arranged to meet my friends, including my gay mates, and she knew that. She wanted me to do this really impractical journey to see her which was stupid, and it was like she was trying to control me and maybe stop me interacting with my bromances.

Of the 20 men interviewed, eight had been involved in romantic relationships lasting more than three months, in the previous 18 months. A year after the conclusion of the study, however, none were still in those relationships. That is not to say that their bromances are to blame for the demise of those romances exclusively, though, some do blame them. It does however indicate that these men's romantic lives are more volatile and unpredictable than their bromantic lives and that relationship longevity in their university years is more certain in bromances.

Bromances require commitment for these men, and any time spent with girlfriends is seen by some as wasteful and can become the subject of argument and jealousy.

Chapter Summary

The men highlighted an unfortunate reality of their social lives that their closest bromances afford them with abuse and insult for being involved in a romantic relationship. Whilst other chapters have shown that the men can emote openly and without judgment in their bromances, there seemingly is judgment if one is upset or troubled over their relationship.

No other cases of judgment among bromances were identified as part of this study. Both bromances and romances required time for their successful maintenance, however, the sometimes demanding, nature of both of these relationship types meant that interpersonal friction could occur.

References

Anderson, E. (2009). *Inclusive masculinity: The changing nature of masculinities.* New York: Routledge

Benenson, J. (2013). The development of human female competition: allies and adversaries. *Philosophical Transactions of the Royal Society B, 368*(1631).

McCormack, M., and Ogilvie, M. F. (2020). Keeping couples together when apart, and driving them apart when together: Exploring the impact of smartphones on relationships in the UK. In Abela, A., Vella, S., and Piscopo, S. (Ed.), *Couple relationships in a global context: Understanding love and intimacy across cultures.* (European Family Therapy Association Series; Vol. 5). Springer. Pp. 245–259.

Rakow, L. (1988). Women and the telephone: The gendering of a communications technology. In Rakow, L (Ed.), *Technology and women's voices: Keeping in touch.* Pp. 207–229.

13

Discussing the Bromance

This research project set out to explore and examine the ways in which young men experience and act out their masculine identities, and homosocial relationships, within the context of a British university sports team. Specifically, the focus was on how men invoked physical tactility, emotionality, and comradery to facilitate and pioneer closer, more intimate, and more loving same-sex friendships than recently observed, known to them as bromances.

This project follows from a conversation between an ex-undergraduate student and his professor, ultimately cumulating in a one-year ethnography of a dodgeball team and accompanying interviews.

The completion of this research shows that Stefan was heavily immersed in this culture. In processes, this research has documented, defined, and clarified the boundaries and operation of the bromance. It highlights that the development of the bromance has been decades in the making. It is here that Stefan's PhD adviser, Eric Anderson played a role in the shape of this research, and the writing of this book.

Eric has previously shown that during epochs of high homohysteria, such as in 1970s–1990s Anglo-American society, men of all ages were socially condemned for expressing same-sex touch and emotional disclosure (Morin and Garfinkle 1978; Connell 1995; Kellner 2003; Pleck 1975). This restrictive environment was maintained through the use of pernicious homophobic narratives that circulated throughout cultural institutions, including sport (Anderson 2005), education (Connell 1989; Mac an Ghaill 1994), government (Ahmed 2013; Boyle 2008), religion (Anderson 2010), and the military (Dunivin 1994).

The state, both institutionally and as a state of mind, rejected emotionality and purged men's emotional and physical freedoms during these decades, leaving a generation of men with a life of non-intimate connections, having never achieved the level of intimacy afforded to women (Connell 1995; Collins and Sroufe 1999; Tognoli 1980). This had drastic consequences for the masculine landscape, as the fear of homosexuality enforced a stratification of the male hierarchy, characterized by intense aggression and homophobia towards those that presented as least heterosexual or homosexual (Connell 1995; Kimmel 1994; Anderson 2010).

Since the publication of these findings, however, there has been an equally dramatic and pervasive shift in the way that young men exhibit and construct their masculine identities (McCormack 2012; Anderson 2014; Magrath 2016) or rather masculinities (Lusher and Robins 2009). Postmillennial research has highlighted a progressive reassessment in the male conscious of the value of oppressive hegemonic hierarchies, as young men advance an appreciation for diverse expression in their own lives, recognizing little value in limiting their own ability to bond and express with one another (McCormack and Anderson 2014a; Anderson 2010; Savin-Williams 2005). Scholars suggest that this has largely been achieved through the successes of multiple social movements throughout the twentieth and twenty-first centuries, broadly advocating for equality and fair treatment by heterosexual men of homosexuals and women (Anderson 2014; Giroux 2001; Gutterman 1994).

This paradigmatic shift in the collective male conscious has recalibrated the masculine realm from a stratified and oppressive structure to a more horizontal range of diverse, soft, and sentient masculinities (Bush et al. 2012; Ripley et al. 2012; Magrath et al. 2013). Newer research has highlighted that young heterosexual men esteem inclusivity towards homosexuality (Adams 2011; McCormack 2012; White and Hobson 2015; Anderson 2005, 2008a, 2010, 2014), and they broadly espouse much more intimate, emotive, and homo-physical behaviors with their friends than previous generations (Drummond et al. 2014; McCormack and Anderson 2014a, b; Adams 2011; Morman et al. 2013; Johansson 2007).

Love, for these men, had real and important meaning in their bromances. During discussions with them and under interview, love for another male was not onflated with femininity or homosexuality, unlike its associations in decade's previous (Fisher 2004; Cancian 1986). The men were passionate, open, and excited to profess their love for their bromances, both publicly and privately. They fundamentally struggled to distinguish the love they felt for their bromances from that of their romances.

The thirty men studied in this research recognized that there was a presence or expectation of sexual desire in their romantic relationships, but many shared a progressive understanding that love existed without sexual desire also; they understood that love and sex can operate as two separate constructs (Diamond 2003; Fisher 1998). As psychology colleagues (Diamond 2003) explain, "The processes underlying sexual desire and affectional bonding are functionally independent" (p. 173).

Under Fishers (2004) three categories of love: romantic, companionate, and lust; bromances occupy the first two forms, with the latter being reserved exclusively mostly for romances. The bromance thus advances emotional romance between men and provides them with strong companionship throughout their time at university. Accordingly, the way in which scholars describe romantic love is synonymous with the love expressed in these bromances.

The presence of emotional dependence, shared interests, shared social networks, and infatuation are all romantic descriptors (Anderson 2012; Hruschka 2010; Fisher 2004) that translate to these men's bromances. Accordingly, if the love in bromances and romances is distinguished only through the experience of sex and recognizing that sexual desire is temporal in romantic relationships (Fisher 2004; Schwartz and Young 2009; Anderson 2012; Ryan and Jethá 2010), then romantic love cannot be exclusive to sexual relationships. Rather, the experience of romance and romantic love operates equally within bromances and is embedded in the operation of the relationship. The only difference between the two relationships is the way in which society perceives the relationships to be different. This is subject to change.

The bonds that these men have created clearly demonstrate a longing for continuous intimate engagement with their bromances that has not been observed in the past century (Anderson 2009; Savin-Williams 2005). However, Rotundo (1989) noted in the nineteenth century that friendships of a bromantic nature existed in their entirety, being emotionally and physically intimate, albeit without a bromantic term being deployed:

> Close male friendship would blossom into something more intimate and intense. Warmth turned into tender attachment, and fondness became romance. An adore developed between young men that would seem unusual outside of gay circles in the twentieth century. (p. 2)

Starkly reflective of Rotundo's (1989) conclusions, the men in this study expected outsiders to consider them to be gay, given the physical ways they interact with one another. Rotundo (1989) continues:

> There were intimate relationships between young men which involved touching, kissing and caressing and their physical expressiveness gave them an extra brush of romance. (p. 4)

Accordingly, in the nineteenth-century period of homoerasure, where the population was incognizant of homosexuality, these intimate same-sex relationships were widely permissible (McCormack and Anderson 2014a, b). After the inception of a homohysteric period in the twentieth century, these same intimate bromantic relationships described by Rotundo (1989) are appearing once more.

However, bromances are now operating under wholly different cultural conditions, scarcely regulated by oppressive institutions that have historically sought to limit same-sex life. Therefore, it cannot be concluded that these relationships are entirely new, though the cultural context in which they are situated is vastly different. Instead, bromances represent a revival of a long-standing sentimentality that has always existed between men, which many of our most cherished institutions have sought to curtail, inhibit, and coach out of men. For these men, bromances are resistant to the same-sex controls that previously functioned to limit their father's friendships.

Enduring Bromances

In a new inclusive world, institutions of marriage, monogamy, and religion have become progressively trivialized (Anderson 2012; Ryan and Jethá 2010): divorce is now a norm (Arnett 2004) and casual sex becomes decreasingly stigmatized and increasingly accessible (Anderson 2012; Grello et al. 2006). Intersecting with and influenced by the declining importance of these institutions, bromances are able to flourish in the everyday lives of young men. This is particularly associated with the men's affectedly positive attitudes towards homosexuality, as many of the participants attributed the physical freedoms in their bromances to the lessening of homophobia.

This change in the way that young men love their friends, and how society has habitually restricted same-sex life, has significant implications for modern relationships when considered alongside the expanding availability of casual sex for young men, and the delayed onset of marriage and cross-sex cohabitation. Given the socio-economic differences between this generation and the last, particularly concerning delayed entry into professional occupations, higher education, fatherhood, and marriage (Arnett 2004; Dermott 2008; Hagestad and Call 2007; Office for National Statistics 2012, 2015, 2016), the idea that these men might maintain their bromantic relationships in their current manner well beyond their university years is tenable. As a *New York Times* article featured American men doing (Howard 2012), our participants might carry on privileging bromances long into their adult lives. Indeed, one articulate participant made explicitly clear that the continued availability of casual sex would extend the longevity of bromances.

The idea of bromances extending into later adulthood could be possible for several reasons. Young men in the United Kingdom today are not afforded the same economic solidarity that their fathers were granted, and are experiencing a housing affordability crisis, whereby the equity of cohabitation with friends has become more appealing (Hilber and Vermeulen 2016). Indeed, the recent passing of same-sex marriage legislation in the United Kingdom would suggest that improved social attitudes exist towards same-sex cohabitation, making the reality of living with same-sex friends altogether more normative.

Moreover, because young men in the twenty-first century can have heterosexual sex without romantic commitment (Anderson 2014; Bogle 2008), and emotional disclosure with male friends (McCormack 2012), unlike in previous generations, they are less pressed to find early attachment with romantic partners. Certainly, the way in which the men in this study trivialized their casual sexual encounters, and privileged their bromantic relationships, suggests that their early desire for cross-sex attachment is limited.

Because data increasingly shows a delayed onset into family life for Anglo-American men (Arnett 2004), it is worthwhile considering that these bromantic cohabitations may already be happening in larger numbers than expected, although more research is needed. Indeed, forthcoming research concludes that men in their post-university years continue to strive for the same emotional intimacy with their male friends that they achieved during their time at university (Magrath and Scoats 2019).

There exists a need for research into the longevity of bromantic relationships. It's possible, yes, that as adulthood extends further into the twenties and thirties, bromantic relationships will play an important part in men's emotional lives. On the other hand, given that heterosexual coupling is in no immediate threat of total-decline—that is to say that men will still look to partner with women out of sexual desire, and emotional (perhaps for fewer men)—the stag due, prior to marriage might very well signal the end of bromances in a practical way.

We feel it is a fair assessment to agree with Thurnell-Read's (2012) work on men emotionally opening to one another and the emotional nature of premarital stag tours in European destinations signals the end of bromances. In his studies of stag dues he showed the importance of intimacy between the men he studied, and the value of group cohesion. So, there is perhaps some mourning, and a lot of drinking (Elliott 2019) that comes with the wedding, it may signal the end of one form of intimate relationship and the start of another.

Emotional Health and Well-Being

Given the depth of the love these men experience for their bromances, this research has other important implications concerning the impact that bromances have on men's emotional health and well-being. It is encouraging to see participants engaging on a deep emotional level with their bromances in order to better theirs, and their significant others, emotional well-being.

Certainly, it is recognized among scholars that sharing emotional and physical closeness with others serves an important purpose in maintaining one's mental well-being (Hruschka 2010; Scourfield 2005). To the extent that the bromance replaces to romance, and which focus of attention might be more advantageous, is not known. But for men without a female lover, the opportunity for male love is remarkable.

Men have traditionally relied on their romantic partners for emotional support more than their friends (Komarovsky 1974; Samaritans 2012) and have managed stress and emotional pain through exercise and outbursts, rather than talking—as women have (Hruschka 2010). However, these findings indicate a decline in this behavior, or at least it indicates that men are actively involved in emotive discussions with other men, and also manage their stress and anxieties through talking. Indeed, scholars have argued that if masculinity can recalibrate to not stigmatize dependence on others for emotional security, then men will simply feel better about themselves and more confident in managing their personal issues (Beasley 2008; Connell and Messerschmidt 2005). The findings of this research would suggest that this greater dependence on others for emotion management is already occurring.

Appropriately, Chandler (2012) calls for a more nuanced perspective of the different ways in which masculinity can now be expressed and suggests that new masculine archetypes may ultimately influence rates of suicidal behavior. The results show that indeed, these new archetypes are being esteemed.

A lack of supportive relationships is well understood as a risk factor for suicide (Samaritans 2012; Chandler 2012; Scourfield 2005), and Stefan noted two instances where men openly discussed their suicidal anxieties with bromances in the research. Moreover, two of the men commented on their ability to discuss depression with their bromances and several identified health concerns and family breakdown as issues for discussion within bromances. These therapeutic narratives are becoming increasingly common among young men (Silva 2013) and will serve them well in maintaining their emotional balance.

Accordingly, in understanding that homohysteria limits emotional disclosure and homosexual freedom (McCormack and Anderson 2014a, b), the below figure may indicate a correlation between cultural antipathy towards homosexuality, and the suicide rate of young men. Simply put, the more inclusive of homosexuality and same-sex touch that society becomes, the less likely young men will be to commit suicide.

Firstly, this is because homosexual men are more at risk of suicide (Lebson 2002) and secondly because men in an inclusive culture (post-millennial) are more inclined to express their feelings to bromances. However, this claim cannot be made definitively at this stage, and further research in establishing these links could be pioneering. We do not suggest that we will see an end to suicide among men of this age; suicide is a complex issue.

However, the trend line of decreasing suicide for men of this age in accord to decreasing homohysteria reminds us that homophobia has always hurt more than just gay men (Fig. 13.1).

In the United Kingdom, young men are nearly four times more likely to commit suicide than women of the same age (Office for National Statistics 2015), and many scholars and organizations attribute this discrepancy partly to restrictive masculine archetypes (Chandler 2012; Cleary 2012; Emslie et al. 2007; Samaritans 2012; Scourfield 2005). This research then indicates one of two things. Firstly, if young men are engaging in highly intimate emotional dialogs with other men, then any continuation in the dramatic rates of suicide in young men cannot be wholly attributed to the pressures of masculinity. Though, it appears

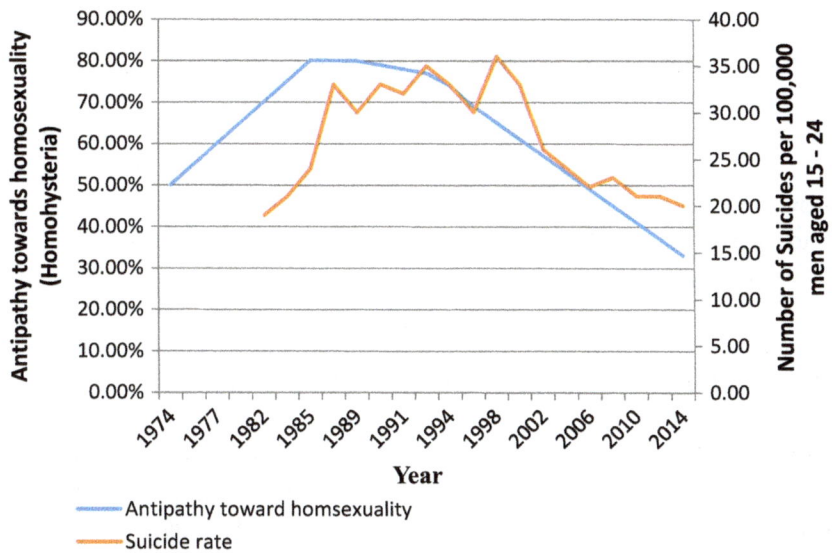

Fig. 13.1 Data collected from the Office for National Statistics (2015) overlaid with Anderson and McCormack's (2014) time series graph concerning the rise and decline of homohysteria

rates are falling in line with the decline of cultural homophobia. Alternatively, it may be that for those not involved in liberal and inclusive sports teams that espouse a bromantic culture like this sample, orthodox masculine pressures still exist to limit their lives. Indeed, one of the limitations of the inclusive masculinities literature is that most, but not all, studies are conducted on white men in university environments.

For the men in this study, however, they were so emotionally engaged with their bromances that they could express their deepest and most troublesome secrets; and often, their bromances were part of the solution. These discussions do not dominate the results in the same way as other findings, but their importance and relevance to young men's lives are likely the most significant.

We argue that this culture of inclusive masculinity, and the bromantic relationships that it permits, positively contributes towards a decreased likelihood of our participants feeling depressed and suicidal, and an increased likelihood of seeking emotional help from a bromance. For those who are dealing with depressive symptoms or social anxieties, bromances offer a way forward and a coping strategy.

This belief is not limited to men on this team alone. Viewers wanting a first-hand account of male athletes at this school discussing how adolescent males do cry, discussing the last time that they have cried and providing support for each other can be found on the video that they made with their student union on the topic. It is worth a watch.

https://www.youtube.com/watch?v=uvirUHmv3Sk.

Inexact Sexualities: "Boys Being Boys"

Anderson (2009) argued that the differences between masculinity and femininity, men and women, gay and straight, would become gradually more difficult to distinguish, as the orthodoxy of late twentieth-century male behavior diminishes. The results in this study give credence to this position, insomuch that the young men are mostly unregulated by peer and outsider expectations of how they should perform their sexuality.

As several of the men put it, they simply "wouldn't give a shit" about what others thought of their sexuality, or whether someone in the team was straight, bisexual, or gay. They recognized that onlookers might be confused about their sexual identity mainly because of the passionate making out, kissing, and cuddling they engaged in. Moreover, they believed that their interests in fashion, hairstyles, women's clothes, and fake tan raised their associations with homosexuality and were unbothered by this. This study provides an extensive response to Anderson and McCormack's (2018) recent request for further investigations into the self-presentation of heterosexuality.

A majority of the men broadly considered their own engagement in same-sex physical behaviors to justify: (1) their acceptance and approval of homosexuality and (2) their inability to identify as exclusively heterosexual, with eight of the 20 self-identifying as mostly heterosexual, and two as between mostly heterosexual and bisexual. Recognizing that these ten participants opted for a non-exclusive, inexact, and partial heterosexuality, the participants show that they understand sexuality to be more subjective, nuanced, and less culture-bound than earlier generations have considered (Summers 2004).

In Savin-Williams and Vrangalova's (2013) review of studies using this scale of sexuality, rarely have results shown more than 10% identifying as anything other than heterosexual. Supporting this, Magrath's (2016) study on slightly younger academy-level football players showed that 59 of the 60 men identified exclusively as heterosexual. Although not published, Anderson recently polled his first-year undergraduate sporting students (anonymously) at the beginning of the academic year and found that 29 of 30 identified as exclusively heterosexual.

However, in this study on bromances we found a 50% split between those who identify as exclusively heterosexual, and those who do not. This may have occurred for several reasons, such as the recognition that the researcher had witnessed the participants same-sex behaviors, the participatory and un-elitist nature of the sport, the strength of the researcher-participant rapport, and/or the uniqueness of this small sample. Further research that adopts a similar methodology and research approach would prove useful in assessing more accurately how young men define their sexuality.

The men in this study were sexually flexible in their behaviors and recognized "everyone's" capacity to behave or "act" bisexual or gay, showing an increased recognition of bisexuality as a legitimate type; an identity that is sometimes overlooked or criticized in mainstream culture (Adams et al. 2010; Anderson and McCormack 2018; Ogilvie and McCormack 2019). They discussed "pulling" their mates, having "close boyfriends," and having respect for young gay men. Accordingly, it is unsurprising that these men kissed and made out with one another with great frequency without embarrassment: having kissed other men 22 times and made out eight times on average in the past year. As opposed to recording whether men have or have not kissed another man, this is the first empirical study that has considered the annual frequency of male same-sex kissing. Furthermore, many had also engaged in other novel behaviors including cock fighting, casual nudity, ice kissing, and MMF threesomes.

The entire nature of same-sex embarrassment had been redefined by these men, best exemplified by their attitudes towards the game "gay chicken," and how they reinterpreted the rules that were previously based on humiliation. Instead, the men aspired to be "alpha male" through pushing the homosexual boundaries of the game, engaging in prolonged instances of making out and aggressive petting. For them, in several cases, it was clear that the incentive of winning outweighed any fear of homophobic associations.

When defining gay chicken, Esterline and Galupo (2013) explain that "the final act of pulling away serves to reinforce and preserve the heterosexuality of the players" (p. 117), but in opposition, these participants were little concerned by this. One participant defended many of the pseudo-sexual behaviors enacted between men in the club as simply "boys being boys." This shows a change in the young male outlook, as this term used to be deployed for justifying violence among men (Anderson 2000).

Whilst some of the behaviors and perspectives expressed in this project align with other recent studies (Peterson and Anderson 2012; Anderson et al. 2012; McCormack 2012; McCormack and Anderson 2010; Magrath 2016), the participants here extend the inclusive masculinities data to reveal more radical, nuanced, and sentimental same-sex relationships. The summation of their behaviors has an entire disregard for Anderson's (2008b) onetime rule of homosexuality that stilted the previous generation.

None of this is to imply that men are becoming more fluid in their sexual attraction; rather, they are just more flexible in their approach to heterosexuality than men have traditionally been allowed to be (Anderson and Robinson 2016; Scoats et al. 2018). The participant's narratives coincide with Dean's (2014) conclusion that in a post-closeted culture, the presumption of heterosexuality is no longer appropriate. The expression of femininity and embracing of gendered and sexual behaviors that were not long ago taboo have set this generation of young, heterosexual men apart, a form of social change unique to millennials and the generation that comes after them.

The participant's self-assessment of their sexuality both expands and limits our knowledge of the concept. The gradual rationalization and classification of sexuality over the past century have legitimized the status of both heterosexual and homosexual identities. However, this simplistic and binate approach has also served to limit our capacity to understand the mosaic of embedded complexities and nuances in the experience of attraction and desire, companionship, and love. Pointedly, the sexual and relational complexities illustrated by the participants in this study denote uncharted territory that challenges the status-quo underpinning many existing, but outdated, scholastic works (Kurzban et al. 2015; Lewis et al. 2015).

Renovating Lad Culture

Some recent research articles, highlighted in the media, have described the culture of men's sports teams in UK universities as being misogynistic, homophobic, and criminal (Jackson, and Sundaram 2015; Phipps and Young 2015); popularly nominated as existing in a "lad culture." As is often the way with mainstream media outlets, there is a preference to focus on negative and antagonistic news stories. We argue that lad culture, as described in the media (BBC 2014) and elsewhere (National Union of Students 2012), has wrongly been portrayed as a norm among university sports teams.

Literature that describes lad culture is often accompanied by a wealth of data on sexual assaults and rapes, without making the necessary empirical connections, yet implying that there is a correlation (National Union of Students 2012). This research project, however, alongside much of the inclusive masculinities data, shows that men's university sports teams can be far more inclusive, respectful, and homo-friendly than often portrayed.

This is not to suggest that sexual assault from males to females does not happen. This is not to suggest that the dodgeball men are puritanical. What we are saying, however, is that these men have redefined lad culture. They are doing the bravado, and hypermasculinity in certain contexts, without doing homophobia, and without intentionally trying to denigrate other males. They do not accept the mistreatment of females. Recognizing this is an important part of further normalizing the behavior and combatting the sexist behavior that remains. (Roberts 2018; Ralph and Roberts 2020).

We thus deploy the concept of the "Bromantic Culture" in this study to illustrate that there is a counternarrative to lad culture, one that receives less media interest but is far more widespread among the male university community. We highlight that, hidden within the lad culture research, Phipps and Young (2015) state:

> … many university men also disidentify with laddism or disapprove of it entirely as a bogus performance of machismo which masks anxiety. (Dempster 2011; Anderson and McGuire 2010)

In other words, these aggressive "lad" groups are minority cultures, but may negatively affect a majority of people. As research has started to document, the focus on specific groups of boys and men at the expense of others can create a partial read of boy's and men's lives (see Roberts 2018). Yes, undisputedly, there have been instances where frenzied groups of young men have cherished harassing and offensive behaviors in their teams. However, the continuity of love and companionship expressed between the men in this study highlights an alternative inclusive culture (McCormack 2011, 2012; Anderson 2009, 2014; Ripley et al. 2012; Adams 2011; Magrath et al. 2013).

The bromantic culture existing among the participants in this study was characterized by:

(1) A unity of association that makes available trust and friendship between all members
(2) A lack of judgment and homophobia
(3) The valuing of humor, diversity, and inclusion, over athleticism and aggression
(4) A condemnation of bullying
(5) The absence of women
(6) The privileging of bromance over romance.

Whilst the men in this study did engage in excessive alcohol consumption and risk-taking, whilst they performed naked displays of homoerotic activities, these behaviors mostly occurred without the presence of women nor did they did not stray into criminal, homophobic, or misogynistic behaviors. They instead esteemed positive attitudes towards women and homosexuality.

The fundamental difference between bromantic and lad cultures, between positive and negative social implications, is that bromantic cultures adopt more elements of inclusive masculinity than lad cultures. Indeed, some of the men identified that rugby and football teams they were a part of had more strict, aggressive, socially exclusive, and hegemonic hierarchies; sports that have been traditionally associated with lad culture (though it should be noted that inclusive masculinity has been widely observed in these settings also).

This is not to say that more mainstream and traditionally masculine sports operate under hegemonic masculinity, but that they may be less inclusive than the participants in this study; most likely owing to the more competitive and elitist nature of these sports (Magrath 2016).

Cross-Sex Socialization and Regulation

The bromantic culture observed and described in this study exemplifies how more inclusive, liberal, and tactile behaviors between men are being incorporated into everyday masculinities. Whilst these behaviors represent better social outcomes when measured against late twentieth-century masculinity, they may not altogether benefit cross-sex relations.

The results show a clear privileging of same-sex friendships over cross-sex relations, and there was no definitive indication that the participants increased appreciation for femininity strengthened their relationships with women. On the contrary, the ability to emote, confide, and cuddle with male friends may reduce the men's appetite for interaction with women, and intensify the exclusivity of their male friendships. Accordingly, Mehta and Strough (2009) suggest that the reinforcement and strengthening of homosocial bonds contribute towards the devaluing and discouraging of cross-sex socialization. Furthermore, the emotion and femininity expressed by the men in this study were said to be unattractive to women.

We propose that, since the late twentieth century, through the decline of homophobia and the rise of inclusive masculinity, this study shows that there have been two binary shifts in the way that masculinity (and thus male behavior) is regulated. Firstly, participants have shown that women have a greater influence than previously observed in regulating and maintaining orthodoxy in men. This is best exemplified by the way in which participants felt compelled to perform stoic and tough masculinities for their girlfriends. As one participant acutely summarized, "No girl is going to fuck a cry-baby." Whatever the research may or may not say about the type of men females desire, these men feel that they can be less-masculine with their bromances than their romances.

Where previously male peers would have regulated one's masculine orthodoxy (Curry 2000; Kellner 1991), women here are increasingly perceived as enforcers of older macho ideals. Indeed, the only person not willing to take part in the research interviews did so out of fear that their girlfriend would find out about their same-sex interactions and disapprove.

Secondly, whilst many men of the 1980s would have entered into cross-sex romantic relationships to secure their socially perceived heterosexual identity (Anderson 2010), young men are now discouraged from engaging in romantic relationships and pressured by their bromances to remain single. The social importance of early romantic commitment has consequently declined, in trend with decreasing homophobia, and quantitative data on the declining number of marriages in the United Kingdom supports this conclusion (Arnett 2004; Office for National Statistics 2012, 2016). Indeed, the intense and hostile nature of jealousy among bromances secures the eventual termination of such romantic relationships, as bromances almost always take precedent.

We highlight that the degradation of heterosexual romances is new to this research, and we cannot generalize that this would occur outside of this setting. We suspect that men having bromances who are not part of a close community, like the team studied, would be permitted more social freedom to engage in romance alongside bromance, but that in this cohesive community pressure ran strong to engage more time with the boys, than their girlfriends.

Gender Equality

The bromance exists because cultural homophobia has waned. The existence of inclusive masculinities, and the emotional and physically tactile relationships exhibited by men in bromantic relationships are domain to their sex, alone. We make no claims about whether the bromance will help unseat patriarchy or promote it. Apart from highlighting variances between romantic relationships with women, and bromantic relationships with men, this is not a treatise on gender equality more fully.

That being said, it seems salient that the bromance promotes equality within the male gender. Whereas masculinity used to be predicated on depriving other males of cultural virtue through the assessment of femininity and assignment of homophobia in response, the adolescent male culture we analyze is not predicated as such. Instead, males look to bond with, not castigate other males. We are not arguing that this is a utopia for all males. But the cultural change we report upon here certainly must be evaluated as promoting the health and well-being, as well as the joie de vivre, of young men in this culture.

We like to think that this might also have some positive impact on the lived experiences of women. Fundamentally, however, work done under the umbrella of Inclusive Masculinity Theory is not about equality between the sexes. So, we leave that for others to research, and hopefully not just speculate about.

Generalizability

Our intention with this book is not to generalize our findings to all adolescent males. A study of thirty people is intended to explore processes rather than to make grand statements of generalizability. It is for this reason that we put the *dynamics* of a bromance under examination, as we find existing in this setting. We do not make claims that it exists everywhere. We do not make claims that homohysteria has decreased enough across all institutions of higher education to enable the bromance to flourish in the first place. Equally, we do not make claims that it would operate precisely the same in another arena.

Conversely, we do not maintain that our results are the outcome of a quirky sample and location, either. We instead highlight that our findings exist within a very large bevy of research which shows that cultural homohysteria is diminishing, and that boys and adolescent males are adopting softer, more gay-friendly (inclusive) attitudes. Other qualitative work finds this, too. For example, Morales and Caffyn-Parsons (2017) show a very similar mechanism of emotional intimacy at play with their study of high school distance runners in America. What this tells us is that these bromantic behaviors are likely to exist elsewhere, perhaps in many social locations. More research needs to be done.

Finally, this manuscript waited for four years before publication. This was to assure that all members of the team investigated had graduated from university to further protect anonymity. In the meantime, it was updated with relevant research.

However, part of this time covered Covid-19 and its subsequent lockdown. Thus, in the final day of work on this manuscript, November of 2021, Professor Anderson anonymously polled 30 of 31 of his fresher/freshman/first-year males to his sporting degree at his university. He wanted to know if two years of lockdown ended the development of bromances for boys who would have been 16 and 17 (crucial adolescent years for friendship development). In asking these questions only 7 weeks into their university experience, the men will not have had time to develop bromances at university, either. The results were as follows.

- 27 identified as exclusively heterosexual, 2 as mostly heterosexual, and one as bisexual
- 29 indicated no intolerance of male homosexuality, 1 indicated minor intolerance
- 23 said that they have vocalized or texted "I love you" to a male friend to 4 or more friends, 6 had done so to 1–3 friends, and 1 had not yet done this.
- 15 had 4 or more bromances, and 15 had 1–3 bromances.
- 22 had cuddled with a boy, 8 had not
- 19 had kissed a boy, 11 had not.

These statistics are drawn from adolescent boys who represent a wide swath of sports. Given that these men have come from around the country the data strongly suggests that having bromances and engaging in the types of behaviors we spell out in this book, is not only commonplace, but is the norm in youth culture. Whilst this data lacks nuance, it certainly highlights that the bromance has risen.

Finally, on the same final day of editing this book, Professor Anderson gave two interviews, one in Germany and the other in Brazil. Both reporters wanted to discuss the operation of the bromance, because they are happening in those locales as well. Thus, the bromance is not germane to the United Kingdom alone.

Theoretical Implications

The findings of this research have important implications in supporting and challenging aspects of leading theories of masculinity, developed since the mid-twentieth century. For most of the late twentieth century, and indeed the brief history of masculinities studies, Hegemonic Masculinity Theory was mainstreamed in academic thought as the leading model for understanding the operation of masculinity (Demetriou 2001; Moller 2007).

Raewyn Connell (1987, 1995) contended that a hegemonic form of masculinity can exist; one that is "culturally exalted above all others" (1995, p. 77), of which its foremost intent was to legitimize men's patriarchal dominion over women. She stressed however that different forms of masculinity could exist simultaneously, but in a stratified social order that glorifies only one form: the hegemon. Particularly during the 1980s and 1990s, it was widely understood that gay men were oppressed victims of the hegemonic system, at the bottom of this hierarchy, and the athletic jock embodied the hegemonic ideal (Consalvo et al. 2013; Anderson 2014).

Whilst the theory has been widely deployed and celebrated within the late twentieth and early twenty-first-century literature, contemporary scholars have become increasingly skeptical of applying Connell's work in a culture where the oppressive binaries of 1980s culture have been abandoned; a culture where masculinities have become more laterally situated, harmonized, and inclusive (Adams 2011; Anderson 2014; McCormack 2012; Ripley et al. 2012).

Critics agree that Connell's theory consistently fails to recognize the more nuanced and complex dynamics of masculinity and male behavior (Beasley 2008; Howson 2006; Roberts 2018). Anderson (2009), among others (Clements and Field 2014), argues that whilst recognizing that Hegemonic Masculinity Theory is applicable to homohysteric cultures, the theory is incompatible with postmillennial Anglo-American cultures. Simply, the theory fails to recognize how improved attitudes towards homosexuality lead to the leveling of masculine hierarchies.

In response to a social evolution of male liberality and same-sex intimacy, the subject cause of a decline in homohysteria, Anderson (2009) developed Inclusive Masculinity Theory. The theory argues that owing to decreasing rates of homophobia, and the consequent expansion of political and social landscapes for gays and lesbians, young men are altogether esteeming more inclusive and emotive masculine identities than previously observed (McCormack and Anderson 2014a, b).

The theory also articulates that a corresponding increase in cultural homophobia would see the opposite. Anderson and McCormack (2014a) explain that cultural attitudes towards homosexuality are intricately linked with constructions of masculinity, and only Inclusive Masculinity Theory is able to "account for decreasing homophobia since the second industrial revolution" (McCormack and Anderson 2014b, p. 153).

The young men in this study expressed strong support, acceptance, and admiration (in light of the stigma they perceived to exist among older generations and religious institutions) for homosexuality. In addition to voicing their support, they were also quick to condemn homophobia, and welcomed the prospect of a fellow teammate coming out as gay, as observed in other recent studies on a similar demographic (Magrath 2016). The evidence of espousing pro-gay attitudes among these men directly coincides with Anderson's (2009) basis of Inclusive Masculinity Theory. In opposition to Connell's proclamation (1987, 1995), the evidence here shows that gay men are no longer marginalized under a hegemonic structure, but instead are recognized and respected by peers.

Importantly, several of the men identified gay men outside of the club that they were in a bromance with, saying that they are not concerned about one's sexuality when it comes to the intimacies of bromances. Whereas gay men were heavily restricted in their social mobility only three decades ago (Meyer 1995), and culturally prohibited from having friendships with heterosexual men (Nardi and Sherrod 1994; Rubin 1985; Weinstock 1998), these men's inclusive attitudes exemplify the liberality in male relations that is permissible under inclusive masculinity.

Inclusive Masculinity Theory regards the decline of homohysteria as a catalyst for improved emotional and physical relations between men. Simply, men are permitted to express more traditionally feminine behaviors that would have otherwise previously coded them as gay (Anderson 2009). Indeed, this study has brought to light a wealth of detailed data to suggest that men are engaged in highly emotional and physical exchanges, expressly within their bromances.

Reflecting the findings of other recent inquiries that support the inclusive masculinities prognosis (Adams 2011; Magrath 2016; McCormack 2012; Roberts, 2018), the men in this study possessed great emotional intelligence and depth when talking to their bromances. Many were able to discuss important issues in their lives through therapeutic narratives (Silva 2013), such as the separation of parents, death of a family member, and even suicidal thoughts. This extends beyond men "just" being emotional in front of one another or talking about their feelings; the bromance has provided a practical utility and coping space for young men dealing with adverse life events.

The data also emphasizes that physical intimacy is progressing to a more radical level, and more frequently, than recorded in other comprehensive literature on inclusive masculinities (McCormack 2012; Anderson 2014; Ralph and Roberts 2020). Namely, passionate and extended kissing in bromances was deeply entrenched as a regular and important social symbol to represent the closeness experienced in the relationship, and this was never confused or conflated with homosexuality. The intense and sexualized performance of these kisses, set against a backdrop of peers with equal esteem of the bro-kiss, is testament to the inapplicability of the onetime rule of homosexuality (Anderson 2008b) in an inclusive culture (Anderson et al. 2012, 2019; Drummond et al. 2014).

Anderson (2014) concludes that young straight men engaging in physically tactile behaviors is a new phenomenon, and this study has answered his request for more research to determine the legitimacy of his early findings. Yet, many other more novel behaviors including the popular desire for MMF threesomes, a lack of stigma around self-administered anal pleasure (Hammers and Sheff 2011; Wignall et al. 2020), cock fighting, highly sexualized games of gay chicken, and dick licking expand our understanding of what same-sex behaviors are increasingly permitted in, at least, this team sport culture.

Indeed, very recent research has shown that varied numbers of young heterosexual men of a similar demographic engage, and aspire to engage in, MMF threesomes (Scoats et al. 2018) and self-anal pleasuring (Branfman et al. 2017). This research shows confidence in these new findings.

Certainly, since the inception of Inclusive Masculinity Theory in 2009, research has tended to focus on the light touch elements of kissing and cuddling. Participants in this study contribute their more radical perspectives to this expanding field, showing that whilst light touch behaviors had symbolic significance in their relationships, more humorous and radical behaviors were also allowed. No other theory we know of can make sense of these data.

References

Adams, A. (2011). Josh wears pink cleats: Inclusive masculinity on the soccer field. *Journal of Homosexuality*, 58(5), 579–596.

Adams, A., and Anderson, E. (2012). Exploring the relationship between homosexuality and sport among the teammates of a small, Midwestern Catholic college soccer team. *Sport, Education and Society*, 17(3), 347–363.

Adams, A., Anderson, E., and McCormack, M. (2010). Establishing and challenging masculinity: The influence of gendered discourses in organized sport. *Journal of Language and Social Psychology*, 29(3), 278–300.

Ahmed, S. (2013). *The cultural politics of emotion.* New York: Routledge
Anderson, E. (2000). *Trailblazing: The true story of America's first openly gay track coach.* New York: Alyson Publications.
Anderson, E. (2005a). *In the game: Gay athletes and the cult of masculinity.* New York: University of New York Press.
Anderson, E. (2008a). Inclusive masculinity in a fraternal setting. *Men and Masculinities,* 10(5), 604–620.
Anderson, E. (2008b). "Being masculine is not about who you sleep with....:" Heterosexual athletes contesting masculinity and the one-time rule of homosexuality. *Sex Roles, 58*(1–2), 104–115.
Anderson, E. (2009). *Inclusive masculinity: The changing nature of masculinities.* New York: Routledge
Anderson, E. (2010). *Sport, theory and social problems: A critical introduction.* New York: Routledge.
Anderson, E. (2012a). *The monogamy gap: Men, love, and the reality of cheating.* Oxford University Press
Anderson, E. (2012b). Inclusive masculinity in a physical education setting. *Journal of Boyhood Studies, 6*(1–2), 151–165.
Anderson, E. (2014). *21st Century Jocks: Sporting Men and Contemporary Heterosexuality.* New York: Macmillan.
Anderson, E., Adams, A., and Rivers, I. (2012). "I kiss them because I love them": The emergence of heterosexual men kissing in British institutes of education. *Archives of sexual behaviour, 41*(2), 421–430.
Anderson, E., and McGuire, R. (2010). Inclusive masculinity theory and the gendered politics of men's rugby. *Journal of Gender Studies, 19*(3), 249–261
Anderson, E., and McCormack, M. (2014). Homohysteria: Definitions, context and intersectionality. *Sex Roles, 71*(3), 152–158.
Anderson, E., and McCormack, M. (2018). Inclusive masculinity theory: Overview, reflection and refinement. *Journal of Gender Studies, 27*(5), 547–561.
Anderson, E., and Robinson, S. (2016). Men's sexual flexibility. In Seidman. S ad Fisher, N. (Ed.), *Introducing the New Sexuality Studies.* New York: Routledge. Pp. 250–258
Anderson, E., Ripley, M., and McCormack, M. (2019). A mixed-method study of same-sex kissing among college-attending heterosexual men in the US. *Sexuality and Culture, 23*(1), 26–44.
Arnett, J. (2004). *A longer road to adulthood.* New York: Oxford University Press.

BBC, 2014. Universities ignoring laddish culture, says NUS leader [Online]. Available at: http://www.bbc.co.uk/news/education-29176844.

Beasley, C. (2008). Rethinking hegemonic masculinity in a globalizing world. *Men and masculinities*, *11*(1), 86-103.

Bogle, K. (2008). *Hooking up: Sex, dating, and relationships on campus.* New York: New York University Press.

Boyle, E. (2008). *Building a body for governance: Embodying power in the shifting media images of Arnold Schwarzenegger.* Illinois: Human Kinetics.

Branfman, J., Stiritz, S. and Anderson, E. (2017) Relaxing the Straight-Male Anus: Decreasing Homohysteria around Anal Eroticism. *Sexualities.* https://doi.org/10.1177/1363460716678560

Bush, A., Anderson, E., and Carr, S. (2012). The declining existence of men's homophobia in British sport. *Journal for the Study of Sports and Athletes in Education*, *6*(1), 107—120.

Cancian, F. M. (1986). The feminization of love. *Signs: Journal of Women in Culture and Society*, *11*(4), 692–709.

Chandler, A. (2012). Exploring the role of masculinities in suicidal behavior. *Men, Suicide and Society*, *111*.

Cleary, A. (2012). Suicidal action, emotional expression, and the performance of masculinities." *Social Science and Medicine*, *74*(4), 498–505.

Clements, B., and Field, C. (2014). Public opinion toward homosexuality and gay rights in Great Britain. *Public Opinion Quarterly*, *78*(2), 523–547.

Collins, W., and Sroufe, L. (1999). Capacity for intimate relationships. In W. Furman., B. Brown., and C. Feiring (Ed.), *The development of romantic relationships in adolescence.* Cambridge: Cambridge University Press. Pp. 125–147.

Connell, R. (1987). *Gender and power: Society, the person and sexual politics.* Berkeley: University of California Press.

Connell, R. (1989). Cool guys, swots and wimps: the interplay of masculinity and education. *Oxford review of education*, *15*(3), 291–203.

Connell, R. (1995). *Masculinities.* Berkeley: University of California Press.

Connell, R., and Messerschmidt, J. (2005). Hegemonic masculinity: Rethinking the concept. *Gender and Society*, *19*(6), 829–859.

Consalvo, M., Mitgutsch, K., and Stein, A. (2013). *Sports videogames.* New York: Routledge.

Curry, T. (2000). Booze and bar fights: A journey to the dark side of college athletics. In McKay, J., Messner, M., and Sabo, D. (Ed.), *Masculinities, gender relations and sport.* London: Sage. Pp. 162–175.

Dean, J. (2014). *Straights: Heterosexuality in post-closeted culture*. New York: New York University Press.

Demetriou, D. (2001). Connell's concept of hegemonic masculinity: A critique. *Theory and society*, *30*(3), 337–361.

Dempster, S. (2011). I drink, therefore I'm man: gender discourses, alcohol and the construction of British undergraduate masculinities. *Gender and Education*, *23*(5), 635-653.

Dermott, E. (2008). Intimate fatherhood: A sociological analysis. New York: Routledge.

Diamond, L. (2003). What does sexual orientation orient? A bio-behavioural model distinguishing romantic love and sexual desire. *Psychological Review*, *110*(1), 173–192.

Drummond, M., Filiault, S., Anderson, E., and Jeffries, D. (2014). Homosocial intimacy among Australian undergraduate men. *Journal of Sociology*, *51*(3), 643–656.

Dunivin, K. (1994). Military culture: Change and continuity. *Armed Forces and Society*, *20*(4), 531–547.

Elliott, K. (2019). Negotiations between progressive and 'traditional' expressions of masculinity among young Australian men. *Journal of Sociology*, *55*(1), 108–123.

Emslie, C., Ridge, D., Ziebland, S., and Hunt, K. (2007). Exploring men's and women's experiences of depression and engagement with health professionals: more similarities than differences? A qualitative interview study. *BioMed Central Family Practice*, *8*(1), 43–61.

Esterline, K., and Galupo, M. (2013). "Drunken curiosity" and "gay chicken": Gender differences in same-sex performativity. *Journal of Bisexuality*, *13*(1), 106–121.

Fisher, H. (1998). Lust, attraction and attachment in mammalian reproduction. *Human Nature*, *9*(1), 23–52

Fisher, H. (2004). *Why we love: the nature and chemistry of romantic love*. New York: Henry Holt and Company.

Giroux, H. (2001). *Public spaces and Private Lives: Beyond the culture of cynicism*. Boston: Rowman and Littlefield Publishers.

Grello, C., Welsh, D., and Harper, M. (2006). No strings attached: The nature of casual sex in college students. *Journal of sex research*, *43*(3), 255–267.

Gutterman, S. (1994). Postmodernism and the interrogation of masculinity. In Brod, H. and Kaufman, M. (ed.), *Theorizing masculinities*. London: Sage Publications. Pp. 219–238

Hagestad, G., and Call, V. (2007). Pathways to childlessness a life course perspective. *Journal of Family Issues, 28*(10), 1338–1361.

Hammers, C., and Sheff, E. (2011). The privilege of perversities: Race, class, and education among polyamorists and kinksters. *Psychology and Sexuality,2*(3), 198–223.

Hilber, C., and Vermeulen, W. (2016). The impact of supply constraints on house prices in England. *The Economic Journal, 126*(591), 358–405.

Howard, H. (2012). A confederacy of bachelors. *New York Times*, August 3.

Howson, R. (2006). *Challenging hegemonic masculinity* (Vol. 10). New York: Routledge.

Hruschka, D. (2010). Friendship: Development, ecology, and evolution of a relationship (Vol. 5). Berkeley: *University of California Press*.

Jackson, C., and Sundaram, V. (2015). *Is 'lad culture' a problem in higher education? Exploring the perspectives of staff working in UK universities.* In International Conference on Research into Higher Education. Pp. 1–8.

Johansson, T. (2007). *The transformation of sexuality: Gender and identity in contemporary youth culture.* Hampshire UK: Ashgate.

Kellner, D. (1991). Film, politics, and ideology: Reflections on Hollywood film in the age of Reagan. *Velvet Light Trap, 27*, 9–24.

Kellner, D. (2003). *Media Culture: Cultural Studies, Identity and Politics between the Modern.* New York: Routledge

Kimmel, M. (1994). *Manhood in America.* New York: Free Press.

Komarovsky, M. (1974). Patterns of self-disclosure of male undergraduates. *Journal of Marriage and the Family, 36*(4), 677–686.

Kurzban, R., Burton-Chellew, M., and West, S. (2015). The evolution of altruism in humans. *Annual Review of Psychology, 66*(3), 575–599.

Lebson, M. (2002). Suicide among homosexual youth. *Journal of Homosexuality, 42*(4), 107–117.

Lewis, D., Al-Shawaf, L., Russell., E., and Buss, D. (2015). Friends and happiness: An evolutionary perspective on friendship. *Friendship and Happiness, 37*.

Lusher, D., and Robins, G. (2009). Hegemonic and other masculinities in local social contexts. *Men and Masculinities, 11*(4), 387–423.

Mac an Ghaill, M. (1994). *Making of men.* Philadelphia: Open University Press.

Magrath, R. (2016). *Inclusive masculinities in contemporary football: Men in the beautiful game.* Routledge.

Magrath, R., and Scoats, R. (2019). Young men's friendships: inclusive masculinities in a post-university setting. *Journal of Gender Studies, 28*(1), 45–56

Magrath, R., Anderson., and Roberts, S. (2013). On the Door- Step of Equality: Attitudes Toward Gay Athletes Among Academy Level Footballers. *International Review for the Sociology of Sport, 50*(7), 804–821.

McCormack, M. (2011). Mapping the terrain of homosexually-themed language. *Journal of homosexuality, 58*(5), 664–679.

McCormack, M. (2012). *The declining significance of homophobia: How teenage boys are redefining masculinity and heterosexuality.* New York: Oxford University Press.

McCormack, M., and Anderson, E. (2010). The re-production of homosexually-themed discourse in educationally-based organised sport. *Culture, Health and Sexuality, 12*(8), 913–927.

McCormack, M., and Anderson, E. (2014a). The influence of declining homophobia on men's gender in the United States: An argument for the study of homohysteria. *Sex Roles, 71*(3-4), 109–120.

McCormack, M., and Anderson, E. (2014b). Homohysteria: Definitions, context and intersectionality. *Sex Roles, 71*(3-4), 152–158.

Mehta, C., and Strough, J. (2009). Sex segregation in friendships and normative contexts across the life span. *Developmental Review, 29*(3), 201–220.

Meyer, I. (1995). Minority stress and mental health in gay men. *Journal of Health and Social Behavior, 36*, 38–56

Moller, M. (2007) Exploiting patterns: A critique of hegemonic masculinity. *Journal of Gender Studies, 16*(3), 263–276.

Morales, L., and Caffyn-Parsons, E. (2017). "I Love You, Guys": A Study of Inclusive Masculinities among High School Cross-Country Runners. *Boyhood Studies, 10*(1), 66–87.

Morin, S., and Garfinkle, E. (1978). Male homophobia. *Journal of Social Issues, 34*(1), 29–47.

Morman, M, Schrodt P, Tornes, M. (2013). Self-disclosure mediates the effects of gender orientation and homophobia on the relationship quality of male same-sex friendships. *Journal of Social and Personal Relationships, 30*(5), 582–605.

Nardi, P., and Sherrod, D. (1994). Friendship in the lives of gay men and lesbians. *Journal of Social and Personal relationships, 11*(2), 185–199.

National Union of Students. (2012). That's what she said: Women students' experiences of 'lad culture' in higher education [Online].

Available at: https://www.nus.org.uk/Global/Campaigns/That's%20what%20she%20said%20full%20report%20Final%20web.pdf.

Office for National Statistics. (2012). *Marriages in England and Wales (provisional)* [Online]. Available at: http://www.ons.gov.uk/ons/dcp171778_366530.pdf.

Office for National Statistics. (2015). Age-specific suicide rates (with 95 per cent confidence limits): By sex and five-year age group, England and Wales, 1981 to 2014 Registrations [Online]. Available at: http://www.ons.gov.uk/ons/about-ons/business-transparency/freedom-of-information/what-can-i-request/published-ad-hoc-data/health/october-2015/age-specific-suicides-rates-by-sex-and-five-year-age-group--england-and-wales.xls.

Office for National Statistics. (2016). Population estimates by marital status and living arrangements in England and Wales: 2002 to 2015 [Online]. Available at: https://www.ons.gov.uk/peoplepopulationandcommunity/populationandmigration/populationestimates/bulletins/populationestimatesbymaritalstatusandlivingarrangements/2002to2015.

Ogilvie, M. F., and McCormack, M. (2019). Conner Mertens and the muted media coverage of the first openly bisexual NCAA American Football Player. In *LGBT athletes in the sports media* (pp. 189–206). Cham: Palgrave Macmillan.

Peterson, G., and Anderson, E. (2012). The performance of softer masculinities on the university dance floor. *The Journal of Men's Studies, 20*(1), 3–15.

Phipps, A., and Young, I. (2015). Neoliberalization and lad cultures in higher education. *Sociology, 49*(2), 305–322.

Pleck, J. (1975). Issues for the men's movement: Summer, 1975. *Changing Men: A Newsletter for Men against Sexism*, 21–23.

Ralph, B., and Roberts, S. (2020). One small step for man: Change and continuity in perceptions and enactments of homosocial intimacy among young Australian men. *Men and Masculinities, 23*(1), 83-103.

Ripley, M., Anderson, E., McCormack, M., and Rockett, B. (2012). Heteronormativity in the university classroom novelty attachment and content substitution among gay-friendly students. *Sociology of Education, 85*(2), 121–130.

Roberts, S. (2018). *Young working-class men in transition*. Routledge.

Rotundo, A. (1989). Romantic Friendship: Male intimacy and middle-class youth in the northern United States, 1800 – 1900. *Journal of Social History, 23*(1), 1–25.

Rubin, L. (1985) *Just Friends*, New York: Harper and Row.

Ryan, C., and Jethá, C. (2010). Sex at dawn. *The prehistoric origins of modern sexuality,* New York.
Samaritans. (2012). *Suicide and Society: Why disadvantaged men in mid-life die by suicide.* Samaritans: London
Savin-Williams, R. (2005). *The new gay teenager* (Vol. 3). Cambridge: Harvard University Press.
Savin-Williams, R., and Vrangalova, Z. (2013). Mostly heterosexual as a distinct sexual orientation group: A systematic review of the empirical evidence. *Developmental Review, 33*(1), 58–88.
Schwartz, P., and Young, L. (2009). Sexual satisfaction in committed relationships. *Sexuality Research and Social Policy, 6*(1), 1–17.
Scoats, R., Joseph, L. J., and Anderson, E. (2018). 'I don't mind watching him cum': Heterosexual men, threesomes, and the erosion of the one-time rule of homosexuality. *Sexualities, 21*(1–2), 30–48
Scourfield, J. (2005). Suicidal masculinities. *Sociological Research Online, 10*(2).
Silva, J. (2013). *Coming up short: Working-class adulthood in an age of uncertainty.* Oxford: Oxford University Press.
Summers, C. (2004). *The queer encyclopaedia of music, dance, and musical theatre.* New Jersey: Cleis Press.
Thurnell-Read, T. (2012). What happens on tour: The premarital stag tour, homosocial bonding, and male friendship. *Men and Masculinities, 15*(3), 249-270.
Tognoli, J. (1980). Male friendship and intimacy across the life span. *Family Relations,* 273–279.
Weinstock, J. (1998). Lesbian, gay, bisexual, transgendered friendships in adulthood. In Patterson, C., and D'Augelli, A (ed.), *Lesbian, Gay, and Bisexual Identities in Families: Psychological Perspectives.* New York: Oxford University Press. Pp. 122–153.
White, A., and Hobson, M. (2015). Teachers' stories: Physical education teachers' constructions and experiences of masculinity within secondary school physical education. *Sport, Education and Society,* 1–14.
Wignall, L., Scoats, R., Anderson, E., and Morales, L. (2020). A qualitative study of heterosexual men's attitudes toward and practices of receiving anal stimulation. *Culture, Health and Sexuality, 22*(6), 675-689.

References

Acker, J. (1990). Hierarchies, jobs, bodies: A theory of gendered organizations. *Gender and Society, 4*(2), 139–158.

Adams, A. (2011). Josh wears pink cleats: Inclusive Masculinity on the Soccer Field. *Journal of Homosexuality, 58*(5), 579–596.

Adams, A., and Anderson, E. (2012). Exploring the relationship between homosexuality and sport among the teammates of a small, Midwestern Catholic college soccer team. *Sport, Education and Society, 17*(3), 347–363.

Adams, A., Anderson, E., and McCormack, M. (2010). Establishing and challenging masculinity: The influence of gendered discourses in organized sport. *Journal of Language and Social Psychology, 29*(3), 278–300.

Adler, P., and Adler, P. (1998). *Peer power: Preadolescent culture and identity.* New Brunswick, NJ: Rutgers University Press.

Afary, J. (2009). *Sexual politics in modern Iran.* Cambridge: Cambridge University Press.

Aggleton, P., Davies, P., Davies, P., and Hart, G. (1992). *AIDS: Rights, risk, and reason* (Preface). London: Taylor & Francis.

Ahmed, S. (2013). *The cultural politics of emotion.* New York: Routledge

Allan, E., and Madden, M. (2008). *Hazing in view: College students at risk. Initial findings from the national study of student hazing* [Online].

Available at: http://www.stophazing.org/wp-content/uploads/2014/06/hazing_in_view_web1.pdf.

Allan, G. (1989). *Friendship: Developing a sociological perspective*. Boulder: Westview Press.

Allan, G. (1996). *Kinship and friendship in Modern Britain*. Oxford: London.

Anderson, E. (2000). *Trailblazing: The true story of America's first openly gay track coach*. New York: Alyson Publications.

Anderson, E. (2002). Openly gay athletes: Contesting hegemonic masculinity in a homophobic environment. *Gender McCormack and Anderson 2014a,b society*, 16(6), 860–877.

Anderson, E. (2005a). *In the game: Gay athletes and the cult of masculinity*. New York: University of New York Press.

Anderson, E. (2005b). Orthodox and inclusive masculinity: Competing masculinities among heterosexual men in a feminized terrain. *Sociological Perspectives*, 48(3), 337–355.

Anderson, E. (2008a). Inclusive masculinity in a fraternal setting. *Men and Masculinities*, 10(5), 604–620.

Anderson, E. (2008b). "Being masculine is not about who you sleep with...:" Heterosexual athletes contesting masculinity and the one-time rule of homosexuality. *Sex Roles*, 58(1–2), 104–115.

Anderson, E. (2009). *Inclusive masculinity: The changing nature of masculinities*. New York: Routledge

Anderson, E. (2010). *Sport, theory and social problems: A critical introduction*. New York: Routledge.

Anderson, E. (2011). Masculinities and sexualities in sport and physical cultures: Three decades of evolving research. *Journal of Homosexuality*, 58(5), 565–578.

Anderson, E. (2012a). *The monogamy gap: Men, love, and the reality of cheating*. Oxford University Press

Anderson, E. (2012b). Inclusive masculinity in a physical education setting. *Journal of Boyhood Studies*, 6(1–2), 151–165.

Anderson, E. (2013). Adolescent masculinity in an age of decreased homohysteria. *Boyhood Studies*, 7(1), 79–93.

Anderson, E. (2014). *21st Century Jocks: Sporting Men and Contemporary Heterosexuality*. New York: Macmillan.

Anderson, E. (2015). Assessing the sociology of sport: On changing masculinities and homophobia. *International Review for the Sociology of Sport*, 50(4–5), 363–367.

Anderson, E., Adams, A., and Rivers, I. (2012). "I kiss them because I love them": The emergence of heterosexual men kissing in British institutes of education. *Archives of Sexual Behaviour, 41*(2), 421–430.

Anderson, E., and Fidler, C. (2018). Elderly British men: Homohysteria and orthodox masculinities. *Journal of Gender Studies, 27*(3), 248–259.

Anderson, E., and Magrath, R. (2019). *Men and masculinities.* Routledge.

Anderson, E., and McCormack, M. (2014). Homohysteria: Definitions, Context and Intersectionality. *Sex Roles, 71*(3), 152–158

Anderson, E., and McCormack, M. (2015). Cuddling and Spooning Heteromasculinity and Homosocial Tactility among Student-athletes. *Men and Masculinities, 18*(2), 214–230.

Anderson, E., and McCormack, M. (2016). *The Changing Dynamics of Bisexual Men's Lives.* New York, NY. Springer

Anderson, E., and McCormack, M. (2018). Inclusive masculinity theory: Overview, reflection and refinement. *Journal of Gender Studies, 27*(5), 547–561.

Anderson, E., and McGuire, R. (2010). Inclusive masculinity theory and the gendered politics of men's rugby. *Journal of Gender Studies, 19*(3), 249–261

Anderson, E., and Robinson, S. (2016). Men's sexual flexibility. In Seidman. S ad Fisher, N. (Ed.), *Introducing the New Sexuality Studies.* New York: Routledge. Pp. 250–258

Anderson, E., Magrath, R., and Bullingham, R. (2016). *Out in Sport: The Experiences of Openly Gay and Lesbian Athletes.* New York: Routledge.

Anderson, E., McCormack., and Lee, H. (2012). Male Team Sport Hazing Initiations in a Culture of Decreasing Homohysteria. *Journal of Adolescent Research, 27*(4), 427–448.

Anderson, E., Ripley, M., and McCormack, M. (2019). A mixed-method study of same-sex kissing among college-attending heterosexual men in the US. *Sexuality and Culture, 23*(1), 26–44.

Aries, E., and Johnson, F. (1983). Close friendship in adulthood: Conversational content between same-sex friends. *Sex Roles, 9*(12), 1183–1196.

Aristotle. (350BC). *Nichomachean Ethics.*

Arnett, J. (2004). *A longer road to adulthood.* New York: Oxford University Press.

Arxer, S. L. (2011). Hybrid masculine power: Reconceptualizing the relationship between

Arxer, S. L. (2011). Hybrid masculine power: Reconceptualizing the relationship between homosociality and hegemonic masculinity. *Humanity & Society, 35*(4), 390–422.

Axelrod, R., and Hamilton, W. (1981). The evolution of cooperation. *Science, 211*(4489), 1390–1396.

Bank, B., and Hansford, S. (2000). Gender and friendship: Why are men's best same-sex friendships less intimate and supportive? *Personal Relationships, 7*(1), 63–78.

Baron, R., and Markman, G. (2003). Beyond social capital: the role of entrepreneurs' social competence in their financial success. *J. Business Venturing, 18*(1), 41–60.

Barrett, T. (2016). Friendships between men across sexual orientation: The management of sexual difference through humour. *Journal of Sociology, 52*(2), 355–370.

Baunach, D. M. (2012). Changing same-sex marriage attitudes in America from 1988 through 2010. *Public Opinion Quarterly, 76*, 364–378.

BBC. (2014). Universities ignoring laddish culture, says NUS leader [Online]. Available at: http://www.bbc.co.uk/news/education-29176844.

Beasley, C. (2008). Rethinking hegemonic masculinity in a globalizing world. *Men and masculinities, 11*(1), 86–103.

Becht, M. and Vingerhoets, A. (2002). Crying and mood change: A cross-cultural study. *Cognition and Emotion, 16*(1), 87–101.

Bell, S. (1981). *Worlds of Friendship*. Newbury Park: Sage Publications

Benenson, J. (2013). The development of human female competition: allies and adversaries. *Philosophical Transactions of the Royal Society B, 368*(1631).

Berger, P. L., and Luckmann, T. (1966). The social construction of reality: A treatise in the sociology of knowledge. *Anchor*.

Berndt, T. (2004). Children's friendships: Shifts over a half-century in perspectives on their development and their effects. *Merrill-Palmer Quarterly, 50*(3), 206–223.

Bishop, J. (1999). Nerd harassment, incentives, school priorities and learning. In Mayer, S., and Peterson, P. (Ed.), *Earning and learning: How schools matter*. Washington: Brookings Institution Press. Pp 231–281.

Blanchard, C., McCormack, M., and Peterson, G. (2017). Inclusive masculinities in a working-class sixth form in northeast England. *Journal of Contemporary Ethnography, 46*(3), 310–333.

Boeckle, M., and Bugnyar, T. (2012). Long-term memory for affiliates in ravens. *Current Biology, 22*(9), 801–806.

Bogle, K. (2008). *Hooking up: Sex, dating, and relationships on campus*. New York: New York University Press.

Borkowska, K. (2018). Approaches to Studying Masculinity: A Nonlinear Perspective of Theoretical Paradigms. *Men and Masculinities*, 1097184X18768376.

Boster, F., Rodriguez, J., Cruz, M., and Marshall, L. (1995). The relative effectiveness of a direct request message and a pregiving message on friends and strangers. *Communication Research, 22*(4), 475–484.

Bourdieu, P. (2001). *Masculine domination*. Stanford University Press.

Boyle, E. (2008). *Building a Body for Governance: Embodying power in the shifting media images of Arnold Schwarzenegger*. Illinois: Human Kinetics.

Boyle, K., and Berridge, S. (2012). I Love You, Man: Gendered Narratives of Friendship in Contemporary Hollywood Comedies. *Feminist Media Studies, 14*(3), 353–368.

Bradford, S., Hills, L., and Johnston, C. (2016). Unintended volunteers: the volunteering pathways of working class young people in community sport. *International Journal of Sport Policy and Politics, 8*(2), 231–244.

Branfman, J., and Ekberg Stiritz, S. (2012). Teaching Men's Anal Pleasure: Challenging Gender Norms with "Prostage" Education. *American Journal of Sexuality Education, 7*(4), 404–428.

Branfman, J., Stiritz, S. and Anderson, E. (2017) Relaxing the Straight-Male Anus: Decreasing Homohysteria around Anal Eroticism. *Sexualities*. https://doi.org/10.1177/1363460716678560.

Bridges, T., (2014). A very "gay" straight? Hybrid masculinities, sexual aesthetics, and the changing relationship between masculinity and homophobia. *Gender & Society, 28*(1), 58–82.

Brim, M., and Ghaziani, A. (2016). Introduction: Queer methods. *WSQ: Women's Studies Quarterly, 44*(3–4), 14–27.

Bryshun, J., and Young, K. (2007). Hazing as a form of sport and gender socialization. In Young., and White., (Ed.), *Sport and Gender in Canada (2nd ed.)*. Oxford: Oxford University Press. Pp. 302–327

Bullingham, R., McGrath, R., and Anderson, E. (2014). 'Changing the game' Sport and a Cultural Shift from Homohysteria. In Hargreaves, J and Anderson, E. (Ed) Handbook of Sport Gender and Sexualities. New York: Routledge. Pp 220–231.

Bullough, V. L. (2019). *Homosexuality: A history (From Ancient Greece to gay liberation)*. Routledge.

Burton-Nelson, M. (1994). *The stronger women get the more men love football*. New York: Avon Books.

Bush, A., Anderson, E., and Carr, S. (2012). The declining existence of men's homophobia in British sport. *Journal for the Study of Sports and Athletes in Education, 6*(1), 107–120.

Buss, D. (2004). *Evolutionary psychology: The new science of the mind (4th ed.)*. Boston: Allyn and Bacon.

Cancian, F. (1990). *Love in America: Gender and self-development*. Cambridge: Cambridge University Press.

Cancian, F. M. (1986). The feminization of love. *Signs: Journal of Women in Culture and Society, 11*(4), 692–709.

Caruso, A., & Roberts, S. (2018). Exploring constructions of masculinity on men's body-positivity blog. *Journal of Sociology, 54*(4), 627–646.

Chan, D. K. S., & Cheng, G. H. L. (2004). A comparison of offline and online friendship qualities at different stages of relationship development. *Journal of Social and Personal Relationships, 21*(3), 305–320.

Chandler, A. (2012). Exploring the role of masculinities in suicidal behaviour. *Men, Suicide and Society*. 111.

Chen, E. (2011). Caught in a bad bromance. *Texas Journal of Women and Law, 21*(2), 241–267.

Cleary, A. (2012). Suicidal action, emotional expression, and the performance of masculinities. *Social Science and Medicine, 74*(4), 498–505.

Clements, B., and Field, C. (2014). Public opinion toward homosexuality and gay rights in Great Britain. *Public Opinion Quarterly, 78*(2), 523–547.

Closson, L. (2009). Status and gender differences in early adolescents' descriptions of popularity. *Social Development, 18*(2), 412–426.

Coad, D. (2008). *The metrosexual: Gender, sexuality and sport*. Albany: State University of New York Press.

Collins, W., and Sroufe, L. (1999). Capacity for intimate relationships. In W. Furman., B. Brown., and C. Feiring (Ed.), *The development of romantic relationships in adolescence*. Cambridge: Cambridge University Press. Pp. 125–147.

Connell, R. (1987). *Gender and power: Society, the person and sexual politics*. Berkeley: University of California Press.

Connell, R. (1989). Cool guys, swots and wimps: The interplay of masculinity and education. *Oxford Review of Education, 15*(3), 291–203.

Connell, R. (1995). *Masculinities*. Berkeley: University of California Press.

Connell, R. (2000). *The men and the boys*. Berkeley: University of California Press

Connell, R. (2005). *Masculinities*. Berkeley: University of California Press

Connell, R., and Messerschmidt, J. (2005). Hegemonic masculinity: Rethinking the concept. *Gender and Society, 19*(6), 829–859.

Consalvo, M., Mitgutsch, K., and Stein, A. (2013). *Sports videogames*. New York: Routledge.

Cosmides, L., and Tooby, J. (2000). Evolutionary psychology and the emotions. In Lewis, M., and Haviland-Jones, J (Ed.), *Handbook of emotions* (2nd ed.). New York: Guilford. Pp. 91–115.

Courtenay, W. (2000). Constructions of masculinity and their influence on men's well-being: A theory of gender and health. *Social Science and Medicine, 50*(10), 1385–1401.

Cullen, F., & Johnston, C. (2018). Playwork goes to school: Professional (mis) recognition and playwork practice in primary school. *Pedagogy, Culture & Society, 26*(3), 467–484.

Curry, T. (2000). Booze and bar fights: A journey to the dark side of college athletics. In McKay, J., Messner, M., and Sabo, D. (Ed.), *Masculinities, gender relations and sport*. London: Sage. Pp. 162–175.

Darwin, C. (1871). 2003. *The descent of man*. London: Gibson Square.

Davies, N. (2014). I love you hombre. In DeAngelis, M (Ed.), *Reading the bromance: Homosocial relationships in film and television*. Detroit: Wayne State University Press. Pp. 109–138.

Davis, L. (1990). Male cheerleaders and the naturalization of gender. In Sabo, D. and Messner, M. (Ed.), *Sport, men and the gender order: Critical feminist perspectives*. Illinois: Human Kinetics. Pp. 153–161.

Dean, J. (2014). *Straights: Heterosexuality in post-closeted culture*. New York: New York University Press.

DeAngelis, M. (2014). *Reading the Bromance: Homosocial relationships in film and television*. Detroit: Wayne State University Press.

Deitcher, D. (2001). *Dear friends: American photographs of men together, 1840-1918*. Michigan: Harry N Abrams Inc.

Demetriou, D. Z. (2001). Connell's concept of hegemonic masculinity: A critique. *Theory and Society, 30*(3), 337–361.

Dempster, S. (2011). I drink, therefore I'm man: Gender discourses, alcohol and the construction of British undergraduate masculinities. *Gender and Education, 23*(5), 635–653.

Derlega, V. J., Lewis, R. J., Harrison, S., Winstead, B. A., and Costanza, R. (1989). Gender differences in the initiation and attribution of tactile intimacy. *Journal of Nonverbal Behavior, 13*(2), 83–96.

Dermott, E. (2008). *Intimate fatherhood: A sociological analysis*. New York: Routledge.

DeScioli, P., and Kurzban, R. (2009). The alliance hypothesis for human friendship. *PloS One, 4*(6), e5802.

Diamond, L. (2000). Passionate friendships among lesbian, bisexual and heterosexual women. *Journal of Research on Adolescence, 10*(2), 191–209.

Diamond, L. (2003). What does sexual orientation orient? A bio-behavioural model distinguishing romantic love and sexual desire. *Psychological Review, 110*(1), 173–192.

Diamond, L. M. (2008). Female bisexuality from adolescence to adulthood: Results from a 10-year longitudinal study. *Developmental Psychology, 44*(1), 5.

Diamond, L., Savin-Williams, R., and Dube, E. (1999). Intimate peer relations among lesbian, gay, and bisexual adolescents: Sex, dating, passionate friendships, and romance. In Furman, W., Brown, B., and Feiring, C. (Ed.), *The development of romantic relationships in adolescence*. Cambridge: Cambridge University Press. Pp. 45–58

Diefendorf, S. (2015). After the wedding night sexual abstinence and masculinities over the life course. *Gender & Society, 29*(5), 647–669.

Domahidi, E., Festl, R., and Quandt, T. (2014). To dwell among gamers: Investigating the relationship between social online game use and gaming-related friendships. *Computers in Human Behavior, 35*, 107–115.

Drummond, M., Filiault, S., Anderson, E., and Jeffries, D. (2014). Homosocial intimacy among Australian undergraduate men. *Journal of Sociology, 51*(3), 643–656.

Dunivin, K. (1994). Military culture: Change and continuity. *Armed Forces and Society, 20*(4), 531–547.

Dunning, E., Murphy, P., and Williams, J. (2014). *The roots of football hooliganism (RLE sports studies): An historical and sociological study* (Vol. 2). New York: Routledge.

Elliott, K. (2019). Negotiations between progressive and 'traditional' expressions of masculinity among young Australian men. *Journal of Sociology, 55*(1), 108–123.

Elliott, K., (2016). Caring masculinities theorizing an emerging concept. *Men and Masculinities, 19*(3), 240–259.

Emslie, C., Ridge, D., Ziebland, S., and Hunt, K. (2007). Exploring men's and women's experiences of depression and engagement with health professionals: More similarities than differences? A qualitative interview study. *BioMed Central Family Practice, 8*(1), 43–61.

Esterline, K., and Galupo, M. (2013). "Drunken curiosity" and "gay chicken": Gender differences in same-sex performativity. *Journal of Bisexuality, 13*(1), 106–121.

Ezzy, D. (1998). Theorizing narrative identity: Symbolic interactionism and hermeneutics. *The Sociological Quarterly, 39*(2), 239–252.

Fagogenis, B. (2010). In defense of Dodgeball. *Physical and Health Education Journal, 76*(2), 32.

Fairhurst, G. T., and Grant, D. (2010). The social construction of leadership: A sailing guide. *Management Communication Quarterly, 24*(2), 171–210.

Fehr, B. (1996). *Friendship processes*. Thousand Oaks, CA: Sage.

Feist, D., Shenton, B., and de Souza, T. (2004). Induction ceremonies in university sport in the UK. Unpublished communication to Athletic Union presidents. *British Universities Sports Association*. London.

Ferber, A. (2007). The construction of black masculinity white supremacy now and then. *Journal of Sport and Social Issues, 31*(1), 11–24.

Ferguson, A. (2001). *Bad boys: Public schools in the making of masculinity*. Ann Arbor: University of Michigan Press.

Fisher, H. (1998). Lust, attraction and attachment in mammalian reproduction. *Human Nature, 9*(1), 23–52

Fisher, H. (2004). *Why we love: The nature and chemistry of romantic love*. New York: Henry Holt and Company.

Fisher, H. (2006). The drive to love: The neural mechanism for mate selection. In Steinberg, R., and Weis, K. (Ed.), *The new psychology of love*. New Haven: Yale University Press. Pp. 87–115.

Floyd, K. (2006). *Communicating affection: Interpersonal behavior and social context*. Cambridge: Cambridge University Press.

Forster, P. (2014). Rad bromance (or I Love You, Man, but We Won't Be Humping on Humpday). In DeAngelis, M. (Ed.), *Reading the bromance: Homosocial relationships in film and television*. Detroit: Wayne State University Press. Pp. 191–212.

Frank, B. (1987). Hegemonic heterosexual masculinity. *Studies in Political Economy, 24*(1),

Freud, S. (1905). *Three essays on the theory of sexuality*. Basic Books 1962.

Galupo, M. P. (2020). Mental health for individuals with pansexual and queer identities. *The Oxford Handbook of Sexual and Gender Minority Mental Health*, 331.

Garfinkel, H. (1967). *Ethnomethodology*. Englewood Cliffs.

Gaston, L., Magrath, R., and Anderson, E. (2018). From hegemonic to inclusive masculinities in English professional football: Marking a cultural shift. *Journal of Gender Studies, 27*(3), 301–312.

Geary, D., Byrd-Craven, J., Hoard, M., Vigil, J., and Numtee, C. (2003). Evolution and development of boys' social behavior. *Developmental Review, 23*(4), 444–470.

General Social Survey. (2010). *Overview of the time use of Canadians*. Statistics Canada [Online]. Available at: http://www.statcan.gc.ca/pub/89-647-x/89-647-x2011001-eng.pdf.

Ghaziani, A. (2010). The reinvention of heterosexuality. *Gay and Lesbian Review, 17*(3): 27–29.

Ghaziani, A. (2011). Post-gay collective identity construction. *Social Problems, 58*(1), 99–125.

Ghaziani, A. (2017). *Sex cultures*. Boston: Polity Press (Cultural Sociology series).

Ghaziani, Amin, and Brim, M. (2019). Queer methods: Four provocations for an emerging field. In Ghaziani, A. and Brim, M. (Ed.), *Imagining queer methods*. New York: NYU Press. Pp. 3–27.

Gill, R., and Hansen-Miller, D. (2011). Lad flicks: Discursive reconstructions of masculinity in popular film: Feminism at the movies: Understanding gender in contemporary popular cinema. In *Feminism at the movies: Understanding gender in contemporary popular cinema*. Routledge. Pp. 36–50.

Giroux, H. (2001). *Public spaces and private lives: Beyond the culture of cynicism*. Boston: Rowman and Littlefield Publishers.

Goldmeier, D., and Richardson, D. (2005). Romantic love and sexually transmitted infection acquisition: Hypothesis and review. *International Journal of STD and AIDS, 16*(9), 585–587.

Gramsci, A. (1971). *Selections from the Prison Notebooks*. London: Lawrence and Wishart.

Greenberg, D. (1988). *The construction of homosexuality*. Chicago: University of Chicago Press.

Grello, C., Welsh, D., and Harper, M. (2006). No strings attached: The nature of casual sex in college students. *Journal of Sex Research, 43*(3), 255–267.

Greif, G. (2008). *Buddy system: Understanding male friendships*. Oxford University Press.

Grindstaff, L., and West, E. (2011). Hegemonic masculinity on the sidelines of sport. *Sociology Compass, 5*(10), 859–881.

Groves, M., Griggs, G., and Leflay, K. (2012). Hazing and initiation ceremonies in university sport: Setting the scene for further research in the United Kingdom. *Sport in Society,* 15(1), 117–131.

Gutterman, S. (1994). Postmodernism and the interrogation of masculinity. In Brod, H. and Kaufman, M. (Ed.), *Theorizing masculinities*. London: Sage Publications. Pp. 219–238

Hagestad, G., and Call, V. (2007). Pathways to childlessness a life course perspective. *Journal of Family Issues,* 28(10), 1338–1361.

Hall, J. (2011). Sex differences in friendship expectations: A meta-analysis. *Journal of Social and Personal Relationships,* 28(6), 723–747.

Halperin, D. M. (2000). How to do the history of male homosexuality. *GLQ: A Journal of Lesbian and Gay Studies,* 6(1), 87–123.

Hammarén, S., and Johansson, T. (2014). Homosociality in between power and intimacy. *SAGE Open,* 4(1), 1–11.

Hammers, C., and Sheff, E. (2011). The privilege of perversities: Race, class, and education among polyamorists and kinksters. *Psychology and Sexuality,* 2(3), 198–223.

Harry, J. (1995). Sports ideology, attitudes toward women, and anti-homosexual attitudes. *Sex Roles,* 32(1–2), 109–116.

Hays, R. (1984). The development and maintenance of friendship. *Journal of Social and Personal Relationships,* 1(1), 75–98.

Hearn, J. (2004). From hegemonic masculinity to the hegemony of me. *Feminist Theory*. London: Sage.

Hearn, J., Nordberg, M., Andersson, K., Balkmar, D., Gottzén, L., Klinth, R., Pringle, K., and Sandberg, L. (2012). Hegemonic masculinity and beyond: 40 years of research in Sweden. *Men and Masculinities,* 15(1), 31–55.

Heath, M. (2003). Soft-boiled masculinity renegotiating gender and racial ideologies in the promise keepers movement. *Gender & Society,* 17(3), 423–444.

Herek, G. M., and McLemore, K. A. (1998). Attitudes toward lesbians and gay men scale. *Handbook of Sexuality-Related Measures,* 392–394.

Herlitz, C. (2001). *HIV/AIDS and society: Knowledge, attitudes and behavior 1989–2000*. Swedish National Institute of Public Health.

Hey, V. (1997). *The company she keeps: An ethnography of girls' friendships*. McGraw-Hill Education (UK).

Heyl, B. (2001). Ethnographic interviewing. In Atkinson, P., Coffey, A., Delamont, S., Lofland, J., Lofland, L. (Eds.), *Handbook of ethnography*. Sage.

Hilber, C., and Vermeulen, W. (2016). The impact of supply constraints on house prices in England. *The Economic Journal,* 126(591), 358–405.

Hill, K., and Hurtado, A. (1996). *Ache life history: The ecology and demography of a foraging people*. New York: Aldine De Gruyter.

Hillebrand, B., Kok, R., and Biemans, W. (2001). Theory-testing using case studies: A comment on Johnston, Leach, and Liu. *Industrial Marketing Management, 30*(8), 651–657.

Holt, N., and Sparkes, A. (2001). An ethnographic study of cohesiveness in a college soccer team over a season. *The Sport Psychologist, 15*(3), 237—259.

Howard, H. (2012). A confederacy of bachelors. *New York Times*, August 3.

Howson, R. (2006). *Challenging hegemonic masculinity* (Vol. 10). New York: Routledge.

Hruschka, D. (2010). Friendship: Development, ecology, and evolution of a relationship (Vol. 5). Berkeley: University of California Press.

Hymel, S., Vaillancourt, T., McDougall, P., and Renshaw, P. (2002). Acceptance and rejection by the peer group. In Smith, P., and Hart, C (Ed.), *Blackwell handbook of childhood social development*. Oxford: Blackwell Publishers. Pp. 265–284.

Ibson, J. (2002). *Picturing men: A century of male relationships in everyday American photography*. Illinois: University of Chicago Press.

Jackson, C., and Dempster, S. (2009). 'I sat back on my computer... with a bottle of whisky next to me'. *Journal of Gender Studies,18*(4), 341–356.

Jackson, C., and Sundaram, V. (2015). *Is 'lad culture' a problem in higher education? Exploring the perspectives of staff working in UK universities*. In International Conference on Research into Higher Education. Pp. 1–8.

Jarvis, N. (2015). The inclusive masculinities of heterosexual men within UK gay sport clubs. *International Review for the Sociology of Sport, 50*(3), 283–300.

Johansson, T. (2007). *The transformation of sexuality: Gender and identity in contemporary youth culture*. Hampshire, UK: Ashgate.

Johnson, H. (2003). *Sleepwalking through history: America in the Reagan years*. London: W. W. Norton and Company.

Johnston, C., and Bradford, S. (2019). Alternative spaces of failure. Disabled 'bad boys' in in alternative further education provision. *Disability & Society, 34*(9–10), 1548–1572.

Joseph, L. J., and Anderson, E. (2016). The influence of gender segregation and teamsport experience on occupational discrimination in sport-based employment. *Journal of Gender Studies, 25*(5), 586–598.

Jourard, S. (1971). *The transparent self*. New York: Van Nostrand.

Keleher, A., and Smith, E. (2012). Growing support for gay and lesbian equality since 1990. *Journal of Homosexuality, 59*, 1307–1326.

Kellner, D. (1991). Film, politics, and ideology: Reflections on Hollywood film in the age of Reagan. *Velvet Light Trap, 27*, 9–24.

Kellner, D. (2003). *Media culture: Cultural studies, identity and politics between the modern*. New York: Routledge

Kimmel, M. (2004). Masculinity as homophobia: Fear, shame, and silence in the construction of gender identity. In Rothenberg, P (Ed.), *Race, class, and gender in the United States: An integrated study*. New York: Worth. Pp. 81–93.

Kimmel, M., and Wade, L. (2018). Ask a feminist: Michael Kimmel and Lisa Wade discuss toxic masculinity. *Signs: Journal of Women in Culture and Society, 44*(1), 233–254.

Kimmel, M. (1994). *Manhood in America*. New York: Free Press.

Kimmel, M. S. (1998). *Manhood in America: A cultural history*. New York: Free Press.

Komarovsky, M. (1974). Patterns of self-disclosure of male undergraduates. *Journal of Marriage and the Family, 36*(4), 677–686.

Kreager, D. (2007). Unnecessary roughness? School sports, peer networks, and male adolescent violence. *American Sociological Review, 72*(5), 705–724.

Kurzban, R., Burton-Chellew, M., and West, S. (2015). The evolution of altruism in humans. *Annual Review of Psychology, 66*(3), 575–599.

Lebson, M. (2002). Suicide among homosexual youth. *Journal of Homosexuality, 42*(4), 107–117.

Lewis, D., Al-Shawaf, L., Russell., E., and Buss, D. (2015). Friends and happiness: An evolutionary perspective on friendship. *Friendship and Happiness, 37*.

Lewis, R. (1978). Emotional intimacy among men. *Journal of Social Research, 34*(1), 108–121.

Lindley, L., Walsemann, K., and Carter, J. (2012). The association of sexual orientation measures with young adults' health related outcomes. *American Journal of Public Health, 102*(6), 1177–1185.

Lipman-Blumen, J. (1976). Toward a homosocial theory of sex roles: An explanation of the sex segregation of social institutions. *Signs, 1*(3), 15–31.

Loftus, J. (2001). America's liberalization in attitudes toward homosexuality, 1973 to 1998. *American Sociological Review, 66*(5), 762–782.

Lugg, C. A. (1998). The religious right and public education: The paranoid politics of homophobia. *Educational Policy, 12*(3), 267–283.

Lusher, D., and Robins, G. (2009). Hegemonic and other masculinities in local social contexts. *Men and Masculinities, 11*(4), 387–423.

Mac an Ghaill, M. (1994). *Making of men*. Philadelphia: Open University Press.

MacLean, S. (2016). Alcohol and the constitution of friendship for young adults. *Sociology*, *50*(1), 93–108
Magrath, R. (2016). *Inclusive masculinities in contemporary football: Men in the beautiful game*. Routledge.
Magrath, R. Batten, J. Anderson, E., and White, A. (2001). Five-year cohort study of White British Male student-athletes' attitudes toward gay men. *Journal for the Study of Sports and Athletes in Education.* https://doi.org/ https://doi.org/10.1080/19357397.2021.1989277.
Magrath, R., Batten, J., Anderson, E., and White, A. J. (2021). White. *Journal for the Study of Sports and Athletes in Education*, 1–15.
Magrath, R., and Scoats, R. (2019). Young men's friendships: Inclusive masculinities in a post-university setting. *Journal of Gender Studies, 28*(1), 45–56.
Magrath, R., Anderson, E., and Roberts, S. (2015). On the door-step of equality: Attitudes toward gay athletes among academy-level footballers. *International Review for the Sociology of Sport, 50*(7), 804–821.
Magrath, R., Cleland, J., and Anderson, E. (2017). Bisexual erasure in the British print media: Representation of Tom Daley's coming out. *Journal of Bisexuality, 17*(3), 300–317.
Maloney, M., Roberts, S., & Caruso, A. (2018). 'Mmm… I love it, bro!': Performances of masculinity in YouTube gaming. *New Media & Society, 20*(5), 1697–1714.
Maloney, M., Roberts, S., and Graham, T. (2019). *Gender, masculinity and video gaming: Analysing Reddit's r/gaming community*. Springer Nature.
Mangan, J. (2000). *Athleticism in the Victorian and Edwardian public school: The emergence and consolidation of an educational ideology*. New York: Psychology Press.
Manley, A., Palmer, C., and Roderick, M. (2012). Disciplinary power, the oligopticon and rhizomatic surveillance in elite sports academies. *Surveillance and Society, 10*(3/4), 303–319.
McCormack, M. (2011). Mapping the terrain of homosexually-themed language. *Journal of homosexuality, 58*(5), 664–679.
McCormack, M. (2012). *The declining significance of homophobia: How teenage boys are redefining masculinity and heterosexuality*. New York: Oxford University Press.
McCormack, M. (2014). The intersection of youth masculinities, decreasing homophobia and class: An ethnography. *The British Journal of Sociology, 65*(1), 130–149.

McCormack, M. (2018). Mostly straights and the study of sexualities: An introduction to the special issue. *Sexualities, 21*(1–2), 3–15.

McCormack, M., and Anderson, E. (2010). The re-production of homosexually-themed discourse in educationally-based organised sport. *Culture, Health and Sexuality, 12*(8), 913–927.

McCormack, M., and Anderson, E. (2014a). The influence of declining homophobia on men's gender in the United States: An argument for the study of homohysteria. *Sex Roles, 71*(3–4), 109–120.

McCormack, M., and Anderson, E. (2014b). Homohysteria: Definitions, context and intersectionality. *Sex Roles, 71*(3–4), 152–158.

McCormack, M., and Ogilvie, M. F. (2020). Keeping couples together when apart, and driving them apart when together: Exploring the impact of smartphones on relationships in the UK. In Abela, A., Vella, S., and Piscopo, S. (Ed.), *Couple relationships in a global context: Understanding love and intimacy across cultures.* (European Family Therapy Association Series; Vol. 5). Springer. Pp. 245–259.

McCormack, M., and Savin-Williams, R. (2018). Young men's rationales for non-exclusive gay sexualities. *Culture, Health and Sexuality, 20*(8), 929–944.

McCormack, M., and Wignall, L. (2017). Enjoyment, exploration and education: Understanding the consumption of pornography among young men with non-exclusive sexual orientations. *Sociology, 51*(5), 975–991.

McCormack, M., Wignall, L., and Anderson, E. (2015). Identities and identifications: Changes in metropolitan bisexual men's attitudes and experiences. *Journal of Bisexuality, 15*(1), 3–20.

McCormack, M., Wignall, L., and Morris, M. (2016). Gay guys using gay discourse: Friendship, shared values and the intent-context-effect matrix. *British Journal of Sociology, 67*(4), 747–767.

McCreary, D. R. (1994). The male role and avoiding femininity. *Sex Roles, 31*, 517–531.

McGuffey, C. S., and Rich, B. L. (1999). "Playing in the gender transgression zone": Race, class, and hegemonic masculinity in middle childhood. *Gender and Society, 13*(5), 608–627.

McKay, B., and McKay, J. (2012). Bosom buddies: A photo history of male affection [Online]. Available at: http://www.artofmanliness.com/2012/07/29/bosom-buddies-a-photo-history-of-male-affection/.

McKay, J. (1993). Marked men and wanton women: The politics of naming sexual deviance in sport. *Journal of Men's Studies, 2*(1), 69–81.

McNair, B. (2002). *Striptease culture: Sex, media and the democratisation of desire.* Routledge.

Mehta, C., and Strough, J. (2009). Sex segregation in friendships and normative contexts across the life span. *Developmental Review, 29*(3), 201–220.

Mercer, J. (2017). *Gay pornography: Representations of masculinity and sexuality.* London: I. B. Tauris.

Messerschmidt, J. W. (2012). Engendering gendered knowledge: Assessing the academic appropriation of hegemonic masculinity. *Men and Masculinities, 15*(1), 56–76.

Messerschmidt, J. W. (2018). *Hegemonic masculinity: Formulation, reformulation, and amplification.* London: Rowman & Littlefield.

Meyer, I. (1995). Minority stress and mental health in gay men. *Journal of Health and Social Behavior, 36*, 38–56.

Millett, K. (1971). *Sexual politics.* London: Granada.

Moller, M. (2007) Exploiting patterns: A critique of hegemonic masculinity. *Journal of Gender Studies, 16*(3), 263–276.

Morales, L., and Caffyn-Parsons, E. (2017). "I Love You, Guys": A study of inclusive masculinities among high school cross-country runners. *Boyhood Studies, 10*(1), 66–87.

Morin, S., and Garfinkle, E. (1978). Male homophobia. *Journal of Social Issues, 34*(1), 29–47.

Morman, M, Schrodt P, Tornes, M. (2013). Self-disclosure mediates the effects of gender orientation and homophobia on the relationship quality of male same-sex friendships. *Journal of Social and Personal Relationships, 30*(5), 582–605.

Morris, M., and Anderson, E. (2015). 'Charlie is so cool like': Authenticity, popularity and inclusive masculinity on YouTube. *Sociology, 49*(6), 1200–1217.

Muir, K., Anderson, E., Parry, K. D., & Letts, D. (2021). The changing nature of gay rugby clubs in the United Kingdom. *Sociology of Sport Journal* (published online ahead of print 2021).

Murray, A., White, A., Scoats, R., and Anderson, E. (2016). Constructing masculinities in the national Rugby League's Footy Show. *Sociological Research Online, 21*(3).

Nardi, P. (1992). *Men's friendships.* London: Sage Publications.

Nardi, P., and Sherrod, D. (1994). Friendship in the lives of gay men and lesbians. *Journal of Social and Personal relationships, 11*(2), 185–199.

National Union of Students. (2012). That's what she said: Women students' experiences of 'lad culture' in higher education [Online]. Available at: https://www.nus.org.uk/Global/Campaigns/That's%20what%20she%20said%20full%20report%20Final%20web.pdf.

Naveed, M., Malal, J., Guisasola, I., and Dunn, A. (2013). Dodgeball: A true sporting story! A typical presentation of an osteochondroma of the scapula. *European Orthopaedics and Traumatology*, *4*(3), 183–185.

Nelson, J. (1988). *The intimate connection: Male sexuality, masculine spirituality.* Westminster: John Knox Press.

Nowak, M. (2006). Five rules for the evolution of cooperation. *Science*, *314*(5805), 1560–1563.

Nuwer, H. (1999). *Wrongs of passage: Fraternities, sororities, hazing and binge drinking.* Bloomington: Indiana University Press.

O'Brien, R., Hunt, K., and Hart, G. (2005). 'It's caveman stuff, but that is to a certain extent how guys still operate': MEN'S accounts of masculinity and help seeking. *Social Science and Medicine*, *61*(3), 503–516.

O'Connor, P. (1998). Women's friendships in a post-modern world. In Adams, R., and Allan, G. (Ed.), *Placing friendship in context.* Cambridge: Cambridge University Press. Pp. 117–135.

Office for National Statistics. (2012). *Marriages in England and Wales (provisional)* [Online]. Available at: http://www.ons.gov.uk/ons/dcp171778_366530.pdf.

Office for National Statistics. (2015b). Age-specific suicide rates (with 95 per cent confidence limits): By sex and five-year age group, England and Wales, 1981 to 2014 Registrations [Online]. Available at: http://www.ons.gov.uk/ons/about-ons/business-transparency/freedom-of-information/what-can-i-request/published-ad-hoc-data/health/october-2015/age-specific-suicides-rates-by-sex-and-five-year-age-group--england-and-wales.xls.

Office for National Statistics. (2016). Population estimates by marital status and living arrangements in England and Wales: 2002 to 2015 [Online]. Available at:https://www.ons.gov.uk/peoplepopulationandcommunity/populationandmigration/populationestimates/bulletins/populationestimatesbymaritalstatusandlivingarrangements/2002to2015.

Ogilvie, M. F., and McCormack, M. (2019). Conner Mertens and the muted media coverage of the first openly bisexual NCAA American Football Player. In *LGBT athletes in the sports media.* Cham: Palgrave Macmillan. Pp. 189–206.

Ogilvie, M. E. (2019). *Masculinities and sexualities of elite male team sport athletes. An ethnographic examination.* Unpublished PhD Thesis. Durham University.

Osborne, C. (1994). *Eros unveiled: Plato and the God of love.* Oxford: Clarendon Press.

Outsports. (2021). https://www.outsports.com/out-gay-athletes/2021/10/4/22706376/out-in-sports-study-lgbtq-athletes-high-school-college-acceptance. October 4th, 2021.
Pahl, R (2000). *On friendship*. Oxford: Blackwell Publishing.
Pahl, R., and Pevalin, D. (2005). Between family and friends: A longitudinal study of friendship choice. *British Journal of Sociology, 56*(3), 433–450.
Parry, K. D., Storr, R., Kavanagh, E. & Anderson, E. (2021). Conceptualising organisational cultural lag: Marriage equality and Australian sport. *Journal of Sociology, 57*(4), 986–1008.
Peralta, R. (2007). College alcohol use and the embodiment of hegemonic masculinity among European American men. *Sex Roles, 56*(11), 741–756.
Peterson, G., and Anderson, E. (2012). The performance of softer masculinities on the university dance floor. *The Journal of Men's Studies, 20*(1), 3–15.
Phipps, A., and Young, I. (2015). Neoliberalization and lad cultures in higher education. *Sociology, 49*(2), 305–322.
Pleck, J. (1975). Issues for the men's movement: Summer, 1975. *Changing Men: A Newsletter for Men against Sexism*, 21–23.
Pleck, J. (1981). *The myth of masculinity*. Massachusetts: MIT Press.
Plummer, D. (1999). *One of the boys: Masculinity, homophobia, and modern manhood*. New York: Routledge.
Pollack, W. (1999). *Real boys: Rescuing our sons from the myths of boyhood*. New York: Macmillan.
Pomerance, M. (2014). *Reading the bromance: Homosocial relationships in film and television*, DeAngelis, M. (Ed.). Detroit: Wayne State University Press. Pp. 255–273.
Pope, H., Phillips, K., and Olivardia, R. (2000). *The Adonis complex: The secret crisis of male body obsession*. New York: Simon and Schuster.
Poplawski, P. (1989). *Psychological and qualitative dimensions of friendship among men: An examination of intimacy, sex-role, loneliness, control and the friendship experience*. PhD diss. Temple University.
Pronger, B. (1990). *The arena of masculinity: Sports, homosexuality, and the meaning of sex*. London: GMP Publishers.
Putnam, R. D. (2000). *Bowling alone: America's declining social capital*. In *Culture and politics*. Palgrave Macmillan, New York. Pp. 223–234
Rakow, L. (1988). Women and the telephone: The gendering of a communications technology. In Rakow, L (Ed.), *Technology and women's voices: Keeping in touch*. Pp. 207–229.

Ralph, B., and Roberts, S. (2020a). One small step for man: Change and continuity in perceptions and enactments of homosocial intimacy among young Australian men. *Men and Masculinities, 23*(1), 83–103.

Ralph, B., and Roberts, S. (2020b). *The Palgrave Handbook of Masculinity and Sport*. Pp. 19–38.

Rands, M., and Levinger, G. (1979). Implicit theories of relationship: An intergenerational study. *Journal of Personality and Social Psychology, 37*(5), 645.

Regan, P. (2004). Sex and the attraction process: Lessons from science (and Shakespeare) on lust, love, chastity, and fidelity. In Harvey, J., Wenzel, A., and Sprecher, S (Ed.), *The handbook of sexuality in close relationships*. New York: Psychology Press. Pp. 115–133.

Reisman, J. (1990). Intimacy in same-gender friendships. *Sex Roles, 23*(1–2), 65–82.

Requena, F. (1995). Friendship and subjective well-being in Spain: A cross-national comparison with the United States. *Social Indicators Research, 35*(3), 271–288.

Rich, A. (1980). Compulsory heterosexuality and lesbian existence. *Signs, 5*(4), 631–660.

Riesman, D. (1953). *The lonely crowd*. New Haven: Yale University press.

Rigauer, B. (1981). *Sport and work*. New York: Columbia University Press

Ripley, M. (2018). The integration of British undergraduate men's public and private masculinities. *Journal of Gender Studies, 27*(3), 288–300.

Ripley, M., Anderson, E., McCormack, M., and Rockett, B. (2012). Heteronormativity in the university classroom novelty attachment and content substitution among gay-friendly students. *Sociology of Education, 85*(2), 121–130.

Roberts, S. (2018). *Young working-class men in transition*. Routledge.

Roberts, S., Anderson, E., & Magrath, R. (2017). Continuity, change and complexity in the performance of masculinity among elite young footballers in England. *The British Journal of Sociology, 68*(2), 336–357.

Roberts, S., Ravn, S., Maloney, M., & Ralph, B. (2021). Navigating the tensions of normative masculinity: Homosocial dynamics in Australian young men's discussions of sexting practices. *Cultural Sociology, 15*(1), 22–43.

Robinson, S., Anderson, E., and White, A. (2018). The bromance: Undergraduate male friendships and the expansion of contemporary homosocial boundaries. *Sex Roles, 78*(1–2), 94–106.

Robinson, S., White, A., and Anderson, E. (2019). Privileging the bromance: A critical appraisal of romantic and bromantic relationships. *Men and Masculinities, 22*(5), 850–871.

Rotolo, T., and Wharton, A. (2004). Living across institutions: Exploring sex-based homophily in occupations and voluntary groups. *Sociological Perspectives, 46*(1), 59–82.

Rotundo, A. (1989). Romantic friendship: Male intimacy and middle-class youth in the northern United States, 1800–1900. *Journal of Social History, 23*(1), 1–25.

Rotundo, A. (1994). *American manhood: Transformations in masculinity from the revolution to the modern era.* New York: Basic Books.

Rubin, L. (1985). *Just friends.* New York: Harper and Row.

Rumens, N. (2017). Postfeminism, men, masculinities and work: A research agenda for gender and organization studies scholars. *Gender, Work and Organization, 24*(3), 245–259.

Rupp, L., Taylor, V., Regev-Messalem, S., Fogarty, A., and England, P. (2014). Queer women in the hookup scene: Beyond the closet. *Gender and Society, 28*(2), 212–235.

Ryan, C., and Jethá, C. (2010). Sex at dawn. *The Prehistoric Origins of Modern Sexuality.* New York.

Sabo, D., and Runfola, R. (1980). *Jock: Sports and male identity.* New Jersey: Prentice Hall.

Samaritans. (2012). *Suicide and society: Why disadvantaged men in mid-life die by suicide.* Samaritans: London.

Savin-Williams, R. (2005). *The new gay teenager* (Vol. 3). Cambridge: Harvard University Press.

Savin-Williams, R. C. (2014). An exploratory study of the categorical versus spectrum nature of sexual orientation. *The Journal of Sex Research, 51*(4), 446–453.

Savin-Williams, R. C. (2017). *Mostly straight: Sexual fluidity among men.* Harvard University Press.

Savin-Williams, R., and Vrangalova, Z. (2013). Mostly heterosexual as a distinct sexual orientation group: A systematic review of the empirical evidence. *Developmental Review, 33*(1), 58–88.

Schwartz, P., and Young, L. (2009). Sexual satisfaction in committed relationships. *Sexuality Research and Social Policy, 6*(1), 1–17.

Scoats, R. (2017). Inclusive masculinity and Facebook photographs among early emerging adults at a British university. *Journal of Adolescent Research, 32*(3), 323–345.

Scoats, R. (2019a). *Understanding threesomes: Gender, sex, and consensual non-monogamy*. Oxford: Routledge.
Scoats, R. (2019b). 'If there is no homo, there is no trio': Women's experiences and expectations of MMF threesomes. *Psychology and Sexuality, 10*(1), 45–55.
Scoats, R., Joseph, L. J., and Anderson, E. (2018). 'I don't mind watching him cum': Heterosexual men, threesomes, and the erosion of the one-time rule of homosexuality. *Sexualities, 21*(1–2), 30–48.
Scourfield, J. (2005). Suicidal masculinities. *Sociological Research Online*, 10(2).
Seiden, A., and Bart, P. (1975). Woman to woman: Is sisterhood powerful? In Glazer-Malbin, N. (Ed.), *Old family/New family*. New York: Van Nostrand. Pp. 189–228.
Sherkat, D. E., Powell-Williams, M., Maddox, G., and De Vries, K. M. (2011). Religion, politics, and support for same-sex marriage in the United States, 1988–2008. *Social Science Research, 40*(1), 167–180.
Shilts, R. (2007). *And the band played on: Politics, people, and the AIDS epidemic, 20th-anniversary edition*. Macmillan.
Silk, J. (2003). Cooperation without counting. In Hammerstein, P (Ed.), *Genetic and cultural evolution of cooperation*. MIT Press. Pp. 37–54.
Silk, J., Beehner, J., Bergman, T., Crockford, C., Engh, A., Moscovice, L., and Cheney, D. (2010). Strong and consistent social bonds enhance the longevity of female baboons. *Current Biology, 20*(15), 1359–1361.
Silva, J. (2013). *Coming up short: Working-class adulthood in an age of uncertainty*. Oxford: Oxford University Press.
Smith, S., Axelton, A., and Saucier, D. (2009). The effects of contact on sexual prejudice: A meta-analysis. *Sex Roles, 61*(3–4), 178–191.
Spencer, L., and Pahl, R. (2006). *Rethinking friendship*: Hidden solidarities today. Princeton University Press.
Spring, G. (1974). Mass culture and school sports. *History of Education Quarterly, 14*(4), 483–499.
Sternberg, R. J. (1986). A triangular theory of love. *Psychological Review, 93*(2), 119.
Stoet, G., & Geary, D. C. (2021). Sex differences in adolescents' occupational aspirations: variations across time and place. https://doi.org/10.1371/journal.pone.0261438.
Stokes, J., Fuehrer, A., and Childs, L. (1980). Gender differences in self-disclosure to various target persons. *Journal of Counseling Psychology, 27*(2), 192.

Su, R., Rounds, J., & Armstrong, P. I. (2009). Men and things, women and people: A meta-analysis of sex differences in interests. *Psychological Bulletin, 135*(6), 859.

Summers, C. (2004). *The queer encyclopaedia of music, dance, and musical theatre*. New Jersey: Cleis Press.

Swain, J. (2006). Reflections on patterns of masculinity in school settings. *Men and Masculinities, 8*(3), 331–349

Swain, S. (1989). Covert intimacy: Closeness in men's friendships. In Risman, B., and Schwartz, P (Ed.), *Gender in intimate relationships*. Belmont: Wadsworth Publishing. Pp. 71–86.

Tennov, D. (1979). *Love and limerance: The experience of being in love in New York*. Stein and Day, New York.

Thibaut, J., and Kelly, H. 1959. *The social psychology of groups*. New York: Wiley

Thomas, R. J. (2019). Sources of friendship and structurally induced homophily across the life course. *Sociological Perspectives, 62*(6), 822–843.

Thompson, L. (2015). Reading the bromance: Homosocial relationships in film and television. *Journal of Gender Studies, 24*(3), 368–370.

Thurnell-Read, T. (2012). What happens on tour: The premarital stag tour, homosocial bonding, and male friendship. *Men and Masculinities, 15*(3), 249–270.

Tognoli, J. (1980). Male friendship and intimacy across the life span. *Family Relations*, 273–279.

Tripp, C. (2005). *The intimate world of Abraham Lincoln*. New York: Free Press.

Trivers, R. (1971). The evolution of reciprocal altruism. *The Quarterly Review of Biology, 46*(1), 35–57.

Tulchin, A. (2007). Same-sex couples creating households in old regime France: The uses of the affrèrement. *The Journal of Modern History, 79*(3), 613–647.

Twenge, J. M., Sherman, R. A., and Wells, B. E. (2016). Changes in American adults' reported same-sex sexual experiences and attitudes, 1973–2014. *Archives of Sexual Behavior, 45*(7), 1713–1730.

Van Duijn, M., Evelien, A., Zeggelink, P., Huisman M., Stokman, F., and Wasseur, F. (2003). Evolution of sociology freshmen into a friendship network. *Journal of Mathematical Sociology, 27*(2–3), 153–191.

Vigil, J. (2007). Asymmetries in the friendship preferences and social styles of men and Women. *Human Nature, 18*, 143–161.

Vrangalova, Z., and Savin-Williams, R. C. (2012). Mostly heterosexual and mostly gay/lesbian: Evidence for new sexual orientation identities. *Archives of Sexual Behavior, 41*(1), 85–101.

Walker, K. (1994). I'm not friends the way she's friends: Ideological and behavioral constructions of masculinity in men's friendships. *Masculinities*, *2*(2), 38–55.
Ward, M. (2015). The chameleonisation of masculinity: Jimmy's multiple performances of a working-class self. *Masculinities & Social Change*, *4*(3), 215–240.
Way, N. (2011). *Deep secrets*. Illinois: Harvard University Press.
Way, N. (2013). Boys' friendships during adolescence: Intimacy, desire, and loss. *Journal of Research on Adolescence*, *23*(2), 201–213.
Weeks, J. (2007). *The world we have won: The remaking of erotic and intimate life*. New York: Routledge.
Weinstock, J. (1998). Lesbian, gay, bisexual, transgendered friendships in adulthood. In Patterson, C., and D'Augelli, A (Ed.), *Lesbian, gay, and bisexual identities in families: Psychological perspectives*. New York: Oxford University Press. Pp. 122–153.
West, C., and Zimmerman, D. H. (1987). Doing gender. *Gender and Society*, *1*(2), 125–151.
Weston, K. (1997). *Families we choose: Lesbians, gays, kinship*. Columbia University Press.
White, A., and Hobson, M. (2015). Teachers' stories: physical education teachers' constructions and experiences of masculinity within secondary school physical education. *Sport, Education and Society*, 1–14.
White, P., and Vagi, A. (1990). Rugby in the 19th-century British boarding-school system: A feminist psychoanalytic perspective. In Messner, M. and Sabo, D. (Ed.), *Sport, men and the gender order: Critical feminist perspectives*. Illinois: Human Kinetics. Pp. 67–78.
Wignall, L. (2019). Pornography use by kinky gay men–A qualitative approach. *Journal of Positive Sexuality*, *15*(1), 7–13.
Wignall, L., and Driscoll, H. (2020). Women's rationales and perspectives on "mostly" as a nonexclusive sexual identity label. *Psychology of Sexual Orientation and Gender Diversity*.
Wignall, L., and McCormack, M. (2017). An exploratory study of a new kink activity: "Pup play". *Archives of Sexual Behavior*, *46*(3), 801–811.
Wignall, L., Scoats, R., Anderson, E., and Morales, L. (2020). A qualitative study of heterosexual men's attitudes toward and practices of receiving anal stimulation. *Culture, Health and Sexuality*, *22*(6), 675–689.
Williams, D. (1985). Gender, masculinity-femininity, and emotional intimacy in same-sex friendship. *Sex Roles*, *12*(5–6), 587–600.

Williams, G. (1966). Adaptation and natural selection. *The American Naturalist*, *100*(916), 687–690.
Winstead, B. (1986). Sex differences in same-sex friendships. In Winstead, B., and Derlega, V. (Ed.), *Friendship and social interaction: An introduction.* New York: Springer. Pp. 81–99.
Winstead, B., and Griffin, J. (2001). Friendship styles. In Worell, J. (Ed.), *Encyclopedia of women and gender.* Boston: Academic Press. Pp. 481–492.
Wood, J. (1868). *Natural history of man: Africa.* New York: George Routeledge and Sons.
Wrangham, R. (1999). Evolution of coalitionary killing. *American Journal of Physical Anthropology, 110*(29), 1–30.
Wright, P. (1982). Men's friendships, women's friendships and the alleged inferiority of the latter. *Sex Roles*, *8*(1), 1–20.
Wright, P. (1998). Toward an expanded orientation to the study of sex differences in friendship. In Canary, D., and Dindia, K (Ed.), *Sex differences and similarities in communication.* Mahwah: Lawrence Erlbaum. Pp. 41–63.
Xue, M., and Silk, J. (2012). The role of tracking and tolerance in relationship among friends. *Evolution and Human Behaviour. 33*(1), 17–25.

GPSR Compliance

The European Union's (EU) General Product Safety Regulation (GPSR) is a set of rules that requires consumer products to be safe and our obligations to ensure this.

If you have any concerns about our products, you can contact us on

ProductSafety@springernature.com

In case Publisher is established outside the EU, the EU authorized representative is:

Springer Nature Customer Service Center GmbH
Europaplatz 3
69115 Heidelberg, Germany

www.ingramcontent.com/pod-product-compliance
Lightning Source LLC
LaVergne TN
LVHW022037260326
834688LV00060B/760

*9 7 8 3 0 3 0 9 8 6 0 9 4 *